# Text, Theology, and Trowel

# Text, Theology, and Trowel
*New Investigations in the Biblical World*

Edited by
LIDIA D. MATASSA
*and*
JASON M. SILVERMAN

☙PICKWICK *Publications* • Eugene, Oregon

TEXT, THEOLOGY, AND TROWEL
New Investigations in the Biblical World

Copyright © 2011 Jason M. Silverman. All rights reserved. Except for brief quotations in critical publications or reviews, no part of this book may be reproduced in any manner without prior written permission from the publisher. Write: Permissions, Wipf and Stock Publishers, 199 W. 8th Ave., Suite 3, Eugene, OR 97401.

Pickwick Publications
An Imprint of Wipf and Stock Publishers
199 W. 8th Ave., Suite 3
Eugene, OR 97401

www.wipfandstock.com

ISBN 13: 978-1-60899-942-2

*Cataloguing-in-Publication data:*

Text, theology, and trowel : new investigations in the biblical world / edited by Lidia D. Matassa and Jason M. Silverman.

xviii + 214 p. ; 23 cm. Includes bibliographical references.

ISBN 13: 978-1-60899-942-2

1. Bible—Criticism, interpretation, etc. 2. Excavations (Archaeology)—Middle East. I. Matassa, Lidia D. II. Silverman, Jason M. III. Title.

BS621.T45.2011

Manufactured in the U.S.A.

Scripture quotations are from New Revised Standard Version Bible, copyright © 1989 National Council of the Churches of Christ in the United States of America. Used by permission. All rights reserved.

# Contents

*List of Illustrations and Tables / vii*

*Preface / ix*

*Acknowledgments / xi*

*Introduction*—A. D. H. Mayes, Trinity College Dublin */ xiii*

*List of Abbreviations / xv*

1. The Divine Designations in Biblical Texts: Towards a Hermeneutical Model—*Máire Byrne, St. Patrick's College, Maynooth / 1*

2. Danger at the King's Table: Insult and Family Conflict at Saul's New Moon Feast—*Killian McAleese, Trinity College Dublin / 24*

3. Life-and-Death Advice from a Conservative Sage: Qohelet's Perspective on Life after Death—*Hans Debel, Katholieke Universiteit Leuven / 39*

4. Two Jewish-American Interpretations of the Book of Job in the Aftermath of the Holocaust: A Short Discussion of the Relationship between Job's Modern Reception and Its Ancient Production—*David C. Tollerton, University of Bristol / 59*

5. Where have all the Female Prophets Gone? Women and Prophetic Communication in Mari—*Jonathan Stökl, University of Oxford / 75*

6. Problems with the Identification of a Synagogue in the Hasmonaean Estate at Jericho: Archaeological and Historiographical Issues—*Lidia D. Matassa, Trinity College Dublin / 95*

7   Iranian-Judaean Interaction in the Achaemenid Period
    —*Jason M. Silverman, Trinity College Dublin* / 133

8   How *Not* to Raise Children: From Adam to David—
    A Contemporary Theological Perspective—*Peter Admirand,
    Trinity College Dublin* / 169

9   Ethics as Cross-Cultural Reaction: Deuteronomic Ethics as a
    Reaction to Manassean Multiculturalism—*Carly L. Crouch,
    University of Oxford* / 182

10  Illuminating Darkness: Mystical Strategies for Biblical
    Interpretation in Judaism and Christianity—*John Robinson,
    Irish School of Ecumenics, Trinity College Dublin* / 204

## Illustrations and Tables

Table 5.1    Professional Prophetesses / 82

Table 5.2    Lay Prophetesses / 84

Table 5.3    Dreamers / 86

Table 5.4.1  Female senders of prophetic letters / 88

Table 5.4.2  Female senders of letters reporting dreams / 89

Figure 6.1   The area of Tulul Abu el-Alayiq —Hasmonaean Jericho / 98

Figure 6.2   View to the north / Showing Cypros (top left), Bedouin Camp (center left) and Herodian palace (foreground) / 99

Figure 6.3   Phase 1—The original courtyard house / 106

Figure 6.4   Comparison of courtyard houses / 110

Figures 6.5 & 6.6   Possible additional rooms at the eastern end of the courtyard house adjoining the industrial area / 113

Figure 6.7   Phase 2—The courtyard-house complex / 115

Figure 6.8   Peristyle courtyard, looking southeast / 118

Figure 6.9   The niche, looking north and burrowing under the Na'aran conduit / 120

Figure 6.10  Phase 3—The triclinium / 123

Figure 6.11　The triclinium (bottom right) and kitchen (bottom center), looking southwest. (Western edge of the peristyle is in left center) / 124

Figure 7.1　Map with locations mentioned in text / 136

# Preface

For various reasons beyond the editors' control, the publication of this collection has been much delayed—so much so, that a second collection of essays from the same conference series preceeded this collection into print (*A Land Like Your Own*; Pickwick Publications, 2010). Despite the unusually long period of abeyance, the editors felt that the overall quality of the work was not marred by age and still had value to offer the scholarly community. The juxtaposition of divergent methods in cognate areas of biblical studies still has the potential to encourage interdisciplinary work. It is in this spirit that we offer this book with the help of a new publisher.

A number of the contributors have changed institutions since the time of the essays' intial submissions; the editors have retained the original information in the interest of non-anachronism. Carly L. Crouch will be at University of Nottingham from this year; David C. Tollerton is currently at University of Wales, Bangor; Jonathon Stökl is at University College London; Killian McAleese is in Edinburgh; and Máire Byrne just finished at Milltown Institute, Dublin.

We would like to thank the publishers at Pickwick Publications for their generous and timely assistance with this project, particularly K. C. Hanson, Christian Amondson, and Patrick Harrison. Working with them has been both professional and an enjoyable experience.

Lidia D. Matassa<br>
Jason M. Silverman<br>
June 2011, Dublin

# Acknowledgments

MANY PEOPLE HELPED WITH the task of putting together this volume, and the editors wish to express their sincerest gratitude to all. We are particularly grateful for the support received from the School of Religions and Theology (Trinity College Dublin [TCD]) and Mediterranean and Near Eastern Studies (TCD) and would like to thank Professors Seán Freyne and Nigel Biggar for their support of the project early on. Professor A. D. H. Mayes has been an enthusiastic supporter throughout the process, and we are especially honored by his participation in this volume. Many eminent scholars helped to evaluate and improve the various contributions to this book, and we are extremely grateful for their time and effort. Additionally, our advisors Professor Catherine Heszer (SOAS) and Dr. Anne Fitzpatrick-McKinley (TCD) deserve special thanks for providing essential feedback on our own contributions.

The hard work of the First Annual Graduate Interdisciplinary Approaches to the Biblical World (GIA) Symposium Committee (Killian McAleese, Damian Bruce, and Máire Byrne) was essential to the completion of this volume. The editors also thank everyone who sent us their papers and regret that not all of them could be included. The task of editing would have been much more cumbersome without the help of Ms. Jane Welch, who solved many logistical and stationary foibles for us.

# Introduction

THE TEN PAPERS COLLECTED here were selected and augmented from among those delivered at a conference held in Trinity College, Dublin in February 2007. The conference was organized by graduate students in the School of Religions and Theology in Trinity College, and the papers were given by many of that group together with graduate students from abroad.

The general heading for the conference was "Interdisciplinary Approaches to the Biblical World." This, however, represented less a theme than a framework within which a wide variety of philosophical, literary, sociological, archaeological, ethical, rhetorical, hermeneutical, and other approaches to the Bible were accommodated. If there was also a theme to the conference, providing some kind of internal link holding the papers together within the given framework, it seemed to be that of cultural identity and self-understanding, how it is created, how it is expressed, how it is transmitted, and how the cultural identities of the past continue to influence—and how they may be appropriated by—the present. In an age such as the present, strongly characterized by uncertainty and insecurity on the issues of identity and self-understanding, it would indeed be surprising if this last concern was not present, either implicitly or explicitly, in our explorations of the past.

Multi-culturalism and the problems it poses for identity and self-understanding may be burning issues for today's world as it strives to accommodate and work through the tensions inherent in our global village. What any given culture's past may contribute to the shape of its present is a source of many conflicts as barriers between peoples are breached and people are exposed to new ways of looking at the world. The physical and material expressions of cultural identity—through buildings, texts, and religious and cultural practices—become the context out of which it is clear that identity is not simply a given but is also a means by which claims and counter-claims are made. From the papers given during the conference, including the selection brought together here, it became evident that these issues, concerns, and problems are not simply phenomena characteristic of our modern world, but are true of every age; the scale may be different but the essence is constant. It may be that the issues became clearer as Israel moved into the world of international conflict, particularly with the eighth-century-BCE rise of Assyria, but even as Israel experienced its own earlier history in relative isolation, the currents of its internal relationships flowed and shifted in response to the same problems.

I should like to commend the graduate students of the School of Religions and Theology for their initiative in establishing what will be, it is hoped, an annual event. This was an expertly organized conference, and the fruits of it, presented here, are a testimony to the value of the exercise.

Professor A. D. H. Mayes<br>
Erasmus Smith's Professor of Hebrew<br>
Head of Department Trinity College Dublin

# Abbreviations

## ANCIENT SOURCES

| | |
|---|---|
| AJ | *Jewish Antiquities* (Josephus) |
| ARM | *Archives royales de Mari* |
| 1 En. | *I Enoch (Ethiopic Apocalypse)* |
| JW | *Jewish War* (Josephus) |
| M. Roš Haš. | M. Rosh Hashshanah |
| M. Sanh. | M. Sanhedrin |
| Spec. | *De specialibus legibus* (Philo) |

## CONTEMPORARY SOURCES

| | |
|---|---|
| AB | Anchor Bible |
| ABD | *The Anchor Bible Dictionary.* 6 vols. Edited by David Noel Freedman. New York: Doubleday, 1992. |
| ACEBT | Amsterdamse Cahiers voor Exegese en bijbelse Theologie |
| AJA | *American Journal of Archaeology* |
| ANES | *Ancient Near Eastern Studies* |
| ANET | *Ancient Near Eastern Texts Relating to the Old Testament.* Edited by James B. Pritchard. 3rd ed. Princeton: Princeton University Press, 1969 |
| AnSt | *Anatolian Studies* |
| AOAT | Alter Orient und Altes Testament |
| BA | *Biblical Archaeologist* |
| BAR | *Biblical Archaeology Review* |
| BASOR | *Bulletin of the American Schools of Oriental Research* |
| BDB | Brown, Francis, S. R. Driver, and Charles A. Briggs. *A Hebrew and English Lexicon of the Old Testament.* Oxford: Clarendon, 1966 |

| | | |
|---|---|---|
| BETL | Bibliotheca ephemeridum theologicarum lovaniensium |
| *Bib* | *Biblica* |
| BibOr | Biblica et orientalia |
| BJS | Brown Judaic Studies |
| *BK* | *Bibel und Kirche* |
| BKAT | Biblischer Kommentar: Altes Testament |
| *BSac* | *Bibliotheca Sacra* |
| *BT* | *The Bible Translator* |
| *BTB* | *Biblical Theology Bulletin* |
| BZAW | Beihefte zur Zeitschrift für altestamentliche Wissenschaft |
| CBC | Cambridge Bible Commentary |
| *CBQ* | *Catholic Biblical Quarterly* |
| ConBNT | Coniectanea biblica: New Testament Series |
| ConBOT | Coniectanea biblica: Old Testament Series |
| CRINT | Compendia rerum Iudaicarum ad Novum Testamentum |
| DJD | Discoveries in the Judaean Desert |
| DMOA | Documenta et monumenta Orientis antiqui |
| EBib | Études bibliques |
| EdF | Erträge der Forschung |
| *ETL* | *Ephemerides theologicae lovanienses* |
| *EQ* | *Evangelical Quarterly* |
| FRLANT | Forschungen zur Religion und Literatur des Alten und Neuen Testaments |
| GBS | Guides to Biblical Scholarship |
| *HR* | *History of Religions* |
| HSM | Harvard Semitic Monographs |
| HThKAT | Herders theologischer Kommentar zum Alten Testament |
| *HTR* | *Harvard Theological Review* |
| *HUCA* | *Hebrew Union College Annual* |
| IBC | Interpretation: A Bible Commentary for Teaching and Preaching |
| ICC | International Critical Commentary |

| | |
|---|---|
| *IDB* | *The Interpreter's Dictionary of the Bible*. 4 vols. Edited by George Buttrick. Nashville: Abingdon, 1962 |
| *IEJ* | *Israel Exploration Journal* |
| ISBE | *International Standard Bible Encyclopedia* |
| JAAR | *Journal of the American Academy of Religion* |
| JANES | *Journal of the Ancient Near Eastern Society* |
| JAOS | *Journal of the American Oriental Society* |
| JBL | *Journal of Biblical Literature* |
| JCS | *Journal of Cuneiform Studies* |
| JETS | *Journal of the Evangelical Theological Society* |
| JHNES | Johns Hopkins Near Eastern Studies |
| JHS | *Journal of Hellenic Studies* |
| JJS | *Journal of Jewish Studies* |
| JJT | *Josephinum Journal of Theology* |
| JNSL | *Journal of Northwest Semitic Languages* |
| JQR | *Jewish Quarterly Review* |
| JR | *Journal of Religion* |
| JRAS | *Journal of the Royal Asiatic Society* |
| JSOT | *Journal for the Study of the Old Testament* |
| JSOTSup | Journal for the Study of the Old Testament Supplemental Series |
| KAT | Kommentar zum Alten Testament |
| LAPO | Littératures anciennes du Proche-Orient |
| LCL | Loeb Classical Library |
| *NABU* | *Nouvelles assyriologiques brèves et utilitaires* |
| NCB | New Century Bible |
| NEchtB | Neue Echter Bibel |
| NICOT | New International Commentary on the Old Testament |
| OBO | Orbis Biblicus et Orientalis |
| OIP | Oriental Institute Publications |
| OLA | Orientalia lovaniensia analecta |
| *OTE* | *Old Testament Essays* |
| OTL | Old Testament Library |
| OtSt | Oudtestamentische Studiën |

| | |
|---|---|
| PSB | *Princeton Seminary Bulletin* |
| RA | *Revue d'assyriologie et d'archéologie orientale* |
| RBL | *Review of Biblical Literature* |
| SBL | Society of Biblical Literature |
| SBLABS | Society of Biblical Literature Archaeology and Biblical Studies |
| SBLDS | Society of Biblical Literature Dissertation Series |
| SBLSMS | Society of Biblical Literature Scholarly Monograph Series |
| SBLSymS | Society of Biblical Literature Symposium Series |
| SBLWAW | Society of Biblical Literature Writngs from the Ancient World |
| SBT | Studies in Biblical Theology |
| ScEs | *Science et Esprit* |
| SEÅ | *Svensk exegetisk årsbok* |
| SJT | *Scottish Journal of Theology* |
| SNTSMS | Society for New Testament Studies Monograph Series |
| SQAW | Schriften und Quellen der alten Welt |
| SSN | Studia semitica neerlandica |
| TCL | Textes Cunéiformes: Musée du Louvre |
| TSAJ | Texte und Studien zum antiken Judentum = Texts and Studies in Ancient Judaism |
| TSJTSA | *Texts and Studies of the Jewish Theological Seminary of America* |
| UF | *Ugarit-Forschungen* |
| USQR | *Union Seminary Quarterly Review* |
| VT | *Vetus Testamentum* |
| VTSup | Supplements to Vetus Testamentum |
| WBC | World Biblical Commentary |
| ZAW | *Zeitschrift für altestamentliche Wissenschaft* |
| ZDMG | *Zeitschrift der Deutschen Morgenländischen Gesellschaft* |

# 1

# The Divine Designations in Biblical Texts
## *Towards a Hermeneutical Model*

### Máire Byrne

St. Patrick's College, Maynooth

### INTRODUCTION

CONSIDER THE SUITABILITY OF using the divine designations that are so prevalent in the Hebrew Bible as a *hermeneutical key* to reading the biblical text. A hermeneutical "key" may be defined here as a means of approach to the biblical text which seeks to "unlock" or understand the text on several levels—for example, grammatically—through exegesis, in a spiritual or historical sense, and on a theological level. Hermeneutics is here understood in the modern sense as the method or art of understanding a piece of written text and interpreting it for a particular audience.

Friedrich Schleiermacher's insistence on the dual aspects of a general hermeneutical theory must be included in the task of formulating a method of approach to the biblical texts.[1] Firstly, there is the grammatical sense of the Hebrew designations and the reader's grasp of the linguistic conventions that are associated with them. Secondly, there is the technical (or psychological) interpretation of the text, namely the comprehension of the overall meaning of the text by its reader, in this case enhanced by a deeper understanding of the divine designations.

---

1. Palmer, *Hermeneutics*, 84–97.

A hermeneutical key is therefore a method of interpretation of a biblical text which attempts to "unlock" that text by seeking to understand the mechanics in a grammatical, linguistic, or stylistic sense. The method would also attempt to interpret the text (normally through exegesis) in its original historical and religious context as well as in the contemporary circumstances of a faith-based community or belief system. The divine designations are ideally suitable to incorporation into this method because the majority of societies in modern and historical situations have placed an emphasis on names and naming. The possibility that this method can be used to speak to people across temporal and religious divides will, therefore, be significant.

The primary stage in this investigation is that of names and naming, including the human perspective of naming and some more complex issues involving the use of names that have been raised by the philosophical approach to language. Continuing in this framework is a focus on the work of Tryggve Mettinger, which has raised some interesting questions with regard to the historical development of Israel's religious institutions and theology with respect to the naming of God in Israelite religious texts.

## THE IMPORTANCE OF NAMES AND NAMING

The question of the importance of names, especially in relation to biblical names, is a complex one. In our everyday lives, names are such an integral part of our thinking and, more vitally, our communication with each other, that their use—much less their importance—is barely noticed. It is essential at the outset to closely examine the human process of allocating names to others—and how these names are used to communicate. Naturally, one must assume the criticism that how humans name each other is entirely different from how they name the divine. In response to this, it may be argued that the divine names are fundamentally an extension of how humans use names, as they are primarily used in a literary context and to communicate an idea of the divine from human to human. The thinking behind the names given to a divine entity is similar, if not identical, to that behind mundane names used in everyday communication.

When linguist A. P. Cohen highlights the "very different kinds of significance which naming has in different societies and cultures," this must be taken as a caution regarding the complexity in a study of names and naming, whether in the purely earthly realm or with divine names.[2] Even within one society, the process of naming can differ between small groups, such as families—or temporally, between generations. A simple modern illustration of this is the common practice in many Western societies of naming a child after a parent or grandparent. Irish families tend to name a first-born child after a parent; in particular, a boy is often given the first name of his father or his grandfather. In America, the practice of giving a male child the identical name to his father is commonplace, with the distinction made between the two by calling the father "senior" and the son "junior." Arab fathers, on the other hand, take the name of their first child with the prefix "the father of . . ." or "*Abu-*."

Placed in a wider cultural realm, there are wide variations to these practices. For example, the custom of firstborn sons taking their father's first name as a memorial name and using it as their first name upon his death is not confined to a particular religion or society. The process of naming therefore must be acknowledged as an inherently complex one that requires a certain degree of anthropological and sociological understanding in order to fully comprehend the possibilities of its communications. We see that even in biblical times there was contact with foreign cultures that could influence names and naming.

Ward Goodenough concludes in his study of names and naming that names communicate ideas of the self and of self-other relationships.[3] His work examines the customary practice in anthropology of naming and identity. This is the assumption of an isomorphism (the identity of form and of operations between two or more groups) between the conclusion of a particular anthropological reading and the means by which they gave meaning to their experience of being named. Therefore, if naming is a way of asserting and maintaining control of something, then it follows that any study of naming has tended to be an illustration of the controlling ways in which people have produced images and cultures from their own thinking—and from this have developed a sense of "selves."

## NAMING—THE HUMAN PERSPECTIVE

The idea of human names is sociologically and anthropologically universal. Names are normally seen as a proper noun, or a word or phrase "con-

2. Cohen, "Naming."
3. Goodenough, "Personal Names and Modes of Address," 275.

stituting the individual designation by which a particular person or thing is known, referred to, or addressed."[4] A *common name* is a name for a plant or animal in the native language of its environment, often describing the item's appearance. For example, *daisy* may describe several unrelated plants with small white flowers in different parts of the world. There are millions of possible objects that can be described in science—too many to create common names for every one. A *personal name* is a proper name attached to a person, such as a given name or a family name. *Identifier* is another term for *name*, used in technical terminology, and generally refers to a name that is unique within a certain namespace. Fredrick Mathewson Denny defines the phenomenon of naming very precisely as being "central to human symbolic and communicative processes. To be human is to name, and to be named, and thereby to possess full being and the ability to relate to the world in meaningful ways."[5]

### *Philosophical Approach to Names*

Proper names operate in a similar way to common nouns in many natural languages (or a person's native language). Philosophers have thus often treated the two as similar in meaning. In the late nineteenth century, the mathematical philosopher Gottlob Frege contended that several perplexing features of both names and nouns could be resolved if the two aspects to the meaning of a name (and, by extension, other nouns) were recognized.[6] The first feature is a "sense," which is equivalent to some sort of description, and the second is a "referent." Frege does not give a precise characterization of the category of "proper names."[7] Rather, in keeping with the idea of "sense," the sense of *dog* might be "domestic canine mammal," and the referent would be all the dogs in this world. Proper names would then be special cases of nouns with only one referent: the sense of *Aristotle* might be, "the author of *de Caelo*," while its referent would be the one person, Aristotle himself.

Bertrand Russell rejected Frege's thinking and instead maintained that "true" names must never be equivalent to a description.[8] Nonetheless,

---

4. *Oxford English Dictionary*, Online Edition, s.v. "Name" (http://www.oed.com/).
5. Denny, "Names and Naming."
6. Sluga, *Gottlob Frege*, 159.
7. Dummett, *Frege*, 54.
8. Beany, "Russell and Frege," 166.

he accepted that most of the "names" in English were actually correspondent to descriptions, particularly definite descriptions or descriptions that only apply to one object. If any real names existed, they were almost certainly more like "this" and "that." This belief is more practically interpreted as the observation that there are two different functions nouns can serve, namely describing (and perhaps indirectly referring) and referring (directly, without description), and that all or almost all names in the English language really do the former. This position came to be known as "Descriptivism" with respect to singular terms, and was prominent through much of twentieth-century analytic philosophy.

Ludwig Wittgenstein, in his *Philosophical Investigations*, sets out his theory of language, namely, that language provides a way of coping with what one might call "everyday purposes," and it works well within that context. However, when everyday language attempts to explain something beyond what it is capable of, problems tend to arise. Primarily, this is what is known as the "say/show distinction": that which can be said can also be shown, but there is that which can only be shown, not said. In other words, that which can only be shown "we must pass over in silence." At the core of Wittgenstein's philosophy, for this work at least, is the idea that "the individual words in language name objects—sentences are combinations of such names. . . . In this picture of language we find the roots of the following idea: Every word has a meaning. This meaning is correlated with the word. It is the object for which the word stands."[9]

Essentially, what Wittgenstein wishes to emphasize is that one may associate the use of a word with the word's referring to an object, but the kind of reference is already agreed.[10] He also reiterates throughout his work the connection between the reference of a name and its bearer. When the bearer of a personal proper name dies, the name does not lose its reference. This has repercussions for the biblical—and indeed the modern—practice of memorial names, where a person takes or gives a name in remembrance of someone who has died. The name lives on.

In 1970, Saul Kripke gave a series of lectures arguing against Descriptivism or "private language," and maintaining, among other things, that names are inflexible designators or expressions that refer

---

9. Wittgenstein, *Philosophical Investigations*, 2e.
10. Kerr, *Theology after Wittgenstein*, 70.

to their objects independently of any properties those objects have.[11] Unquestionably, descriptions are often used to select references, to explain to others what object is being talked about, by reference to some property or characteristic that both parties agree it has, but it does not follow that any of these characteristics represent the meaning of the name. Kripke's work led to the development of various versions of the causal theory of reference, which in various forms, claims that our words mean what they do, not because of descriptions that are associated with them, but because of the causal history of our acquisition of that name in our vocabulary.

### A Christian Approach

A more recent philosophical report on the use of divine names in the particular setting of Christian dialogue is useful to introduce at this point. Carlo Huber follows the lines of the philosophical methods known in linguistic analysis and phenomenology to address the theological problem of "the meaningfulness and reasonability of that which Christians say about God."[12] Huber identifies "three distinct linguistic levels: the human, the religious, the Christian."[13] The human level refers to the significance for the lay community, the religious level has consequences for the transcendent significance, and finally there is significance that is particular to the Christian experience.

Huber's work is essential here as it is yet another layer of context that must be recognized when analyzing the divine designations. This designation is one that is present outside of the text itself and is more correctly connected with the reader and the reader's response to the text as well as the meaning of designation for a wider community. With the level of the "lay" significance, Huber highlights how the religious meaning is only indirectly introduced into human language.[14] He discusses an important point that must be included in this study, namely that there are negative as well as positive implications. This is relevant in particular with familial terms such as *father*, but may also hold true for expressions such as *king* or *judge*.

---

11. Kripke, *Wittgenstein on Rules and Private Language*, 1.
12. Huber, *Speaking of God*, 1.
13. Ibid., 57.
14. Ibid., 59.

In relation to the religious transcendent meaning, Huber stresses that "the meaning of a phrase to be used in speaking about God must be capable of being gradually stretched to infinity."[15] In this instance, infinity is a sense of the everlasting property of the name, and the name cannot be taken away once it is designated. It also signifies the fact that the name designates an absolute. If God is termed the father, for example, he is *the* father, above all others.

In terms of the attributes of God, Huber intends them to be seen in "a logical sense . . . as any *predicate* (function) that can be united with the subject 'God.'"[16] Huber also emphasizes the need to use our own human language when we speak of God. These words already have a meaning, through their everyday use. Huber calls the change that they undergo when used as a designation for God "specific shading," and ultimately the "*non-religious significance* of a word constitutes the *model* for its use in speaking about God."[17] The terms used for God must have three characteristics:

- A *positive* connotation, by which Huber means that it must express a meaning of a moral, social, or economic order. Terms that are not positive must be in the negative, expressed simply. They should be of the form "God is not evil."
- "A horizontally analogical meaning" at the human or "lay" level of significance, where only expressions that can be used analogically in dialogue that is not religious can be used as designations for God.
- Graduations of significance already existing at the level of human use. This is associated with the notion that the meaning of the word must be able to exist and be comprehended for all time.[18]

### The Function of a Name

A human name essentially has two functions in Western culture. The first is to distinguish one person from another. Shakespeare famously wrote: "What's in a name? That which we call a rose/ By any other word would

15. Ibid., 60.
16. Ibid., 49.
17. Ibid., 50.
18. Ibid.

smell as sweet." In the West, names have no connection with meaning, so that if each human were given a number, this number would serve the same purpose as a name—to tell us apart from one another and, in terms of oral communication, to signify ourselves as an entity to others. The second function of the name has the opposite task from distinguishing ourselves from others, that is, to form an association with a familial group or a community or a lineage. A clear example of this is in northern European languages where the patronymic was indicated by adding the father's given name to -*son* and -*dotter* in Sweden, -*son* and -*datter* in Danish and Norwegian. The importance of this association can be seen in the tradition of females taking their husband's family name on marriage as a designation of joining a new family unit.

Linguistic scholars who have studied proper names usually emphasize that such names have referential, denotative meaning, but no connotative meaning. In the circle of people we are familiar with, we know who is meant by *Mary* or *Peter* as the names have a reference value. We also know who *Mr. Smith*, *The Minister for Foreign Affairs*, and *the President* are if our communicative context is taken into account. For example, George Bush would be "the President" if we were American, or if one were a newscaster reading a piece on American politics. To change the context is to shift the referential meaning of a name. This simple example is well worth keeping in mind when the biblical texts are examined. The context from which the text is taken needs to be appreciated, otherwise we run the risk of failing to deduce the meaning of the name—either deducing incorrectly or failing to realize it at all.

Ordinarily, there is no special significance placed on the names themselves. Some may choose to name their children after a family member or a person they admire. Some may choose to create their own name, usually by altering the spelling of an existing name or amalgamating two or even three names. The names themselves are very rarely significant in themselves; the referent makes them important. Only those who study onomastics or etymology would have an interest in the word that is the signifier.

It is worth noting that in Hebrew, the situation is changed somewhat and there is one more characteristic of a name—that is, a name may denote some feature considered fundamental to what is designated. For example, the root meaning of a given Hebrew word is often apparent, no matter how the word is inflected. Therefore, in the majority of cases,

Israelite proper names were fully comprehensible to the Israelites. In the ancient world in general, a name "was not merely a convenient collocation of sounds by which a person, place or thing could be identified; rather a name expressed something of the very essence of that which was being named."[19]

Moreover, names included more than simple reference content. Normally, these names would have had a connotative meaning, and it is easy to divide them into their linguistic component parts and, as a result, to settle on their meaning. *Isaiah*, for example, would have been fully understandable to Israelites as "the Lord saves." This also applies to Hebrew divine names. The result of this is that any attempt to determine their linguistic derivation and etymology is well founded and allows for a thorough examination of the name. Furthermore, it is a logical belief that the etymology of a divine name would have had clear associative potential for the people of Israel and would be necessary in disclosing the true essence of the person to whom the name referred.

## *Names and Naming in a Biblical Context*

There has been a considerable amount of written work based on the significance of names and naming in the Bible, and in the Hebrew Bible in particular. As Wesley Fuerst prompts the reader, it is important to remember that, "how Israel conceived of and addressed God, and how God was conceived of and addressed in the Hebrew Bible, are two quite distinct questions."[20] Discerning the meanings of names in the Bible, much like counting them, is difficult. The meanings of names are sometimes doubtful or contested. Occasionally the text itself provides more than one meaning for a name. Alternately, more often, no meaning at all is provided, forcing us to depend on our knowledge of biblical languages, as well as their cognates, for derivation of a name's meaning. In addition, a certain name may have originally had a specific allusion attached to it that is now lost, or it may have had none at all.

Given these difficulties, caution must be taken in examining the names in the biblical context. Although precise details cannot always be provided, general patterns and trends can be identified with some conviction. In general, it is seen that "in biblical thought a name is not a mere

---

19. Bohmbach, "Names and Naming," 944.
20. Fuerst, "How Israel Conceived of and Addressed God," 61.

label of identification."[21] Names "often carry enormous significance, being inextricably connected to the very nature of that which is named. Hence, to know the name is to know something of the fundamental traits, nature or destiny of the name's bearer."[22]

With so much importance placed on the giving of a name, the study of onomastics, the science of names, should be discussed at this point. This branch of social science covers a wide range of names such as personal, place, brand, pet, yacht, and team. Within the Bible, onomastics, though it is rarely termed as such, concentrates on place names, personal names (both given and family names), and the divine designations. Through this research, a vast amount of work on the science of onomastics can be found, but very little on this discipline actually is applied as such to the Bible, much less the Hebrew Bible.

There is a consensus among onomatologists that proper names can be derived, both semantically and morphologically, from an appellative (or common noun) or some other "per-individualizing" ground form.[23] Initially, the proper name and the ground form from which it is derived are homophones. The range of their use, however, is markedly different. Any appellative has both a content and an area of employment. The more precise the semantic content of the word, the more reserved its use is. Since a proper name has an exceedingly rich content, its range of applicability is reduced to a minimum.

In English, names are usually associated with nouns, both common and proper. A common noun is one that does not state the name of a specific person, place, or thing. In English, a common noun begins with a lower-case letter. These nouns are sometimes termed substantive. A proper noun is one that states the name of a specific person, place, or thing. In English, this type of noun is capitalized. Nouns generally have the same function in Biblical Hebrew as they do in English. Since capitalization is not a phenomenon in Biblical Hebrew, common and proper nouns are not distinguished in writing. This is relatively simple, and there is little argument over those names or titles that are designated by a noun. Those titles that are formed using an adjective or a verb usually cause disagreement among commentators and as such deserve significant consideration.

---

21. Abba, "Name," 500.
22. Bohmbach, "Names and Naming in the Biblical World."
23. Layton, *Archaic Features of Canaanite Personal Names*, 1.

An important point, on which many commentators do not focus, is that if the name of a person or deity is known, they may be summoned or "invoked." In this context, if awareness of the name indicates a level of influence over the person, then the person's name also has corresponding effect and can be used both for good as well as evil objectives. John Sawyer also notes, "There is often a perceived connection between bearing a name and existing."[24] He refers to the ancient Sumerian creation epic *Enuma elish*, in particular the opening words of the first tablet: "When on high the heaven had not been named, Firm ground below has not been called by name."[25] He sees the term *named* as representing the creation of the heavens and the earth. Sawyer infers that the process of naming, especially in terms of naming newborns and children, ensures "their very existence as well as their identity."[26]

## NAMING THE DIVINE

The exercise of examining the divine designations is naturally quite complex, though not as difficult as commentators such as Herbert Chanan Brichto might presume. Brichto sees the "problem" of examining the names as "so complex that movements toward the solution may be impeded, distorted, or even blocked by its formulation in the singular."[27] Admittedly, the task is large, as both literal and metaphorical terminology is dealt with.[28] In the Hebrew Bible, as well as in other traditions, the name of the deity is believed to have special significance. Firstly, it is important to remember in relation to the name of God that the people of Israel probably "did not think in any fundamentally different way than in respect to *human* personal names."[29] A second point to take into account is that the Israelites would have been heavily influenced by neighboring cultures and societies as well as by other religions in how they chose names to designate their deity.

---

24. Sawyer, "Names: Religious Beliefs."
25. Speiser, "The Creation Epic," 61.
26. Sawyer, "Names: Religious Beliefs."
27. Brichto, *The Names of God*, 3.
28. Gabel et al., *The Bible as Literature*, 313.
29. Rose, "Names of God in the Old Testament," 1002 (emphasis original).

Martin Rose highlights how Israel's God could be referred to by using a number of "names, titles, and epithets in the Hebrew Bible."[30] Some of the designations are used in both the generic and specific sense. Others are used only as the personal name for Israel's God. Most of these terms were also used by the Canaanites in reference to their pagan gods. This is not surprising as the early Israelites "spoke the language of Canaan" (Isa 19:18). The designations are significant as indicators of the developments in the course of Israel's religious history and as expressions of concepts of the divine held by the ancient Israelites.

Othmar Keel describes how these early Israelites would have also borrowed from surrounding cultures their "conceptions of the cosmic system, the institutions of temple and kingship, and numerous cultic forms."[31] Keel is keen to point out that, even though the Israelites would naturally have put their own stamp on these traditionally held views and would have adapted them for their own language and religious viewpoints, the Israelites would have had their own experiences and, consequently, their own concepts of God that they would have brought to this new setting.

### *Limits of Language*

"Nothing in the world—no kin, no animal (bull!), no constellation of stars—can adequately embody Yahweh."[32] Repeatedly the texts of the Hebrew Bible raise objections to any ideas that God can fully be comprehended through images of him as father, king, judge, etc. The Hebrew Bible is a collection of texts that are written by humans for communication to humans. The texts may be inspired, but that does not diminish the limitations that humans will have in expressing their thinking and representations of the divine. Describing God is similar to recounting a color to a blind person. Other senses can be elaborated on; *green* may be associated with the feel and taste of fresh shoots, but it cannot be described accurately, as it is a concept that is unique to each person and a result of their lived experience.

Humans have limits in the use of language in describing something that is not physically concrete and not visually experienced. No human possesses anything that could be remotely seen as a universal language,

---

30. Ibid., 1001.
31. Keel, *The Symbolism of the Biblical World*, 178.
32. Ibid.

and even within our own language, we have a limited vocabulary and are technically inadequate in our use of this vocabulary. For example, the poet Seamus Heaney may have more success in describing the color green than someone else, but the description and explanation would still be specific to him and his experience. How would a Bedouin tribesman who lived a nomadic life in a desert describe green? The same difficulty would be present in a writer who lived in a republic with a democratically elected government describing his god as a king. It is also true that humans "have the unwitting conviction that if something is there, we should see it, that if something is explained, we should understand it."[33] It follows, inversely, that if something cannot be understood, then its significance tends to be diminished.

### Anthropomorphism

This limitation of language gives rise to the problem of anthropomorphism, applying to God the meaning of words as they apply to us, as we are the only beings of whom we have firsthand knowledge. This is trying to understand God as if God were patterned on us rather than the other way around. Nonetheless, we *are* made in the image of God, as Gen 1:27 states "so God created humankind in his image, in the image of God he created them; male and female he created them." In the same way as we can find out something about the artist by looking at that artist's work, by understanding the essence of humanity, we can try to form a clearer idea of God. God is, therefore, not anthropomorphic; rather, as human beings, we are theomorphic. When we consider the elements in human nature that make us distinct from animals, then we can begin to develop a remote insight into God. In fact, the Hebrew Bible never speaks of God without attributing human traits to him. Additionally, there is scarcely any anthropomorphism in the Hebrew Bible that cannot be paralleled in other Semitic literature, as the gods of other ancient Semitic groups were personifications of natural forces or social realities to which human features and behavior were attributed.

Edwin Yamauchi investigates the contrasting concepts of deity that are visible in the Hebrew Bible through use of anthropomorphisms. He uses an examination of mainly pagan religions, in particular Egyptian, to illustrate his argument, and his work provides a good insight into how

---

33. O'Malley, *God: The Oldest Question*, 13.

"foreign" worship would have influenced the authors of the texts of the Hebrew Bible, particularly with respect to designations that would indicate a monotheistic belief.[34] This is important as "the epithets which the Egyptians applied to their gods also bear valuable testimony concerning the ideas which they [the Egyptians] held about God."[35]

## CATEGORIZING THE DESIGNATIONS

In order to systematically study the use and distribution of divine designations in the Hebrew Bible, it is necessary to comprehensively categorize the designations that have been located in a particular text under three headings: name, title, and epithet. This is essential. A systematic study of designations cannot be conducted without identifying which heading they come under, as each category will have its own theological implications as well as a different approach in terms of etymological and grammatical analysis. The insistence on this cataloging also comes from the fact that many discussions and surveys of the divine designations do not succeed in communicating a successful argument—as a direct result of ambiguity with regard to defining to which appellations they refer in their study. Often there are examples of arbitrary usage of the terminology, and some commentators switch back and forth between the categories, for example, referring to "Yahweh Sabaoth" as a name for Yahweh in one section and a title in another. Many even switch intermittently between the three classifications even when talking about divine designations in general. Having previously discussed the implications of the term *name*, it is now necessary to explore the grammatical and historical uses of *title* and *epithet*.

### Title

In modern societies a title is normally viewed as a formal appellation in the form of a prefix or suffix to the name of a person or family by virtue of their office, rank, hereditary privilege, noble birth, or attainment. It is usually seen as a mark of respect, and the list of titles present in different historical periods and societies is extensive. To give a short example in current usage, titles for a head of state can be divided into those for appointed heads of state, those elected or popularly proclaimed (chair-

---

34. Yamauchi, "Anthropomorphism in Ancient Religions," 34.
35. Budge, *Egyptian Religion*, 17.

person, colonel, pope, regent), and those that are inherited (chief, duke, emperor, king, and prince).

It is noteworthy that there is varied usage of these titles with the person's name. For example, the president of a country is usually given their title in conjunction with their family name. Modern monarchical systems work with the title and the person's first (given) name. This classification goes against the grain of the usual use of the family name, as monarchies are based on an inherited position and, therefore, the family name is taken as given, as in the Windsor family of Great Britain. In relation to what this example can bring to the examination of divine titles, it makes any examination and definition of the titles more straightforward.

## Epithet

An epithet (from the Greek ἐπίθετος and Latin *epitheton*, literally meaning "imposed") is a descriptive word or phrase. It has various degrees of meaning when applied to linguistics and religion.

In linguistics, an epithet is often metaphoric, essentially a reduced or condensed appositive. Epithets are sometimes attached to a person's name, as what might be described as a glorified nickname. Not every adjective is an epithet—not even worn clichés. An epithet is linked to its noun by long-established usage, and some are not otherwise employed. Some epithets are known as *epitheton necessarium* because they are required to distinguish the bearers, for example, an alternative to ordinals after a king's name, such as Richard *the Lionheart*. The same epithet can be used repeatedly, in different spheres of life or joined to different names, a common example being *the Great* in *Alexander the Great* and *Catherine the Great*. Other epithets, *epitheton ornans* can easily be omitted without serious risk of confusion. Thus Virgil systematically called the arms-bearer of Aeneas, his principal hero, *fidus Achates*—the epithet being *fidus*, which means loyal or faithful.

In ancient pagan religions—for example, Greek, Roman, and Egyptian—a deity's epithet (or rather each one, as the principal gods often had many) generally reflected a particular aspect of that god's myth and role. For example, Apollo *Musagetes* is "Apollo, [as] leader of the Muses," and therefore patron of the arts and sciences, while *Phoebos* Apollo is the same deity, but as a sun god. The epithet may also identify a particular and localized aspect of the god, such as a reference to the mythological place of birth or another origin. It often appears to refer simply to a main center of worship and possibly some cultic tradition there, but often this is actually the result of an intercultural equation of a divinity with another one who is usually older. Therefore, most Roman gods and goddesses, especially the twelve principal gods, had traditional counterparts in Greek, Etruscan, and most other Mediterranean pantheons. For example, Jupiter, as father of the Olympian gods, is identified with Zeus, but in specific cult places there may even be a different equation, based on one specific aspect of the divinity.

## TRYGGVE METTINGER

Mettinger is the Professor Emeritus of Old Testament at Lund Universitet and is one of the few scholars to place any great emphasis on a systematic study of the divine designations. He primarily looks at the designations within both their biblical and extra-biblical contexts, not merely in one particular text. While his focus principally rests on the contribution to "name theology,"[36] his work is important in this piece as it allows a prototype of how the designations may be successfully studied (once the emphasis is placed on the particular context), and how this study can bring a meaningful contribution to the study of a theology.

The idea of contextualized study is a prevailing theme through much of Mettinger's work on the divine designations, not only in the medium of the biblical text but on external influences, such as historical and cultural settings. For example, in terms of the book of Isaiah, Mettinger has focused his work on this text predominantly on the subject of the Servant Songs,[37] though of course he does refer to the text in other works, particularly in his work on Yahweh as King in Deutero-Isaiah.[38]

In this latter work, he examines the idea of a text (such as 52:7–10) being a part of a "macro-context."[39] By examination of the designation

---

36. The theory of "name theology" originated with Von Rad, *Studies in Deuteronomy*, 33–44. Von Rad suggests an evolutionary development, whereby material presence of Yahweh was replaced by a more sophisticated tendency toward hypostasis for all these concepts: the ark, the angel of the Lord, the face of the Lord, the glory and name of God are presented as representations and pledges of Yahweh's presence. A modern study is Richter, *The Deuteronomistic History*.

37. Mettinger, *A Farewell to the Servant Songs*.

38. Mettinger, "In Search of the Hidden Structure."

39. Ibid., 145.

king, not just in its immediate context, but in the context of the immediate text, a fuller understanding of the term may be determined. This is a useful lesson to eventually take to a more focused look at a particular text of the Hebrew Bible. Two of Mettinger's principal works will now be examined with a view to locating a model of hermeneutical approach to the divine designations in a biblical text.

### The Dethronement of Sabaoth

The principal issue addressed by Mettinger in *The Dethronement of Sabaoth: Studies in the Shem and Kabod Theologies* is why the term *Yahweh Sabaoth*, which was the principal divine designation used in the temple theology of the Jerusalem cult tradition, was substituted in the deuteronomistic and priestly materials and in the book of Ezekiel by the *shem* and *kabod* theologies respectively. Mettinger surmises that this "dethronement" or substitution was the result of "cognitive dissonance"[40] that was created by the circumstances affecting the exiles, where the idea of the enthronement of Yahweh in the temple was no longer a satisfactory one.

Mettinger focuses on an overview of the Zion-Sabaoth theology of the Jerusalem cult tradition with the fundamental theory of the enthroned God and his actual presence in the temple. He associates the cultic symbols of the cherubim (whose wings made Yahweh a throne) and the ark (his footstool) with the "original and complete title," or the essential term for the divine presence. Mettinger also asserts that "the enthroned king and the coming God" were originally, "two diametrically apposed aspects of God," but that they were combined into "a *complementary*, rather than a contradictory, relationship" with the temple theology and consequently "are by no means to be played off against each other."[41]

Mettinger goes on to discuss the "name theology" of the Deuteronomistic School, and the *kabod* theology of the Priestly source and of Ezekiel. He reviews the biblical name formulae and preceding critical work of von Rad and van der Woude, among others, asserting that there is a systematic "name theology" in the deuteronomistic history, which is a determined amendment to the Zion-Sabaoth theology. The Deuteronomist is conceptual in comparison to other biblical writers, emphasizing the

---

40. Mettinger, *The Dethronement of Sabaoth*.
41. Ibid., 36 (emphasis original).

transcendence of Yahweh.[42] The Deuteronomistic version of the ark and the cherubim represents a "conscious suppression of the notion of the God who sat enthroned in the Temple."[43]

Mettinger uses the texts of 1 Kgs 8:14–66 and 2 Sam 7:5, 13 as evidence to support his claims. He considers that the development of the name theology occurred after the Babylonian takeover of Jerusalem in 597 BCE[44] and that there is no evidence for a pre-exilic name theology in Jer 62–66. Proposals are also made that the "dethronement of Sabaoth" as articulated in the name theology is also echoed liturgically, in the change in prominence from the autumn festival to Passover that occurred during the Josianic era. The move represents a swing from the mythical concept of divine kingship (*Chaos kampf* and creation) to one of *Heilsgeschichte* (exodus and the formation of a nation).

Mettinger builds on the "Yahweh Sabaoth—the Heavenly King of the Cherubim Throne" philosophy, or more accurately the term *Sabaoth* which he views as the key indicator of this profound theological shift of ideas in ancient Israel. The *Sabaoth* designation "played an important role during the Davidic-Solomonic era"[45] but is rare in the literature that is concerned with the history of the monarchy, as it is principally associated with the ark traditions. The term is "the pre-eminent term employed in the Jerusalem tradition for the God who dwelt in the Temple ... indeed the key-word in the classical Jerusalemite theology of the Presence."[46]

This specific realization of the divine presence is fundamentally altered in the "programmatically abstract" deuteronomic tradition which "shattered this unitary conception by emphasizing the transcendence of God," so that "God became 'relocated' to the heavens above."[47] In the work of the Deuteronomist, "it is only the Name which 'is' in the Temple, and ... the Temple was constructed 'for the name of the Lord,' and not as a dwelling place for the enthroned God himself."[48]

---

42. Ibid., 46–47.
43. Ibid., 51.
44. Ibid., 61.
45. Ibid., 13.
46. Ibid., 15.
47. Ibid., 46–47.
48. Ibid., 49–50.

## In Search of God

This book is a theological work that builds on Mettinger's previous historical work. The text is not directed to a purely academic audience (for example, there is a glossary of technical words and phrases) but it presents the reader with a thorough argument as to the historical and theological importance of the divine designations in the Old and New Testaments. Its aim is to "offer an exegetical treatment of the most representative divine names, with a view to revealing the underlying theological conceptions."[49] The first half of the book focuses on the importance of names in ancient Israel and in particular the divine name, Yahweh. He moves chronologically from the divine designations in the patriarchal narratives, such as "the god of the fathers," through designations that were created in reaction to the Canaanite religion, such as "the living God." The latter half of the book focuses on the roles of Yahweh, as a king, as the Lord of the Hosts (which Mettinger associates with the term *king*), Redeemer, Savior, and Creator. Prominence is always placed on the dynamic and contextual characteristics of the Hebrew Bible's understanding of God.

Mettinger notes that the ultimate concern of biblical texts is to understand theologically the divine plan. These biblical (con)texts provide the framework for a proper understanding of the divine designations. He observes the clear differences between Yahweh and other deities (such as those of the Canaanite religion). For example, Yahweh does not die and he is not portrayed as having sexual relationships. Mettinger poses the question as to whether this is something that is ingrained in the Israelite religion or whether it is a later development of Israel's understanding of Yahweh.[50] This particular aspect of Mettinger's work is somewhat problematic as he does not appear to compare "like with like,"[51] namely the Canaanite religion was a fertility religion (and therefore sexually charged images of the deity would not be unusual), whereas the Israelite religion was very much a historical one.

Mettinger's work is very important for this study, especially in relation to its historical and archaeological aspects. The book makes use of non-biblical texts and iconographical materials from the ancient Near

---

49. Mettinger, *In Search of God*, xi.
50. Ibid., 122.
51. Mark Smith in his review, 314.

East. Mettinger often makes use of Israel's adaptations of symbols, ideas, and ideologies that were prominent in other contemporary cultures.

### Mettinger's Contribution to the Hermeneutical Model

Mettinger primarily establishes the importance of the divine designations in biblical literature and theology. This is mainly done with a view to the exploration of name theology, but his study validates the theory that the designations may be used as a valid hermeneutical key for an examination of a biblical text. His assertion that it is "a reasonable supposition that the etymology of a divine name held certain associative possibilities for the Israelites"[52] underlines the need for an etymological study to be an inherent part of the hermeneutical model, at least at the groundwork level. Mettinger also allows for a preliminary idea of the importance of studying the divine designations not only in the "macro-context" of the chapters and verses that surround it, but also in the context of the historical, cultural, and political influences that may have been prevalent at the time of writing and redaction.

## CONCLUSION

The use of the divine designations as a hermeneutical key for the exegesis and general study of the Hebrew Bible may only be fully evaluated by applying the methodology to a biblical text, an exercise that may not be attempted here. It may be assumed, however, that any information that may be gained from studying the divine designations, in their etymological and historical contexts, their setting in the context of the Hebrew Bible as a whole, and their position in the religious and cultural world of the ancient Near East, promises to be only beneficial to a study of a text.

With this information to hand, a fuller significance of the text may be uncovered, which is often largely left untreated in previous studies, as the divine designations were not regarded as particularly significant in the text as a whole. This idea of "dimensional influence" of the study may be furthered by the inclusion of the hermeneutical perspective of Mettinger concerning the significance of the divine designations and the structure of the text.

The methodology would seem to seek to avoid the common problem in biblical exegesis of an uneven focus, either on the individual words

---

52. Mettinger, *In Search of God*, 122.

and verses, or on the greater part of the text in question. When the significance of the divine designations is evaluated, both in terms of their impact on the literary style of the text and on the view of God that their use conveys, it may be concluded that the use of the designations brings a new dimension to the study of the text.

## BIBLIOGRAPHY

Abba, Raymond. "Name." In *IDB* 3:500–508.
Beany, Michael. "Russell and Frege." In *The Cambridge Companion to Bertrand Russell*, edited by Nicholas Griffin, 128–70. Cambridge Companions. Cambridge: Cambridge University Press, 2003.
Bohmbach, Karla. "Names and Naming." In *Eerdmans Dictionary of the Bible*, edited by David Noel Freedman et al., 944–46. Grand Rapids: Eerdmans, 2000.
———. "Names and Naming in the Biblical World." In *Women in Scripture: A Dictionary of Named and Unnamed Women in the Hebrew Bible, the Apocryphal/ Deuterocanonical Books, and the New Testament*, edited by Carol Meyers, 33–99. Grand Rapids: Eerdmans, 2001.
Brichto, Herbert Chanan. *The Names of God: Poetic Readings in Biblical Beginnings*. New York: Oxford University Press, 1998.
Budge, Ernest Wallis. *Egyptian Religion: Egyptian Ideas of the Future Life*. New York: Bell, 1975.
Cohen, A. P. "Naming." In *The Encyclopaedia of Language and Linguistics*, edited by Brian Riley, 5:536–42. 12 vols. New Delhi: Cosmo, 2002.
Denny, Frederick Mathewson. "Names and Naming." In *The Encyclopedia of Religion*, edited by Mircea Eliade, 10:300–307. New York: Macmillan, 1987.
Dummett, Michael. *Frege: Philosophy of Language*. London: Duckworth, 1973.
Fuerst, Wesley. "How Israel Conceived of and Addressed God." In *Our Naming of God: Problems and Prospects of God-Talk Today*, edited by Carl Braaten, 54–72. Minneapolis: Fortress, 1989.
Gabel, John et al., editors. *The Bible as Literature: An Introduction*. 4th ed. New York: Oxford University Press, 2000.
Goodenough, Ward. "Personal Names and Modes of Address in Two Oceanic Societies." In *Context and Meaning in Cultural Anthropology*, edited by Melford Spiro, 260–76. New York: Free Press, 1965.
Huber, Carlo. *Speaking of God*. Cultural Heritage and Contemporary Change, Series 1: Culture and Values. Cultural Heritage and Contemporay Change, Series 4: West Europe 4. Washington DC: Council for Research in Values and Philosophy, 2000.
Jenni, Ernst, and Claus Westermann, editors. *Theological Lexicon of the Old Testament*. Translated by Mark Biddle. 3 vols. Peabody, MA: Hendrickson, 1997.
Keel, Othmar. *The Symbolism of the Biblical World: Ancient Near Eastern Iconography and the Book of Psalms*. Translated by Timothy Hallet. New York: Seabury, 1978.
Kerr, Fergus. *Theology after Wittgenstein*. 2nd ed. London: SPCK, 1997.
Kripke, Saul. *Wittgenstein on Rules and Private Language: An Elementary Exposition*. Oxford: Blackwell, 1982.
Layton, Scott. *Archaic Features of Canaanite Personal Names in the Hebrew Bible*. HSM 47. Atlanta: Scholars, 1990.
Mettinger, Tryggve N. D. *The Dethronement of Sabaoth: Studies in the Shem and Kabod Theologies*. ConBOT 18. Lund: Gleerup, 1982.
———. *A Farewell to the Servant Songs: A Critical Examination of an Exegetical Axiom*. Scripta Minora 1982–1983: 3. Lund: Gleerup, 1983.
———. *In Search of God: The Meaning and Message of the Everlasting Names*. Translated by Frederick H. Cryer. Philadelphia: Fortress, 1988.

———. "In Search of the Hidden Structure: YHWH as King in Isaiah 40–55." In *Writing and Reading the Scroll of Isaiah: Studies of an Interpretative Tradition*, edited by Craig Broyles and Craig Evans, 1:143–54. 2 vols. VTSup 70. Formation and Interpretation of Old Testament Literature 1–2. Leiden: Brill, 1997.

———. "In Search of the Hidden Structure: YHWH as King in Isaiah 40–55." *SEÅ* 51–52 (1986–1987) 148–57.

O'Malley, William. *God: The Oldest Question*. Chicago: Loyola, 2000.

Palmer, Richard E. *Hermeneutics: Interpretation Theory in Schleiermacher, Dilthey, Heidegger, and Gadamer*. Northwestern University Studies in Phenomenology & Existential Philosophy. Evanston, IL: Northwestern University Press, 1969.

Pritchard, James B., editor. *Ancient Near Eastern Texts Relating to the Old Testament*. 3rd ed. Princeton: Princeton University Press, 1969.

Rad, Gerhard von. *Studies in Deuteronomy*. Translated by David Stalker. SBT 9. London: SCM, 1961.

Richter, Sandra. *The Deuteronomistic History and the Name Theology: leš akken šēmo šām in the Bible and the Ancient Near East*. BZAW 318. Berlin: de Gruyter, 2002.

Rose, Martin. "Names of God in the Old Testament." In *ABD* 4:1001–11.

Sawyer, John. "Names: Religious Beliefs," In *The Encyclopaedia of Language and Linguistics*, edited by Brian Riley, 5:345–47. 12 vols. New Delhi: Cosmo, 2002.

Sluga, Hans D. *Gottlob Frege*. London: Routledge & Kegan Paul, 1980.

Smith, Mark. Review of Tryggve Mettinger, *In Search of God: The Meaning and Message of the Everlasting Names*. *JBL* 109 (1990) 313–16.

Speiser, E. A., translator. "The Creation Epic." In *ANET*, 60–72. 3rd ed. Princeton: Princeton University Press, 1969.

Wittgenstein, Ludwig. *Philosophical Investigations*. Translated by G. E. M. Anscombe. 2nd ed. Oxford: Blackwell, 1997.

Yamauchi, Edwin. "Anthropomorphism in Ancient Religions." *BSac* 125 (1968) 29–44.

# 2

## Danger at the King's Table

*Insult and Family Conflict at Saul's New Moon Feast*

KILLIAN MCALEESE

Trinity College Dublin

### INTRODUCTION

IN THIS ESSAY IT is argued that engaging with ethnographic material on the role of feasting in traditional societies enhances our understanding of the significance of the events recounted in 1 Sam 20. This is especially evident when the events are considered within the broad context of the narrative describing David's rise and eventual succession to the kingship of Israel.

It is demonstrated here that some of the main roles which ethnographers and archaeologists commonly ascribe to feasting in traditional societies are not only evident in this episode, whose story unfolds around the focus of a feast, but they also emerge as some of the text's most important themes. It is hoped that the preliminary conclusions herein attest to the potential fruitfulness of such interdisciplinary approaches in biblical studies.

Ethnographic and archaeological studies of feasting record a variety of occasions for special food consumption events in different societies. As Wright summarizes, these include "events from birth to death which people choose to celebrate" such as a birth, a wedding, a new house, to honor ancestors, or to announce the New Year.[1]

For our case, we can briefly recount the occasion for Saul's feast described in 1 Sam 20. The cultic calendar of ancient Israel and Judah, like that of much of the ancient Near East over successive periods of time, seems to have been reckoned primarily by a luni-solar system; the solar year of 365¼ days was divided by and reconciled with twelve lunations, or lunar months, of 29 or 30 days in length. The lunar month, along with the week, the year, and the day were, for much of Israel's history, the determinative temporal units in relation to ritual activity. This view is not unanimously agreed upon, but whatever the exact nature of the Israelite and Judaean calendars, and particularly their months, it is the ritual aspect of this repetitive, monthly occasion with which we are concerned.[2]

This paper is concerned with the ritual which occurred variously over the first and second days of each month, referred to in the Hebrew Bible variously as חדש, ראש חדש, and יום החדש.[3] By the Hellenistic period, the timing of this feast corresponded with the return of the crescent moon in the sky after one or two days of invisibility from earth, marking the beginning of each lunar month.[4] It is likely that it was marked by the

---

1. Wright, "Introduction," 5. Wright draws these particular examples from Clarke's study of Akha feasts: "Akha Feasting: An Ethnoarchaeological Perspective."

2. Sacha Stern describes the issue of pre-exilic time reckoning as "extremely controversial" (Stern, *Calendar and Community*, 2). Jaubert presents the hypothesis that the 364-day schematic calendar of Jubilees and Qumran, which is not a lunar calendar, dates to early biblical times. Cf. Jaubert, "Le Calendrier des Jubilés et de la Secte de Qumrân"; Jaubert, *The Date of the Last Supper*. Other scholars, however, argue for a lunar calendar in the monarchic period. Cf. de Vaux, *Ancient Israel: Its Life and Institutions*, 179ff.; Herr, "The Calendar." Jaubert's theories have recently been refuted in Wacholder and Wacholder, "Patterns of Biblical Dates and Qumran's Calendar."

3. חֹדֶשׁ alone is the most common designation. The form רֹאשׁ חֹדֶשׁ appears only twice in the Hebrew Bible (Num 10:10; 28:11); in both cases the plural form is used. The form יוֹם הַחֹדֶשׁ is used in Ezek 46:1, where is it paired with יוֹם הַשַּׁבָּת.

4. Despite evidence for certain contexts in which this was not the case, most notably the Qumran library and the book of Jubilees, the geographical and chronological dispersal of Jewish sources which attest to the practice of sighting the lunar crescent suggests that this had become a normative Jewish practice. See, for example, Ps 104:19; Ben Sira 43:6–8; Philo *Spec*. II 41, 140ff.; Josephus *AJ* III 248; *AJ* IV 78; *1 En*. 73:4; M. Roš. Haš. 1:3ff. Two first-century BCE/CE Jewish inscriptions from Berenike in Cyrenaica also refer to the new moon. Cf. Stern, *Calendar and Community*, 25, 34, 58–61, 120–21. Recently Jan A. Wagenaar has argued that the beginning of the month in pre-exilic Israel and Judah may have reflected the Egyptian custom of reckoning from the first day of

same astronomical event in earlier times. The beginning of the month was observed in the sanctuary, with a ritual gathering, animal sacrifices, and grain and drink offerings (Isa 1:12–14; Num 28:11–14). In this paper, we understand חדש, the days at the beginnings of months, as regularly occurring constellations of rites, or "festivals," pertaining to a large group, on a fixed cycle. This understanding corresponds approximately to what the anthropologist Victor Turner called "calendrical rites," which, in his view, "almost always refer to large groups and quite often embrace whole societies."[5]

## SAUL'S TABLE AT THE NEW MOON

First Samuel 20 differs from the majority of biblical sources for חדש in that its purpose is not specifically to describe or prescribe any aspect of the ritual; it is not a "ritual" text in the sense of being a list of cultic instructions bereft of narrative or significant protagonists. Rather, it is rich in narrative and characters. The events in 1 Sam 20 constitute a turning point in the relationship between David and Saul.[6] The prevailing theme is one of loyalty—specifically, interrupted social reciprocity.

The chapter begins with David's fleeing from Naioth to Jonathan to ask about Saul's anger with him, after two previous attempts by Saul on David's life (1 Sam 18:10; 19:9–10). Unsatisfied with Jonathan's assurances, David devises a plan to test Saul's feelings towards him.[7] The setting is the חדש feast at Saul's table which David, Jonathan, Saul, and Abner (we infer) are expected to attend.

---

the moon's obscuration from earth at the end of its cycle, approximately one or two days before its reappearance as the new crescent. Wagenaar, *Origin and Transformation of the Ancient Israelite Festival Calendar*, 139–46.

5. Turner, *The Ritual Process*, 168–69. The other main group of rites delineated in Turner's work is that of "Life-crisis rites," in which his main interest lies. Ibid. 168. These are similar to what scholars following Van Gennep refer to as "rites of passage." Van Gennep, *The Rites of Passage*. Cf. Gross, "Measurement of Calendrical Information in Food-Taking Behaviour," 222–23. Gross defines three classes of "culturally significant occurrences that precipitate food events": "astronomical and meteorological phenomena, life-cycle phenomena, and reciprocity phenomena."

6. After this episode, according to McCarter, *1 Samuel*, 345, "Saul now knows that David stands in the way of his establishment of a dynasty."

7. The idea of David "testing" Saul is taken up in Philbeck: "1–2 Samuel," 62; cf. Gehrke, *Concorida Commentary*, 166–68, which also refers to a "new moon test."

As part of his plan, David will not attend the meal. He asks leave of Jonathan so that he can hide in a field or open countryside (1 Sam 20:5).[8] Jonathan is to go to the feast and offer Saul a fabricated excuse for David's absence: that he went to Bethlehem for a special family sacrifice (זבח הימים). If Saul is angered and David's life is truly in danger, Jonathan is to give David a sign: a planned signal involving the shooting of three arrows, followed by a coded message.

Likewise a similar but distinct sign is to indicate that David is not in danger from Saul (1 Sam 20:20–23). Two days of feasting are subsequently described. On the first day, Saul remains silent regarding David's absence, but we are told that Saul noticed that David's place was empty and that Saul guessed that this absence was due to some ritual impurity on David's part (1 Sam 20:26). On the second day, however, Saul is angered by David's repeated absence and attempts to strike Jonathan with his spear, supposedly recognizing David as a threat to his dynasty (1 Sam 20:27–33).

### Three Problems with Saul's New Moon Feast

There are three main areas of discrepancy between the basic conclusions which some of the main commentaries on this text have reached regarding the principal event around which the action takes place. 1) There is disagreement as to whether this setting indeed justifies the term *feast*, or was just an ordinary meal. 2) There is some disagreement as to the length of the feast—whether it lasted two or three days. 3) It has also been suggested, inaccurately in my opinion, that women were excluded from this feast. Before introducing some ideas from ethnographic literature, I will briefly address these three discrepancies.

First, are we justified in referring to this event as a feast? According to Dietler and Hayden, the term *feasting* as used with respect to eating and table fellowship implies "special food consumption events."[9] This terminology is useful in the distinction it draws between feasts as special events on the one hand, and everyday subsistence on the other. This view does not deny the social significance of everyday eating, but it does single out feasting for special consideration. To conflate these two categories, in Dietler and Hayden's view, "precludes both understanding feasts as a spe-

---

8. Cf. *BDB* 961. The term שָׂדֶה, in Gen 25:29; 27:3, 5, and, probably also in this context, implies a "hunting ground."

9. This is the terminology used by Dietler and Hayden, in "Digesting the Feast," 3.

cific social practice and understanding the important semiotic and functional relationships between feasts and these other kinds of practices."[10]

H. P. Smith, S. R. Driver, and J. Mauchline, in their respective commentaries on this text, suggest that this episode reflects David's everyday attendance at Saul's table, Mauchline adding that the obligations to Saul's table emerging in this episode apply at all times.[11] This is not a widely held view, however, and many other scholars have not demonstrated the same reluctance to attribute the feast and its obligations to their coincidence with the beginning of the lunar month, thus equating it fully with the new moon festival.[12] There are several features of the episode and its portrayal in 1 Sam 20 which support the latter view.

The author refers to the event in question as חדש five times in the chapter, each time in direct association with this eating event. For example, in verse 24, the narrator tells us (1 Sam 20:24b), ויהי החדש וישב המלך על־הלחם לאכול "When the new moon came, the king sat at the feast to eat."

In verse 5, David says to Jonathan, הנה־חדש מחר "Behold, tomorrow is the new moon." This usage implies that the term should be read here as a reference to the feast of חדש, and *not* to the term's more generic meaning of month, as the phrase, "tomorrow is a month" seems less suitable a translation. This, with the repeated reference to חדש in relation to the event at Saul's table in this chapter, implies that the text refers to a specific occasion for David's presence at Saul's table, not his everyday attendance, pointing to a "special food consumption event," which had special obligations attached to it. There is also evidence for a cultic/sacrificial aspect to this eating event, which would also point away from its being an ordinary or everyday meal: When David fails to appear on the first day, Saul concludes that he was not clean, טהור, and does not pursue the matter further for the rest of that day (1 Sam 20:26). It is only after the first day, when temporary ritual impurity was no longer a viable explanation, that

---

10. Ibid.

11. Smith, *A Critical and Exegetical Commentary*, 187; Driver, *Notes on the Hebrew Text*, 161; Mauchline, *1 and 2 Samuel*, 145. Interestingly, however, Mauchline adds that attendance was compulsory at Saul's table, "especially on a feast day" without developing this evident distinction that he draws (ibid., 145).

12. Cf., for example, Gandz, "Studies in the Hebrew Calendar," 157–72, 251–77; de Vaux, *Ancient Israel*, 179ff.; Alter, *The David Story*, 124.

Saul's anger is kindled. We will return to the cultic aspect of the event presently.

Regarding the second discrepancy, some commentators exhibit uncertainty as to the length of the feast as recounted in 1 Sam 20, variously suggesting that the festivities lasted two or three days. In verse 5, the phrase "until the third evening" עד הערב השלשית has raised complications, with some concluding that this remark implies a three-day aspect to the ritual.[13] This is not suggested in any other source for the feast and is an unnecessary conclusion. The text does not refer to a third day of feasting, or of new moon observance of any kind. Also, the phrase עד הערב השלשית is grammatically problematic, due to an inappropriate gender suffix.

Various resolutions to this grammatical problem have been suggested. Several commentators omit הַשְּׁלִשִׁית altogether, ascribing the term's inclusion to a later glossator, anticipating the subsequent narrative, which indeed proceeds to refer to a third evening.[14] Robert Alter, on the other hand, suggests an amendment to text, from "*ha'erev hashelishit*" to "*'erev hashleshit*."[15] The sequence of events in the chapter, in any case, nowhere implies that the feast itself lasted three days, and any conclusion that this was the case should certainly not be based on this text. Indeed, to the current author's knowledge, there are no biblical, Israelite, Judahite, or later sources at all which suggest that חדש lasted more than two days.

Now that we have ruled out a third day of feasting, clear evidence for a *second* day should be acknowledged. As we have seen, the events of this episode between David and Saul depend on a second day of feasting, and necessarily one which had the same obligations as the first day. For example, two days of feasting are clearly referred to unambiguously in Saul's question in verse 27: מדוע לא־בא בן־ישי גם־תמול גם־היום אל־הלחם "Why has the son of Jesse not come to the feast, either yesterday or today?"

A second day of eating in association with the feast of חדש is corroborated in other contexts: the Hellenistic period book of Judith, and perhaps later rabbinic literature.[16] There are two possible explanations for

---

13. McCarter, *1 Samuel*, 341; Ackroyd, *The First Book of Samuel*, 163.

14. Driver, *Notes on the Hebrew Text*, 161–62; Mauchline, *1 and 2 Samuel*, 146; Hertzberg, *I & II Samuel*, 168.

15. Alter, *The David Story*, 124 (transliteration original).

16. Judith is described as breaking her fast on the day before the new moon, and on the new moon (Jdt 8:5): two days. A reference in *M. Sanh.* 8:2 to eating on the occasion of the intercalation of a month may also indicate two days, as according to the Mishnah's

this sequence of days. Firstly, it has recently been suggested by J. Wagenaar, as we have noted, that in the pre-exilic Israelite calendar, the month began with the disappearance of the "old moon"—when the moon ends its cycle by disappearing from visibility from the earth for approximately one or two days, after which it reappears as the crescent moon ("new moon"). Thus, the feast of חדש may have spanned this astronomical two-day period—between the moon's disappearance in the morning of the last day of this month and its reappearance in the evening, one or two days later.[17]

It is more often concluded, however, that the feast *began* with the latter astronomical event: the appearance of the lunar crescent after this period of obscuration from earth.[18] Moreover, later traditions regarding the technical reckoning of this event provide a plausible two-day sequence of ritual, associated with feasting, which occurred at the start of approximately every second month, when the outgoing month was empirically deemed thirty days long, rather then twenty nine, and the feast of חדש, in such circumstances, spanned the first two days of the month.[19]

Finally, as to the conclusion of at least one of the major commentaries on this text, that this kind of monthly feast was a men-only affair, the evidence in favor of this is circumstantial. According to H. W. Hertzberg, "Only four men are expected at the festal meal; women, as still today in the East, have no part in it."[20] This is argued mainly on the basis that only four men are referred to in the text.[21] This conclusion is problematic regarding

---

calendar, such occasions occurred approximately every second month and the associated procedures lasted two days (Cf. M. Roš Haš 3–4).

17. Wagenaar, *The Origin and Transformation*, 139–46.

18. This argument is implicitly supported by the meaning of the term חֹדֶשׁ and its association with the verb חָדַשׁ "renew, repair" and the adjective חָדָשׁ "new" (cf. *BDB*, 293–94). This association with renewal points to the renewal of the moon's illumination after a period of darkness. Thus, the feast occurs with the appearance of the crescent. Stern, *Calendar and Community*, 3 observes this association, but with caution.

19. In fact, the Targum Jonathan of the Former Prophets suggests, translating and commenting on 1 Sam 20:26, that this two-day period was precisely because of the intercalation of the previous month (that is, the previous month was counted as thirty days long, and חדש lasted two days instead of one). The Turgumic author also adds that it was the intercalation of the *second* month, although this may simply result from the textual difficulties in the original version. Cf. Harrington and Saldarini, *Targum Jonathan of the Former Prophets*, 141.

20. Hertzberg, *I & II Samuel*, 175.

21. Hertzberg's use of ethnographic analogue is also implied from several references to "the East," or "the Arabian East" (ibid., 174 n. a; 175, 175 n. a), but his comparative methodology remains undeveloped in relation to this episode.

the biblical text because examples of similar occasions of feasting, such as at Shiloh, described in 1 Sam 1, include the participation of female family members. The presence of women at such occasions is suggested by the fact that mixed-sex meals find their way into pentateuchal ritual prescription, for example in Deut 12:17–18.

In the present author's opinion, the idea of Saul remaining silent regarding David's absence on the first day suggests that a greater number of diners than the four referred to were expected to be present at such an occasion. Remaining silent about such a matter in the presence of only two other diners seems excessively awkward! It is therefore suggested here that there would have been considerably more than four diners expected at the king's table/court and that women may well have been among them—even if we cannot discern any details regarding their specific location or role at the event.

To summarize: 1 Sam 20 describes a series of events which develop around a feast which took place at the beginning of the lunar month, held monthly, at the table of the king. This event corresponds with the monthly festival referred to as ראש חדש, חדש, or יום החדש in the Hebrew Bible and probably began at some point after, or coincident with, the crescent moon's appearance in the western sky. The feasting lasted two days in this episode, and there are parallels for this two-day sequence in other texts, as we have seen. Based on parallel biblical texts, we have no compelling reason to conclude that women were specifically excluded from the event.

## ETHNOGRAPHIC STUDY OF FEASTING AND THE RIFT BETWEEN SAUL AND DAVID

I shall proceed now to describe some ways in which we can employ modern ethnographic studies of feasting to better read this text. Upon even a cursory reading of almost any modern case study of feasting, it will quickly become clear that there is an enormous amount, by comparison, that we do *not* know about Saul's new moon feast. In particular, much of the material and visual aspect will remain entirely unknown to us: accouterments, types of food consumed, exact nature of the locus, number of guests, and decorative or costume elements.[22] While we might draw some conclusions regarding these details from archaeological assemblages or

---

22. Cf. Dietler and Hayden, "Digesting the Feast," 8–9, on archaeological indicators of feasting with parallels from ethnographic studies.

iconographic evidence for ancient Near Eastern parallels,[23] we nevertheless lose any insight into the specific new moon feast as an occasion unto itself. And indeed, a general picture of dining habits in ancient Israel based on such evidence does not render any of the special nuances of the event of the new moon over against any other meal, special or otherwise, for us. This unfortunate reality may sound somewhat familiar to many studying the social life of ancient Israel and Judah. I would stress, however, that this should not discourage us, because, interestingly, several of the key themes raised by ethnographic work on feasting emerge very clearly in 1 Sam 20, despite the almost complete lack of material details for this particular episode.

Hayden, in identifying the benefits of most types of feasting across numerous societies, states that, apart from certain limited circumstances, "all other benefits of feasting revolve around *the creation or maintenance of important social relationships.*"[24] This idea summarizes a range of economic and social roles which a feast can play in a society. It is the social role of feasting that we shall focus on in this paper. The social roles of feasting identified by Hayden include these:

- The creation of cooperative relationships within groups or, conversely, the exclusion of other groups.
- The creation of cooperative alliances between social groups, including political support between households.
- The creation of political power (control over resources and labor) through the creation of a network of reciprocal debts.[25]

Saul's feast reflects in varying degrees all of these roles. If we look at Saul's חדש feast as a theater for expression of social relationships with an eye for the symbolic expression of political power and loyalty, we find some hints as to how this was expressed in the spatial arrangement of the diners.

---

23. See, for example, Schmandt-Besserat, "Feasting in the Ancient Near East," 391–403.

24. Hayden, "Fabulous Feasts," 30. The emphasis is Hayden's.

25. Several of the roles identified by Hayden, including those listed above, are summarized in Wright, "Introduction," 6.

According to Dietler and Hayden, "spatial segregation" is one of several criteria that can serve to "define and inculcate social categories,"[26] and indeed, in the feast described in 1 Sam 20, each individual described has his specific place referred to distinctively in the text, even if not always in a manner which is particularly clear to the modern reader. Verse 25 clearly states that the king had a fixed place at the feast, and it also seems implied that Abner, Jonathan, and David had fixed positions: וישב המלך על־מושבו כפעם בפעם אל־מושב הקיר ויקם יהונתן וישב אבנר מצד שאול ויפקד מקום דוד: "The king sat upon his seat, as at other times, upon the seat of the wall. Jonathan stood, while Abner sat by Saul's side; but David's place was empty (1 Sam 20:25)."[27]

The narrative description of the feast is confined to the roles and positions of these four characters. It is clear who has authority in this context and this is overtly represented in the spatial reality of the meal; the center of activity is "the king's table" שלחן המלך (20:29). Saul has the best position, which is his regular place, presumably with his back to the wall מושב הקיר (20:25). This is a position of honor: from here, as well as being more secure, he can survey all of the proceedings in the room.[28] From this position, he was likely to have been visible to all of the other diners, favoring a display of wealth and suzerainty. This position seems also to have both expressed and optimized his personal security. Abner, Saul's military commander, is described as being by his side. It also becomes evident, from the narrative that follows, that Saul kept a spear by his side, as it is available to throw at Jonathan during the second day's feasting (1 Sam 20:33). The other diners were most likely in front of Saul at this feast, seemingly in positions of lesser import, and with less personal security.

The admittedly scanty details above serve to paint a picture of a feast that would have served to express Saul's political power, while his guests, in this context, may well have presented themselves as military, political,

---

26. Dietler and Hayden, "Digesting the Feast," 10.

27. Regarding Jonathan's location, several commentators amend וַיָּקָם, after LXX, to ויקדם, to render translations variously approximating "Jonathan confronted/preceded/was opposite." See Smith, *A Critical and Exegetical Commentary*, 193; McCarter, *1 Samuel*, 338; Alter, *The David Story*, 127.

28. This is, according to Hertzberg, "the best (and safest) place." Hertzberg, *I & II Samuel*, 175. Ackroyd describes Saul's position by the wall as "a position of safety and no doubt honour" (Ackroyd, *The First Book of Samuel*, 167).

or economic allies. As previously suggested, it is likely that other people were assumed to have been present on such an occasion, but that remains in the realm of speculation, and is therefore somewhat beyond the scope of analysis, except to conclude that any other guests were likely in positions of lesser honor than that of the king. It also remains a possibility that the author envisages the mentioned figures at such a feast to have been collectively located in a prominent location, such that the king sat at the most honored position, followed by prominent guests, and then more numerous unmentioned guests—but this must also remain speculation for the above context.

It seems quite clear that this feast, in the episode between David and Saul, serves in the creation and maintenance of "cooperative alliances between social groups, including political support between households."[29] And this is certainly taken up in the case of David's "clan," or משפחה.[30] David's excuse, while fabricated in the story, emphasizes the rupture between him and Saul at a family, or "clan" level. When Saul finds out, only on the second day in fact, that David has supposedly gone to Bethlehem for a sacrifice with his own family, rather than fulfill his obligations to Saul, he is furious. It is at this point that Saul flings his spear at Jonathan in rage (20:33), and this is the "insult" that is referred to in the title of this paper.

The decisiveness of this moment in the rupture at the family level between these two figures is emphasized, according to Green, by Saul's calling David בן־ישי "son of Jesse" (1 Sam 20:11). Saul's using David's patronym disparagingly, in Green's opinion, "names his failure to make David his own son."[31] We thus conclude that the feast itself carries with it themes which are well suited to this particular point in the overall narrative of the growing enmity between Saul and David—and David's eventual succession to the throne.

Despite the paucity of detail, we may deduce something about the ritual status of the location in which the new moon feast took place from an apparent ritual requirement for purity. This also helps us to contrast new moon meals as *special* events with regular subsistence meals. Dietler and Hayden, in relation to archaeological indicators of feasting, as well

---

29. Wright "Introduction," 6.

30. On the Mishpahah, see, for example, de Vaux, *Ancient Israel*, 21; de Geus, *The Tribes of Israel*.

31. Green, *How Are the Mighty Fallen?*, 342.

as ethnographic analogues, note that identified feasting locations "are often associated with notable ritual structures."³² So, before we conclude, I would like to suggest, after several other commentators, that Saul's חדש feast had a cultic and sacrificial aspect to it.³³ This has been suggested on account of Saul's thoughts regarding David's absence on the first day, as recounted in the narrative: that he was not "clean" טהור.³⁴ We know from other texts that sacrifices were associated with the new moon through successive periods of Israel's history, and although that aspect of this particular episode remains obscure, it is present nonetheless.³⁵

Several scholars have hypothesized reasons for a potential uncleanness in such a context, and have suggested that texts such as Deut 23:10 and Lev 15:16 provide plausible reasons, such as recent contact with a corpse, or a seminal emission.³⁶ These suggestions are actually quite plausibly applied to the scene in 1 Sam 20, because it is only during the first day of David's absence that Saul remains pacified. We are told that he concluded that David was not clean and that he remained silent regarding the matter. It was on the *second* day however, that Saul spoke out and eventually struck out, in anger at David's absence. This, we can conclude, happened because temporary uncleanness would no longer have been a viable option after a full day and night had already passed, if we go by these texts in Leviticus and Deuteronomy.

## CONCLUSION

The episode briefly examined includes a play on the tension created by a character who refuses to "play by the rules" in precisely the kind of feasting environment that is often recounted in modern literature describing ethnographic analogues. Not only does David test Saul's feelings by

32. Dietler and Hayden, "Digesting the Feast," 8–9. These structures may be for the specific purpose of feasting in some cases, or a variety of rituals, including feasts, in others (see Hayden, "Fabulous Feasts," 57–58).

33. Cf. Smith, *A Critical and Exegetical Commentary*, 192; McCarter, *1 Samuel*, 343.

34. Later, Josephus takes up this aspect of the feast in his description of it, and adds that before the first day's feast, Saul himself customarily purified himself (Josephus, *AJ* VI 235). Later still, *M. Sanh.* 8 indicates that attending certain meals around the new moon constituted the fulfilment of a religious obligation. Cf. Neusner, *A History of the Mishnaic Law of Damages, Part Three*, 203.

35. The new moon's sacrificial aspect is well attested in several texts: for example, Num 28:11–14; 2 Chr 2:4; Isa 1:12–14; Ezek 46:6–7.

36. McCarter, *1 Samuel*, 343.

failing to play by conventional rules, but the inclusion of this episode as the turning point in the relationship between David and Saul seems to symbolize and indeed stress the rupture that occurs between David and Saul—expressed in David's symbolic rejection of the cooperative alliance and political support between these two parties.

We have not been overly concerned here with the historicity of the particular events described, but I suggest that we here have presented for us an opportunity to engage with some of the traditional paradigmatic ritual practices and categories of both the authors of the text and its intended audience. Special food consumption associated with חדש, as we have previously noted, emerges once again in the Hellenistic period book of Judith, and later still in the text of the Mishnah; the association might also be corroborated for the period at the end of Monarchic Judah, by Ostracon number 7 from Arad.[37]

The observance of חדש, the festival of the new moon, consistently emerges as a feature of Israelite religion from this early period, if not earlier still,[38] through Second Temple times, to beyond the destruction of 70 CE. First Sam 20 constitutes a unique source for the feast, particularly regarding the light the text sheds on the social obligations attached to its observance. In fact, in the sources now extant, the feast's special social ramifications do not receive such a vivid treatment until the completion of Mishnah, whose authors record certain inevitable changes in the character of the observance, but also remarkable continuities.[39]

This brief study has emerged from a preliminary examination of a biblical context which is decidedly lacking in the intense scrutiny which marks much ethnographic research, but the reason for my choosing to present it is this: the little available from the text of 1 Sam 20 corresponds very comfortably with many of the cross-cultural aspects of feasting evident from other literature available to us, such that this case testifies to the potential usefulness such an interdisciplinary approach can have in our present field of biblical studies.

---

37. Cf. for example, Loewenstamm, "Ostracon 7."
38. Cf. Isa 1:12–14; Amos 8:4–5; Hos 2:11.
39. Cf. *M. Roš Haš*; *M. Sanh* 8.

## BIBLIOGRAPHY

Ackroyd, Peter R. *The First Book of Samuel.* CBC. Cambridge: Cambridge University Press, 1971.

Alter, Robert. *The David Story: A Translation with Commentary of 1 and 2 Samuel.* New York: Norton, 1999.

Clarke, Michael. "Akha Feasting: An Ethnoarchaeological Perspective." In *Feasts: Archaeological and Ethnographic Perspectives on Food, Politics, and Power*, edited by Michael Dietler and Brian Hayden, 144–67. Washington, DC: Smithsonian Institute Press, 2001.

Dietler, Michael, and Brian Hayden, "Digesting the Feast: Good to Eat, Good to Drink, Good to Think: An Introduction." In *Feasts: Archaeological and Ethnographic Perspectives on Food, Politics, and Power*, edited by Michael Dietler and Brian Hayden, 1–20. Washington, DC: Smithsonian Institute Press, 2001.

Driver, S. R. *Notes on the Hebrew Text and the Topography of the Books of Samuel.* 2nd ed. Oxford: Clarendon, 1913.

Gandz, Solomon. "Studies in the Hebrew Calendar: II. The Origin of the Two New Moon Days." *JQR* 40 (1950) 157–72, 251–77.

Gehrke, Ralph David. *Concordia Commentary: 1 and 2 Samuel.* Concordia Commentary. St. Louis: Concordia, 1968.

Gennep, Arnold van. *The Rites of Passage.* Translated by Monika B. Vizedom and Gabrielle L. Caffee. Chicago: University of Chicago Press, 1960.

Geus, C. H. J. de. *The Tribes of Israel: An Investigation into some of the Presuppositions of Martin Noth's Amphictyony Hypothesis.* SSN 18. Assen: Van Gorcum, 1976.

Green, Barbara. *How Are the Mighty Fallen? A Dialogical Study of King Saul in 1 Samuel.* JSOTSup 365. London: Sheffield Academic, 2003.

Gross, Jonathan L. "Measurement of Calendrical Information in Food-Taking Behaviour." In *Food in the Social Order: Studies of Food and Festivities in Three American Communities*, edited by Mary Douglas, 219–77. Collected Works 9. London: Routledge, 2003.

Harrington, Daniel J., and Anthony J. Saldarini. *Targum Jonathan of the Former Prophets: Introduction, Translation and Notes.* The Aramaic Bible 10. Wilmington, DE: Glazier, 1987.

Hayden, Brian. "Fabulous Feasts: A Prolegomenon to the Importance of Feasting." In *Feasts: Archaeological and Ethnographic Perspectives on Food, Politics, and Power*, edited by Michael Dietler and Brian Hayden, 23–64. Washington, DC: Smithsonian Institute Press, 2001.

Herr, M. D. "The Calendar." In *The Jewish People in the First Century: Historical Geography, Political History, Cultural and Religious Life and Institutions*, edited by S. Safrai and M. Stern, 834–64. CRINT, sec. 1. Assen: Van Gorcum, 1976.

Hertzberg, H. W. *I & II Samuel: A Commentary.* Translated by J. S. Bowden OTL. Philadelphia: Westminster, 1964.

Jaubert, Annie. "Le Calendrier des Jubilés et de la Secte de Qumran: Ses Origines Bibliques." *VT* 3 (1953) 250–64.

———. *The Date of the Last Supper.* Translated by Isaac Rafferty. Staten Island, NY: Alba House, 1965.

Loewenstamm, Samuel E. "Ostracon 7 from Arad Attesting to the Observance of the New Moon Day." In *From Babylon to Canaan: Studies in the Bible and Its Oriental*

*Background*, 131–35. Publication of the Perry Foundation for Biblical Research in the Hebrew University of Jerusalem. Jerusalem: Magnes, 1992.

Mauchline, John. *1 and 2 Samuel*. NCB. London: Oliphants, 1971.

McCarter, P. Kyle. *1 Samuel: A New Translation with Introduction, Notes, and Commentary*. AB 8. Garden City, NY: Doubleday, 1980.

Neusner, Jacob. *A History of the Mishnaic Law of Damages, Part Three: Baba Batra, Sanhedrin, Makkot, Translation and Explanation*. Studies in Judaism in Late Antiquity 35. Leiden: Brill, 1984.

Philbeck, B. F. *1–2 Samuel*. In *The Broadman Bible Commentary*. Vol. 3, *1 Samuel–Nehemiah*, edited by Clifton J. Allen et al., 1–145. London: Marshall, Morgan & Scott, 1970.

Rost, Leonhard. "Die Überlieferung von der Thronnachfolge Davids." In *Das kleine Credo und andere Studien zum alten Testament*. Heidelberg: Quelle and Meyer, 1965.

Schmandt-Besserat, Denise. "Feasting in the Ancient Near East." In *Feasts: Archaeological and Ethnographic Perspectives on Food, Politics, and Power*, edited by Michael Dietler and Brian Hayden, 391–403. Washington, DC: Smithsonian Institute Press, 2001.

Smith, Henry Preserved. *A Critical and Exegetical Commentary on the Books of Samuel*. ICC. Edinburgh: T. & T. Clark, 1899.

Stern, Sacha. *Calendar and Community: A History of the Jewish Calendar Second Century BCE–Tenth Century CE*. Oxford: Oxford University Press, 2001.

Taggar-Cohen, Ada. "Political Loyalty in the Biblical Account of 1 Samuel XX–XXII in the Light of Hittite Texts." *VT* 55 (2005) 251–68.

Turner, Victor. *The Ritual Process: Structure and Anti-Structure*. The Lewis Henry Morgan Lectures 1966. New York: de Gruyter, 1995.

Vaux, Roland de. *Ancient Israel: Its Life and Institutions*. Translated by John McHugh. London: Darton, Longman & Todd, 1965.

Wacholder, B. Z., and S. Wacholder. "Patterns of Biblical Dates and Qumran's Calendar: The Fallacy of Jaubert's Hypothesis." *HUCA* 66 (1995) 1–40.

Wagenaar, Jan A. *Origin and Transformation of the Ancient Israelite Festival Calendar*. Wiesbaden: Harrasowitz, 2005.

Wright, James C. "Introduction." In *The Mycenaean Feast*, edited by J. C. Wright, 1–12. Princeton, NJ: American School of Classical Studies at Athens, 2004.

# 3

# Life-and-Death Advice from a Conservative Sage

*Qohelet's Perspective on Life after Death*

HANS DEBEL

Katholieke Universiteit Leuven

## INTRODUCTION

THE BOOK OF QOHELET, commonly known as Ecclesiastes, is a striking appearance in the Hebrew Bible. Qohelet's gloomy thoughts and sceptical attitude towards traditional Israelite wisdom have yielded him nicknames such as "a gentle cynic."[1] The theme of death takes up a prominent place in these considerations, to such a degree that only the complaints of Job are comparable to Ecclesiastes.[2] In this respect, A. Schoors observes, in the second volume of his outstanding and exhaustive study of the language of Qohelet, that although the verb מות and the noun מָוֶת can only be found nine and six times, respectively, throughout the book, and that both lexemes often simply refer to the fact of dying or the state of death, it appears from the contexts in which they occur that death plays

---

1. Cf. Jastrow, *A Gentle Cynic*.

2. See Burkes, *Death in Qoheleth*, 74–75; Fox, "Aging and Death in Qohelet 12," 67; Gretler, *Zeit und Stunde*, 134; Kutschera, "Kohelet: Leben im Angesicht des Todes," 364–65; Lauha, *Kohelet*, 150; Lohfink, *Kohelet*, 51; Schwienhorst-Schönberger, *Kohelet*, 542; and Zimmer, *Zwischen Tod und Lebensglück*, 45.

a major role in Ecclesiastes.³ Moreover, speculations about a rescue from death had become apparent in Israelite wisdom of Qohelet's day. It seems as if Qohelet is interfering in an ongoing intellectual debate on the possibility of overcoming human mortality.

The present paper aims at exploring the position of Qohelet in this controversy. In the first part, attention will be paid to the question of dating the book as a whole, in particular with respect to the linguistic evidence presented by eminent scholars such as Schoors and Seow. Secondly, I will offer a brief presentation of the so-called doctrine of retribution as it can be found in several biblical writings. Thirdly, the objections of Qohelet raised against this doctrine will be dealt with. Finally, Qohelet's own perspective will be presented.⁴

## THE DATING OF ECCLESIASTES

Although the author of Ecclesiastes, to whom I will refer as *Qohelet*, presents himself as King Solomon in the first chapters, it is highly unlikely that Solomon has made any contribution to the composition of the book. It is remarkable that any allusion to his kingship is absent from the third chapter on, and parallels with the Mesopotamic genre of the fictional autobiography render it more plausible that Qohelet's allusions to King Solomon are a "subtle playing with his identity."⁵ However, the pivotal argument concerning the date of Ecclesiastes is the language of the book. It is accepted as the "most objective and thus the most significant contributory premise,"⁶ and, in the case of Qohelet, is characterized as Late Biblical Hebrew—perhaps even the latest Hebrew in the Bible and the closest approximation to Mishnaic Hebrew.⁷ Already in 1875, F. Delitzsch

---

3. Cf. Schoors, *The Preacher Sought to Find Pleasing Words*, 205.

4. Some insights in this chapter have been partially published in Dutch as part of my contribution, Debel, "Gedenk, o mens."

5. See Longman, *The Book of Ecclesiastes*, 8. I have borrowed the expression "subtle playing with the identity" from Krüger, *Qoheleth*, 40.

6. Quoted from Fredericks, *Qoheleth's Language*, 269.

7. See Gordis, *Koheleth*, 65. Gordis argued vigorously for this characterization of the language of Qohelet when contesting the so-called Aramaic-translation hypothesis. For the main contributions to the controversy in question, see, in chronological order, Burkitt, "Is Ecclesiastes a Translation?"; Fernández, "¿Es Eclesiastes una versión?"; Zimmermann, "The Aramaic Provenance of Qohelet"; Gordis, "The Original Language of Qohelet"; Torrey, "The Question of the Original Language of Kohelet"; Zimmermann, "The Question of Hebrew in Qohelet"; Gordis, "The Translation Theory of Qohelet Re-

stated that if the Book of Qohelet were of old solomonic origin, then there is no history of the Hebrew language.[8]

Generally speaking, the exile is put forward as a *terminus post quem* for the language of Qohelet.[9] Since one of the two copies of Qohelet found in Qumran, 4Q109 (4QQoh[a]), is supposed to belong to the community's oldest biblical manuscripts,[10] scholars agree upon the middle of the second century BCE as the *terminus ante quem*.[11] This is confirmed by the orthography of MT Qohelet, which, according to Schoors, represents a somewhat middle stage in the development of *plene* writing.[12] Seow affirms that, whereas Qohelet makes ample use of internal vowel letters, which were only sparingly used before the sixth century, his spelling is still more conservative than what is found in the evidence from Qumran, Wadi Murabba'at, and in the Bar Kochba letters. Therefore, it should be

---

Examined"; Ginsberg, *Studies in Koheleth*; Gordis, "Koheleth—Hebrew or Aramaic?"; Muilenburg, "A Qoheleth Scroll from Qumran," 24; Dahood, "Qoheleth and Recent Discoveries," 303–4. An overview of this controversy is given in Bianchi, "The Language of Qohelet: A Bibliographical Survey," 213–16; Kroeber, *Der Prediger*, 42–45; and Schoors, *The Preacher Sought to Find Pleasing Words*, 6–8. Schoors's conclusion on the translation hypothesis is scathing (p. 8): "This is a self-destructive theory, for why should somebody want to translate an Aramaic text into Hebrew when he neither properly understands the Aramaic original nor sufficiently masters the Hebrew language to offer a flawless translation. For a few mistranslations can betray the translational character of a text, but in the theory under consideration, there are too many of them and they are too fundamental."

8. Cf. Delitzsch, *Hoheslied und Koheleth*, 197: "Wenn das buch Koheleth altsalomonisch ware, so gäbe es keine Geschichte der hebraïschen Sprache."

9. Pace Fredericks, *Qoheleth's Language*.

10. See Muilenburg, "A Qoheleth Scroll," 23, 27; Cross, "The Oldest Manuscripts from Qumran," 152–59, 162; Seow, "Linguistic Evidence and the Dating of Qohelet," 643; Tov, *Textual Criticism of the Hebrew Bible*, 106. Both manuscripts, 4Q109 (4QQoh[a]) and 4Q110 (4QQoh[b]), have been published in Ulrich et al., *Qumran Cave 4, Vol. 11: Psalms to Chronicles*, 221–27. See also Nebe, "Qumranica I," 312–13; and Ulrich, "Ezra and Qohelet Manuscripts from Qumran (4QEzra and 4QQoh[a,b])," 142–48.

11. The book of Ben Sira, which was written around 190 BCE, is also often put forward as *terminus ante quem*, especially since Podechard has argued for a dependence of Ben Sira upon Qohelet; see E. Podechard, *L'Ecclésiaste*, 55–65. Nevertheless, Whitley concluded that Qoheleth was dependent on Ben Sira; see Whitley, *Koheleth*, 122–31, 162–64. Therefore, it is probably better to agree with Middendorp, who states that dependence in either direction cannot be shown; see Middendorp, *Die Stellung Jesu Ben Siras*, 85–90. See also Murphy, *Ecclesiastes*, xlv–xlvi; and Schwienhorst-Schönberger, "Kohelet: Stand und Perspektiven der Forschung," 24.

12. See for example Schoors, "The Use of Vowel Letters in Qoheleth," 285; and Schoors, *The Preacher Sought to Find Pleasing Words*, 1:32, 221.

dated between the beginning of the sixth century and the end of the third century BCE.[13]

It makes a difference to know whether the book originated in the Persian or the Hellenistic period,[14] but at this point, the above-mentioned scholars do not reach a consensus. In Seow's view, Qohelet belongs to the Persian period, specifically between the second half of the fifth century and the first half of the fourth.[15] He argues that the two Persian loanwords in the book, פרדס (Eccl 2:5) and פתגם (Eccl 8:11), suggest that the book should not be dated in the sixth century, since they are both for the first time attested in the Persepolis Fortification Tablets, which date back to around 500 BCE.[16] Moreover, he points out that the highly frequent Aramaisms in the book, which corroborate once again its post-exilic origins, significantly all occur in fifth- and fourth-century documents,[17] and that other terms that may not be Aramaisms belong to the socio-economic vocabulary of this period.[18] At the same time, Seow denies the presence of Greek loanwords and linguistic Graecisms in the book, as a consequence of which no linguistic argument is left to place the book in the Hellenistic period.[19] He concludes that Qohelet's language "represents

---

13. See Seow, "Linguistic Evidence," 645–46.

14. As remarked in Schoors, "Qoheleth," 68.

15. Seow is thereby in agreement with Delitzsch, *Hoheslied und Koheleth*, 222; and Kugel, "Qohelet and Money," 46–49. Schoors attributes the same conclusion to D. Castelli, *Il libro del Cohelet, volgarmente detto Ecclesiaste*, Pisa, 1866, 138–41, but I did not have access to this work. See Schoors, "Qoheleth," 69.

16. See Seow, "Linguistic Evidence," 646–50.

17. He discerns אריה, בטל, גומץ, זמן, חסרון, חשבון, יתרון, כאחד, כשר, מדינה, נכסים, סוף, קרב, רעות, רעיון, שלט, שלטון, תקן, תקף, and תקיף. See Seow, "Linguistic Evidence," 650–54.

18. Notably כף, חפן, טחנה, חלק and בית הסורים. See Seow, "Linguistic Evidence," 665.

19. See Seow, "Linguistic Evidence," 657–60. Seow also pays attention to the suggestion of Dahood that Qohelet was a Phoenician writing in Hebrew but with a clear Canaanite-Phoenician influence (pp. 654–57). Nevertheless, Seow comes to the conclusion that this Phoenician influence can neither be ruled out nor be demonstrated, and hence no conclusions can be drawn from it concerning the dating of Qohelet. Likewise, Schoors observes that Dahood's theory relies upon superfluous textual emendations and dubious proof texts; cf. Schoors, "The Use of Vowel Letters," 284: "Practically all of Dahood's suggestions concerning the use of *matres lectionis* must be rejected. When they are not completely conjectural, they are mostly based on a mechanical reference to textual variants which have to be explained otherwise, e.g., by the characteristics of the ancient version under consideration or by textual corruption in the *Vorlage* (*lectio facilitans*) or in the version." A comparable assessment of Dahood's theory can be found in Schoors, *The Preacher Sought*, (vol. I) 223. It should be remarked that Dahood himself

the literary deposit of the everyday Hebrew of Persian-period Palestine, with its large number of Aramaisms and whatever jargon and vernacular elements one may find in the marketplace."[20]

On the basis of a thorough examination of the grammar and the vocabulary of the Hebrew of Qohelet, Schoors agrees on the one hand that the language must be post-exilic,[21] but on the other hand he refutes a date in the Persian period, because the socio-economic connotation of the terms mentioned by Seow is often unwarranted in his view.[22] Furthermore, although he admits that there are no compelling arguments to prove an important Greek influence on Qohelet, he finds it impossible to reject all

---

was building upon the suggestions of Albright, *From the Stone Age to Christianity*, 243 and Gordon, *Ugaritic Literature*, 133. Dahood elaborated his theory in "Canaanite-Phoenician Influence in Qoheleth," 30–52, 191–221; "The Language of Qoheleth," 227–32; "Qoheleth and Recent Discoveries," 302–18; "Qoheleth and Northwest Semitic Philology," 349–65; "The Phoenician Background of Qoheleth," 264–82; "Three Parallel Pairs in Eccl. 10:18," 84–87 and "Northwest Semitic Philology and Three Biblical Texts," 17–22, but he too was opposed by Gordis; see Gordis, "Was Koheleth a Phoenician?," 103–14; Gordis, "Qoheleth and Qumran," esp. 396–97; and Gordis, "On Methodology in Biblical Exegesis," esp. 100–101. For an overview of the Phoenician controversy, see Bianchi, "The Language of Qohelet," 216–19; and Schoors, *The Preacher Sought to Find Pleasing Words*, 1:8–10.

20. Quoted in Seow, "The Socioeconomic Context of 'the Preacher's' Hermeneutic," 171. Cf. Seow, "Linguistic Evidence," 666.

21. In the interim conclusion of the first volume of his study of Qohelet's language, Schoors lists an impressive number of grammatical features in order to prove the language of Qohelet to be close to post-exilic books such as Chr, Ezr, Neh, Dan, or Sir. Among these features are some Aramaisms (a larger usage of nouns ending in ־וֹת, nouns of the *qetāl* type, the particle אֲלוּ, a more frequent use of שֶׁ/אֲשֶׁר as a conjunction, and a high concentration of composite conjunctions); see Schoors, *The Preacher Sought*, (vol. I) 221–23. In the second volume, devoted to Qohelet's vocabulary, he confirms the late character of the book by discerning some 30 lexemes typical of Late Biblical Hebrew or used with a meaning that is found in late texts only. Furthermore, he adds חוּץ מִן, עִנְיָן, עָבַד, מַדָּע, (עָשָׂה), לָהֶם, כָּל־אֲשֶׁר יַחְפֹּץ עָשָׂה ("plausible but not proven"), שֶׁבַח, שָׂדֶה ("accepting the Aramaic etymology of שָׂדֶה, 'to pour'") and שׁוּק ("a trans-Aramaic borrowing of Akkadian") to Seow's inventory of Aramaisms (see note 18), although he does not agree upon יִתְרוֹן ("Heb יִתְרוֹן is a normal development of West-Semitic *yutrān*, so that the from of the noun must not be ascribed to Aramaic influence," p. 423), see Schoors, *The Preacher Sought*, (vol. II) 499–501.

22. See Schoors, *The Preacher Sought to Find Pleasing Words*, 2:501–2. Rudman likewise observes that the use of the root שׁלט in its technical sense survived throughout the Hellenistic era and consequently concludes that its parallels in fifth- and fourth-century documents are not decisive for the dating of Ecclesiastes. See Rudman, "A Note on the Dating of Ecclesiastes," 52.

suggested Graecisms and accepts a few Greek parallels.[23] Hence a date in the Hellenistic period is favored by him. Moreover, he asserts that it cannot be excluded a priori that some passages allude to historical events, and on these grounds he suggests the Ptolemaic reign (301–198 BCE) as the socio-political background of Ecclesiastes.[24] In this way, he finds himself in a position to confirm the date commonly accepted by most scholars, namely the second half of the third century BCE.[25]

## THE DOCTRINE OF RETRIBUTION

Bearing these observations in mind, we can take a closer look at the so-called doctrine of retribution, which is particularly present in the later writings of the Hebrew Bible, although its traces can be found throughout the entire Hebrew Bible.[26] This doctrine, also known as the *Tun-Ergehen-Zusammenhang*, expresses the expectation of a connection between what people do and how they fare. Pious and righteous behavior was supposed to bring about wealth, old age, and numerous offspring. This threefold expectation is exemplified in the epilogue of the book of Job (Job 42), in which the repenting Job of the frame-narrative is rewarded because he has spoken of God what is right:

> [10] And the LORD restored the fortunes of Job when he had prayed for his friends; and the LORD gave Job twice as much as he had before. [11] Then there came to him all his brothers and sisters and all who had known him before, and they ate bread with him in his house; they showed him sympathy and comforted him for all the evil that the LORD had brought upon him; and each of them gave him a piece of money and a gold ring. [12] The LORD blessed the latter days of Job more than his beginning; and he had fourteen

---

23. Notably לעשות טוב (Gr. εὖ πράττειν); עשה הימים (Gr. ποιεῖν χρόνον); תחת השמש (Gr. ὑπ' ἡλίῳ) and תור with the denotation of "explore mentally" (Gr. σκέπτεσθαι). See Schoors, *The Preacher Sought*, 2:501.

24. See Schoors, "Qoheleth," 68–72.

25. See, for example, Burkes, *Death in Qoheleth*, 36–39; Crenshaw, *Ecclesiastes*, 50; Gilbert, *Les cinq livres des Sages*, 117; Gordis, *Koheleth*, 59–68; Krüger, *Kohelet (Prediger)*, 39; Lauha, *Kohelet*, 3; Longman, *Ecclesiastes*, 9–11; Michel, *Qohelet*, 114; Murphy, *Ecclesiastes*, xxii; Schwienhorst-Schönberger, *Kohelet*, 103; Vinel, *L'Ecclésiaste*, 24; and Whybray, *Ecclesiastes*, 4, 15.

26. For an overview of these traces, see, for example, Ginsburg, *The Song of Songs and Coheleth*, 21–22. With respect to the doctrine of retribution, see in particular Van Hecke, "'Wie goed doet, goed ontmoet,'" 47–63.

thousand sheep, six thousand camels, a thousand yoke oxen, and a thousand donkeys. [13] He also had seven sons and three daughters . . . [16] After this, Job lived one hundred and forty years, and saw his children, and his children's children, four generations. [17] And Job died, old and full of days.[27]

Moreover, in Qohelet's day, wisdom seems to have been added to this threefold expectation, and, most probably under the influence of Hellenistic dualism of body and soul,[28] the doctrine of retribution had even aroused hope that the wise man could possess eternal life and that his merits would not perish, whereas the fool would suffer eternal punishment in the desperate state of Sheol. For example, it is stated in the book of Proverbs:

[10:27] The fear of the LORD prolongs life, but the years of the wicked will be short.

[13:14] The teaching of the wise is a fountain of life, so that one may avoid the snares of death.

[15:24] For the wise, the path of life leads upward, in order to avoid Sheol below.

## Qohelet's Objections

Nevertheless, Qohelet's observations lead him to the rejection of the doctrine of retribution. In his opinion, none of the three indications of a praiseworthy life imply any advantage when it comes to life and death. In 5:14–15, he relates the fate of the so-called rich fool[29] and his son, both of whom cannot escape death despite their wealth:

[14] As they came from their mother's womb, so they shall go again, naked as they came; they shall take nothing for their toil, which they may carry away with their hands.[30] [15] This also is a

27. Biblical quotations are taken from the New Revised Standard Version.

28. See Berlejung, "Was kommt nach dem Tod?" 5; Burkes, *Death in Qoheleth*, 88; Custer, "Qohelet and the Canon," 20; Janowski, "Sehnsucht nach Unsterblichkeit," 35; Kutschera, "Kohelet," 365; and Whitley, *Koheleth*, 136.

29. See Seow, *Ecclesiastes*, 221.

30. It should be noted that this verse almost literally echoes Job 1:21, in which Job piously accepts the loss of his wealth. In both verses, the verbs יצא and שוב play an important role, along with the adjective ערום/ערם and the construction מבטן אמי/ו. However, they disagree insofar as the verbs take a different form (3rd-person singular in Ecclesiastes,

grievous ill: just as they came, so shall they go; and what gain do they have from toiling for the wind?

In these verses death appears as the absolute boundary and annihilation of human earnings. Nevertheless, it could be argued that Qohelet has only the particular situation of the rich fool in mind, but at the beginning of the following chapter, he maintains in more general terms that neither old age nor progeny can grant a man a happy life or a peaceful death:

> [6:3] A man may beget a hundred children, and live many years, but however many are the days of his years, if he does not enjoy life's good things, or has no burial, I say that a stillborn child is better off than he.

Contrary to the teachings of his contemporaries, Qohelet denies in these chapters the advantage of the rich over the poor: despite their wealth, the rich die as the poor. Likewise, Qohelet calls into question the advantage of the wise over the fool when death is at stake, as for example in 2:15–16:

> [15] Then I said to myself, "What happens to the fool will happen to me also; why then have I been so very wise?" And I said to myself that this also is vanity. [16] For there is no enduring remembrance of the wise or of fools, seeing that in the days to come all will have been long forgotten. How can the wise die just like fools?

---

1st-person singular in Job) and depend upon each other in a different way (subordinate clause in Ecclesiastes, ordinate clauses in Job). See Bergant, *Job, Ecclesiastes*, 258; Crenshaw, *Ecclesiastes*, 123; Delsman, *Die Datierung des Buches Qoheleth*, 56; Galling, "Der Prediger," 103; Gordis, *Koheleth*, 253; Krüger, *Kohelet*, 229; Lauha, *Kohelet*, 111; Laurent, *Les biens pour rien*, 202–8; Levy, *Das Buch Qoheleth*, 97; Longman, *Ecclesiastes*, 166–67; Murphy, *Ecclesiastes*, 52; Ogden, *Qoheleth*, 84; Schoors, "(Mis)use of Intertextuality in Qoheleth Exegesis," 47; Schwienhorst-Schönberger, *Kohelet*, 334; Seow, *Ecclesiastes*, 221; Siegfried, *Prediger und Hoheslied*, 13; Whybray, *Ecclesiastes*, 101. In this respect, Lohfink raises the question whether it is correct to interpret the verb הלך (in ללכת) as referring to the process of dying. He suggests that the symbolic beginning of a new life after a bad transaction fits better into the financial context of 5:12–16: the rich fool has to "go on" with his life. See Lohfink, "Kohelet und die Banken." Although there seems to be evidence that the monetary system of the Ptolemaic Empire was quite developed (see Schwienhorst-Schönberger, "Nicht im Menschen gründet das Glück," 145; Seow, "The Socioeconomic Context," 173–74; and Whybray, *Ecclesiastes*, 10), it is difficult to exclude the possibility of הלך used as a euphemism for dying in Eccl 1:4 and 6:6, as this was one of the common meanings of this verb in Hebrew (see Tromp, *Primitive Conceptions of Death*, 167).

Furthermore, he makes a comparable observation with respect to the righteous and the wicked in 8:12–14. After having concluded that the sentence against an evil deed is not executed speedily and that the human heart is full of evil, he bitterly observes that death is not inflicted as a punishment upon the sinners, and that wise men even have to undergo the supposed fate of the sinners:

> [12] Sinners do evil a hundred times and prolong their lives. Truly, I know that it will be well with those who fear God, because they stand in fear before him, [13] and that it will not be well with the wicked, neither will they prolong their days, like a shadow, because they do not stand in fear before God. [14] There is a vanity that takes place on earth, that there are righteous people who are treated according to the conduct of the wicked, and there are wicked people who are treated according to the conduct of the righteous. I said that this also is vanity.[31]

In verses 12 and 13, Qohelet puts the doctrine of retribution in a nutshell: it will be well with those who fear God, whereas the wicked will not prolong their days. Some scholars consider these verses as an orthodox gloss from a pious editor, meant to weaken Qohelet's almost heretical scepticism.[32] However, an analysis of the rhetorical structure of this pericope renders their efforts superfluous. After having recapitulated what he has learned about sinners, possibly quoting the teachings of his opponents or of his own teachers,[33] Qohelet confronts their insights with his actual observations of reality and comes to the conclusion that in some cases the doctrine of retribution proves to be inadequate.[34]

---

31. Because the NRSV does not fully reflect MT, I have made a few emendations to its translation of this pericope.

32. See Crenshaw, *Ecclesiastes*, 155; Galling, "Der Prediger," 111–12; Lauha, *Kohelet*, 154; Schwienhorst-Schönberger, *Kohelet*, 425; van der Ploeg, *Prediker*, 54; and Whybray, *Ecclesiastes*, 135.

33. In this respect, it should be remarked that the unusual use of the participle יודע can be viewed as a signal that the following argument is not Qohelet's own. As Gordis notes, quotation marks were not available to the ancient writers. See Gordis, *Koheleth*, 95; Longman, *Ecclesiastes*, 219; and Murphy, *Ecclesiastes*, 85.

34. Cf. Beentjes, "'Who Is Like the Wise?'" 314: "This structure, with Qohelet's own observations at the beginning and at the end, and the classical doctrine of retribution at the centre, is proof enough to fully disagree with those scholars who consider just that traditional point of view (8,12b–13) as a *gloss*." Cf. likewise Van Niekerk, "Response," 101: "Such an exposition of the traditional doctrine of retribution can, here, be nothing more than a quotation by Qoheleth. Its strategic position, between two contradictory flanks,

Although his conclusion might seem nothing more than a marginal note to the doctrine of retribution,[35] Qohelet implicitly casts fundamental doubts on it,[36] since the doctrine of retribution can only be legitimate as a principle when no exceptions are allowed. By focusing on the exceptions that he has observed, Qohelet demonstrates that the principle of retribution lacks any credibility at all and that it tends to arbitrariness. The universal justice postulated by the doctrine of retribution proves to be neither universal nor just, since it is possible to point to exceptions.

### Qohelet's Alternative

These examples make it clear that Qohelet disapproves the innovations of his contemporaries concerning humanity's possibility of overcoming death and that he does not share their ideas on retribution. Yet standing in the same sapiential tradition, he draws attention to the physical reality of death.[37] Even if there may be some advantages of being wise over being foolish, death is the one certainty to all, from which neither the wise man nor the fool can escape.[38]

In his description of the dissolution of the body at the time of death in 12:7, Qohelet even reverses the modelling of man as related in the second creation narrative—when God formed man from the dust of the ground and breathed into his nostrils the breath of life (Gen 2:7). Still, Qohelet does not mention the literal expression נשמת חיים to denote the breath of life, but rather רוח, the word commonly used by his contemporaries to designate the "soul" of man, potentially able to survive death. In his view, however, the רוח of man does not consist of an immaterial entity carrying the inner personality, as it is in Jewish-Hellenistic philosophy,

---

emphasises the irony of a doctrine which Qoheleth's opponents cling to, but which does not function." See also Gordis, "Quotations in Wisdom Literature," 137; "Quotations as a Literary Usage in Biblical, Oriental and Rabbinic Literature," 163–64; Levy, *Qoheleth*, 115; and Zimmer, *Zwischen Tod*, 205.

35. As is suggested in Fox, *A Time to Tear Down*, 286; Krüger, *Kohelet*, 289; Ogden, *Qoheleth*, 137–38; Scwhienhorst-Schönberger, *Kohelet*, 425–26; and Seow, *Ecclesiastes*, 288.

36. See Gordis, *Koheleth*, 282–83, 287; Longman, *Ecclesiastes*, 219; Murphy, *Ecclesiastes*, 87; Scott, *Proverbs, Ecclesiastes*, 242–43; and Whybray, *Ecclesiastes*, 135.

37. See Seow, *Ecclesiastes*, 145.

38. See Davis, "Ecclesiastes 12:1–8," 300.

but merely of the general principle of life stripped of every peculiarity of its individuality.

According to Qohelet, the obliterating power of death allows no individual consciousness to survive, and it is therefore depicted as the absolute boundary of human existence.[39] Qohelet clings thus to the holistic anthropology of his ancestors in which man is not regarded as the addition of body and soul but as an inseparable unity of the principle of life and flesh, dissolving at the hour of death, after which both components return to their sources—being God, the giver of life, on the one hand, and the dust of the earth on the other.[40] Qohelet takes up a somewhat conservative stance with respect to death and can in this respect be considered as a conservative sage.[41]

Furthermore, Qohelet goes beyond criticizing the innovative view of other sages by developing an alternative outlook on life. Contrary to the line of thinking evolved in the footsteps of the doctrine of retribution, he does not focus on the afterlife, but rather on life before death. In Qohelet's considerations, death does not appear as the necessary access to everlasting life, which is in all respects superior to earthly life, but as a dehumanizing,[42] and, to put it in Qohelet's own words, "vain" (הבל) phenomenon.[43] Hence he ironically asserts that a living dog is better than

---

39. See Burkes, *Death in Qoheleth*, 75; Fox, *A Time to Tear Down*, 332; Hossfeld, "Die theologische Relevanz des Buches Kohelet," 385; Kutschera, "Kohelet," 363; Lauha, *Kohelet*, 115; Longman, *Ecclesiastes*, 128; and Schoors, "Koheleth."

40. See Fox, *A Time to Tear Down*, 331; Schoors, "Koheleth," 304; and Schweizer, "Body," 768.

41. An exemplification of this assertion is to be found in Qohelet's disbelief of a corporal resurrection, which he shares with the majority of Old Testament writings. The Hebrew Bible contains only one explicit reference to a raising of the dead in the future, notably Dan 12:2–3, an apocalyptic vision that obviously stands at the end of the above-depicted evolution in Jewish thinking: "Many of those who sleep in the dust of the earth shall awake, some to everlasting life, and some to shame and everlasting contempt. Those who are wise shall shine like the brightness of the sky, and those who lead many to righteousness, like the stars forever and ever." In the Christian Old Testament, only 2 Macc 7:9 bears witness to a similar belief: "And when he was at his last breath, he said, 'You accursed wretch, you dismiss us from this present life, but the King of the universe will raise us up to an everlasting renewal of life, because we have died for his laws.'" See in this respect, Burkes, *Death in Qoheleth*, 83–84; Janowski, "Sehnsucht," 35.

42. See Burkes, *Death in Qoheleth*, 71.

43. Other translations of הבל have been suggested in recent exegesis, such as "absurd(ity)" or "ephemeral(ity)." For a discussion of הבל, see Albertz, "הבל *hebel*"; Drijvers, "Alles is lucht?"; Ehlrich, "הבל – Metaphern der Nichtigkeit"; Fox, "The Meaning of *Hebel*

a dead lion (9:4),[44] which is an extremely ironic proverb. The dog, considered to be one of the lowest animal species, is better off alive than the already dead lion, even though the latter is looked upon as the king of the animals, associated with courage and royal power.[45]

After all, as long as people are alive, they have the possibility of enjoying the good things of life. In this way, Qohelet's observations are not purely negative, but lead to a positive alternative. His deconstruction of the doctrine of retribution ultimately turns out to be an appreciation of the pleasures in life and hence a reconstruction of wisdom, be it of a somewhat more modest nature than the teachings of the adherents of the doctrine of retribution. Even though the merits of wisdom are limited, wisdom is still preferable to foolishness in Qohelet's view.

This reconstruction of alternative wisdom teachings is exemplified in the ninth chapter, when Qohelet once again emphasizes that one and the same fate will come to all, to both the righteous and the wicked, both the good and the evil (9:2). Subsequently, he recommends that his audience enjoy everyday life as long as they have the opportunity to do so:

> [9:7] Go, eat your bread with enjoyment, and drink your wine with a merry heart; for God has long ago approved what you do. [8] Let your garments always be white; do not let oil be lacking on your head. [9] Enjoy life with the wife whom you love, all the days of your vain life that are given you under the sun, because that is your portion in life and in your toil at which you toil under the sun. [10]

---

for Qohelet"; Fox, *A Time to Tear Down*, 27–42; Lauha, "Omnia vanitas"; Loretz, *Qohelet und der alte Orient*, 218–46; McKenna, "The Concept of *Hebel*"; Michel, *Untersuchungen zur Eigenart*, 40–51; Miller, "Qohelet's Symbolic Use of הבל"; Ogden, "'Vanity' It Certainly Is Not"; Schoors, *The Preacher Sought to Find Pleasing Words*, 2:119–29; Seybold, "הבל hebhel"; and Zimmer, *Zwischen Tod*, 25–32.

44. Some commentators argue that this aphorism could have existed before Qohelet; see Crenshaw, *Ecclesiastes*, 161; Lauha, *Kohelet*, 165; Lavoie, "Vie, mort et finitude," 77–78; and Michel, *Untersuchungen*, 176.

45. Examples of the inferiority of the dog can be found in Deut 23:19; 1 Sam 17:43; 24:15; 2 Sam 9:8; 16:9; 2 Kgs 8:13; Ps 22:17; 59:7, 15; Prov 26:11; Sir 26:25; and Isa 56:10–11; examples of the royalty and courage attributed the lion in Gen 49:9; 2 Sam 17:10; 1 Chr 12:9; 1 Macc 3:4; 2 Macc 11:11; Prov 19:12; 28:1; 30:30; Hos 5:14; 13:7; and Ezek 32:2. See in this respect Beek, *Prediker*, Hoogleed, 111; Bergant, *Ecclesiastes*, 275; Brown, *Ecclesiastes*, 92; Crenshaw, "The Shadow of Death in Qoheleth," 209; Firmage, "Zoology," 1143–44; Gordis, *Koheleth*, 295; Lavoie, "Vie, mort et finitude," 78; Krüger, *Kohelet*, 305; Lauha, *Kohelet*, 167–68; Lohfink, *Kohelet*, 66; Longman, *Ecclesiastes*, 228; Murphy, *Ecclesiastes*, 92; Schwienhorst-Schönberger, *Kohelet*, 449; Seow, *Ecclesiastes*, 301; van der Ploeg, *Prediker*, 56–57; and Whybray, *Ecclesiastes*, 142.

Whatever your hand finds to do, do with your might, for there is no work or thought or knowledge or wisdom in Sheol, to which you are going.[46]

In these verses, Qohelet no longer speaks in reflective considerations, but directly addresses his audience in order to convince them that they should make the most of every opportunity to enjoy life. The short imperative forms that he uses create a sense of urgency, which is in fact hardly surprising, because death annihilates the ability to enjoy life, and Qohelet wants people to avoid wasting the opportunities given to them "under the sun" by not grasping them immediately. In verse 10, he stresses that one should not expect to enter a superior life beyond death in which the same opportunities will be given in abundance: in Sheol every hope and aspiration has gone to waste. Contrary to what had been taught in Prov 15:24 (see above), he suggests that even the wise cannot avoid Sheol, where their wisdom is lost forever.

In verses 7 to 9, however, Qohelet provides some examples of opportunities to enjoy life on earth. All of these examples refer to everyday life—eating, drinking, and loving "a" wife[47]—with the possible exception of the oil and the white clothes in verse 8, which were both expensive goods in ancient Israel and were therefore only used on special occasions.[48] Still, the position of this verse between two references to everyday life and the words בכל־עת at the beginning of the verse seem to indicate that Qohelet rather advises his audience to consider every day that they may live as a special occasion worth celebrating.[49] As a consequence, I consider this

---

46. It has been suggested that Qohelet's reference to Sheol would be a metaphor for man's grave. See Levy, *Qoheleth*, 119.

47. It should be noted that the Hebrew text lacks the definite article in אשה. Hence it has been argued, particularly in Yeong-Sik Pahk, "A Syntactical and Contextual Consideration," that Qohelet disdains marriage and favours promiscuity. However, Qohelet's point is not to discuss marriage as a social institution, but rather to consider the pleasures in life, of which living alongside a woman is part. See also Ehrlich, *Randglossen zur Hebräischen Bibel*, 94; Krüger, *Kohelet*, 307; Lavoie, "Bonheur et finitude humaine," 319–21; Lohfink, *Kohelet*, 70; Seow, *Ecclesiastes*, 301; Whybray, *Ecclesiastes*, 144; and Zimmer, *Zwischen Tod*, 120–21.

48. See Hertzberg, *Der Prediger*, 179; Lavoie, "Bonheur et finitude humaine," 318–19; Levy, *Qoheleth*, 118; Longman, *Ecclesiastes*, 230; Murphy, *Ecclesiastes*, 93; Scott, *Proverbs, Ecclesiastes*, 246; van der Ploeg, *Prediker*, 57; and Whybray, *Ecclesiastes*, 144.

49. It should be remarked that Lohfink explicitly opposes this interpretation of Eccl 9:7–9; cf. Lohfink, *Kohelet*, 70: "Die bisher einzigen konkreten Motive 'Essen' und 'Trinken' werden durch andere erweitert, die aber alle in den Kreis des Festefeierns ge-

pericope as a whole to be focused on the small pleasures of everyday life. Similar advice had already been given by Qohelet in the previous chapters of his book:

> [2:24] There is nothing better for mortals than to eat and drink, and find enjoyment in their toil. This also, I saw, is from the hand of God; [25] for apart from him who can eat or who can have enjoyment?
>
> [3:13] Moreover, it is God's gift that all should eat and drink and take pleasure in all their toil.
>
> [5:18] This is what I have seen to be good: it is fitting to eat and drink and find enjoyment in all the toil with which one toils under the sun the few days of the life God gives us; for this is our lot.
>
> [8:15] So I commend enjoyment, for there is nothing better for people under the sun than to eat, and drink, and enjoy themselves, for this will go with them in their toil through the days of life that God gives them under the sun.

In other words, it would do Qohelet wrong to label him as a pessimist, since this is only one side of the picture. Next to his pessimistic considerations about the fate of every man and the impossibility to overcome this fate, there is also a remarkable optimism towards the opportunities to enjoy everyday life in his book, although this optimism should not be exaggerated.[50] Even if humankind is undoubtedly heading for the ultimate vanity of death, and even if no one's merits will endure the course of time, it is, according to Qohelet, still possible for the individual to cope with the apparent futility of a life limited in time, particularly by enjoying the pleasures of eating, drinking, toiling, and loving. Qohelet's gloomy thoughts on the theme of death or *memento mori* turn out to be a kind of *via negationis* for his *carpe diem*, his appeal to leap at every opportunity to enjoy life.[51]

---

hören. Kohelet ist kein Prediger der 'kleinen Freuden des Alltags', wie manche Moralisten möchten. Er denkt an große Gelage."

50. See, for example, Schoors's assessment of the root שמח, which appears in all Qohelet's recommendations of enjoyment, in *The Preacher Sought*, 2:176–80. Cf. Van Hecke, "'Wie goed doet, goed ontmoet,'" 61.

51. Cf. Schwienhorst-Schönberger, *"Nicht im Menschen gründet das Glück,"* 331: "Das Thema Tod ist im Buch allgegenwärtig, aber nicht als Ausdruck von Melancholie und Pessimismus, sondern als die via negationis der Begründung des Aufrufs zur Freude." Cf. Zimmer, *Zwischen Tod*, 155: "Bei der hier vorausgesetzten Annahme, daß die Reflexionen

## CONCLUSION

This essay has briefly explored the considerations of Qohelet concerning human mortality. It has demonstrated that Qohelet does not give approval to the doctrine of retribution that had been received by many of the sages of his day. Being extremely sceptical of their postulations about a rescue from death, he highlights the physical reality of death. At the same time, he offers some practical advice to his readers and recommends that they seize the opportunities to enjoy everyday life—despite its iniquities—as long as possible. For Qohelet, life on earth is not a mere prelude to the afterlife, but rather and above all a unique event of which man should take advantage whenever God allows him to, even if the same life is full of injustice and sorrow.

---

des Kohelet-Buches weitgehend auf die Erkenntnis der eigenen Sterblichkeit und die daraus resultierende Auseinandersetzung mit traditionellen Weltvorstellungen zurückgehen, ergibt sich, daß das *memento mori* in diesem Erkenntnisprozeß Kohelets chronologisch vor dem *carpe diem* steht."

## BIBLIOGRAPHY

Albertz, Rainer. "הבל hebel." In *Theological Lexicon of the Old Testament*, edited by E. Jenni and C. Westermann, 1:351–53. Translated by Mark E. Biddle. Peabody, MA: Hendrickson, 1997.

Albright, William Foxwell. *From the Stone Age to Christianity: Monotheism and the Historical Process*. Baltimore: Johns Hopkins University Press, 1946.

Beek, M. A. *Prediker, Hooglied*. De Prediking van het Oude Testament. Nijkerk: Callenbach, 1984.

Beentjes, Panc. "'Who Is Like the Wise?' Some Notes on Qohelet 8,1–15." In *Qohelet in the Context of Wisdom*, edited by A. Schoors, 303–15. BETL 136. Leuven: Peeters, 1998.

Bergant, Dianne. *Job, Ecclesiastes*. Old Testament Message 18. Wilmington, DE: Glazier, 1982.

Berlejung, A. "Was kommt nach dem Tod? Die alttestamentische Rede von Tod und Unterwelt." *BK* 61 (2006) 2–7.

Bianchi, Francesco. "The Language of Qohelet: A Bibliographical Survey." *ZAW* 105 (1993) 210–23.

Brown, William P. *Ecclesiastes*. Interpretation. Louisville: Westminster John Knox, 2000.

Burkes, Shannon. *Death in Qoheleth and Egyptian Biographies of the Late Period*. SBLDS 170. Atlanta: Society of Biblical Literature, 1999.

Burkitt, F. C. "Is Ecclesiastes a Translation?" *JTS* 23 (1922) 22–28.

Crenshaw, James L. *Ecclesiastes: A Commentary*. OTL. London: SCM, 1988.

———. "The Shadow of Death in Qoheleth." In *Israelite Wisdom: Theological and Literary Essays in Honor of Samuel Terrein*, edited by John G. Gammie, et al., 205–16. Homage Series 3. Missoula, MT: Scholars, 1978.

Cross, Frank Moore. "The Oldest Manuscripts from Qumran." *JBL* 74 (1955) 147–72.

Custer, John S. "Qohelet and the Canon: The Dissenting Voice in Dialogue." *JJT* 1:2 (1994) 15–24.

Dahood, Mitchell J. "Canaanite-Phoenician Influence in Qoheleth." *Bib* 33 (1952) 30–52, 191–221.

———. "The Language of Qoheleth." *CBQ* 14 (1952) 227–32.

———. "Northwest Semitic Philology and Three Biblical Texts." *JNSL* 2 (1972) 17–22.

———. "The Phoenician Background of Qoheleth." *Bib* 47 (1966) 264–82.

———. "Qoheleth and Northwest Semitic Philology." *Bib* 43 (1962) 349–65.

———. "Qoheleth and Recent Discoveries." *Bib* 39 (1958) 302–18.

———. "Three Parallel Pairs in Eccl. 10:18: A Reply to Prof. Gordis." *JQR* 62 (1971–72) 84–87.

Davis, Barry C. "Ecclesiastes 12:1–8: Death, an Impetus for Life." *BSac* 148 (1991) 298–318.

Debel, Hans. "Gedenk, o mens, dat je zult sterven... Het perspectief van het boek Prediker op het leven vóór en na de dood." In *Bijbelse wijsheid aan het woord*, edited by Hans Ausloos and Bénédicte Lemmelijn, 85–119. Leuven: VBS–Acco, 2007.

Delitzsch, Franz. *Hoheslied und Koheleth. Biblischer Commentar über die nachexilischen Geschichtsbücher* IV, 4. Leipzig: Dürffling und Franke, 1875.

Delsman, Wilhelmus Cornelis. *Die Datierung des Buches Qoheleth: eine Sprachwissenschaftliche Analyse*. Nijmegen: Nijmegen University Press, 2000.

Drijvers, Pius. "Alles is lucht? De betekenis van het woord הֶבֶל in het bijbelboek Prediker." In *Prediker*, edited by G. J. Venema, 51–61. ACEBT 21. Maastricht: Shaker, 2004.

Ehrlich, Arnold B. *Randglossen zur Hebraïschen Bibel: Textkritisches, sprachliches und sachliches* 7. Hildesheim: Olms, 1968 (= Leipzig, 1914).
Ehlich, Konrad. "הבל—Metaphern der Nichtigkeit." In *"Jedes Ding hat seine Zeit . . .": Studien zur israelitischen und altorientalischen Weisheit: Diethelm Michel zum 65*, edited by Anja A. Diesel et al., 49–64. BZAW 241. Berlin: de Gruyter, 1996.
Fernández, A. "¿Es Eclesiastes una versión?" *Bib* 3 (1922) 45–50.
Firmage, E. "Zoology." In *ABD* 6:1109–67.
Fox Michael V. "Aging and Death in Qohelet 12." *JSOT* 42 (1988) 55–77.
———. "The Meaning of *Hebel* for Qohelet." *JBL* 105 (1986) 409–27.
———. *A Time to Tear Down and a Time to Build Up: A Rereading of Ecclesiastes*. Grand Rapids: Eerdmans, 1999.
Fredericks, Daniel C. *Qoheleth's Language: Re-Evaluating Its Nature and Date*. Ancient Near Eastern Texts and Studies 3. Lewiston, NY: Mellen, 1988.
Galling, Kurt. "Der Prediger." In *Die Fünf Megilloth*, edited by Ernst Würthwein et al., 73–125. Handbuch zum Alten Testament 18. Tübingen: Mohr, 1969.
Gilbert, Maurice. *Les cinq livres des Sages: Proverbes, Job, Qohélet, Ben Sira, Sagesse*. Lire la Bible. Paris: CERF, 2003.
Ginsberg, Harold Louis. *Studies in Koheleth*. TSJTSA 17. New York: Jewish Theological Seminary of America, 1950.
Ginsburg, Christian D. *The Song of Songs and Coheleth, Commonly Called the Book of Ecclesiastes: Translated from the Original Hebrew, with a Commentary, Historical and Critical* (1861), edited by S. H. Blank. New York: KTAV, 1970.
Gordis, Robert. "Koheleth—Hebrew or Aramaic?" *JBL* 71 (1952) 93–109.
———. *Koheleth: The Man and His World*. 2nd, aug. ed. TSJTSA 19. New York: Bloch, 1955.
———. "On Methodology in Biblical Exegesis." *JQR* 61 (1970–71) 93–118.
———. "The Original Language of Qohelet." *JQR* 37 (1946–47) 67–84.
———. "Qoheleth and Qumran: A Study of Style." *Bib* 41 (1960) 395–410.
———. "Quotations as a Literary Usage in Biblical, Oriental and Rabbinic Literature." *HUCA* 22 (1949) 157–219.
———. "Quotations in Wisdom Literature." *JQR* 30 (1939–40) 123–47.
———. "The Translation Theory of Qohelet Re-Examined." *JQR* 40 (1949–50) 103–16.
———. "Was Koheleth a Phoenician? Some Observations on Methods of Research." *JBL* 74 (1955) 103–14.
Gordon, Cyrus H. *Ugaritic Literature: A Comprehensive Translation of the Poetic and Prose Texts*. Scripta Pontificii Instituti Biblici 98. Rome: Pontificium Institutum Biblicum, 1949.
Gretler, Trix. *Zeit und Stunde: Theologische Zeitkonzepte zwischen Erfahrung und Ideologie in den Büchern Kohelet und Daniel*. TVZ Dissertationen. Zürich: Theologischer, 2004.
Hertzberg, Hans Wilhelm. *Der Prediger*. KAT 17.4. Gütersloh: Mohn, 1963.
Hossfeld, Frank-Lothar. "Die Theologische Relevanz des Buches Kohelet." In *Das Buch Kohelet: Studien zur Struktur, Geschichte, Rezeption und Theologie*, edited by Ludger Schwienhorst-Schönberger, 377–89. BZAW 254. Berlin: de Gruyter, 1997.
Janowski, Bernd. "Sehnsucht nach Unsterblichkeit: Zur Jenseitshoffnung in der Weisheitlichen Literatur." *BK* 61 (2006) 34–39.

Jastrow, Morris, Jr. *A Gentle Cynic: Being a Translation of the Book of Koheleth, Commonly Known as Ecclesiastes, Stripped of Later Additions, also its Origin, Growth and Interpretation*. Philadelphia: Lippincott, 1919.

Kroeber, Rudi. *Der Prediger*. SQAW 13. Berlin: Akademie, 1963.

Krüger, Thomas. *Kohelet (Prediger)*. BKAT 19. Neukirchen: Neukirchener, 2000.

———. *Qoheleth*. Hermeneia. Minneapolis: Fortress, 2004.

Kugel, James L. "Qohelet and Money." *CBQ* 51 (1989) 32–49.

Kutschera, Franz von. "Kohelet: Leben im Angesicht des Todes." In *Das Buch Kohelet: Studien zur Struktur, Geschichte, Rezeption und Theologie*, edited by Ludger Schwienhorst-Schönberger, 363–76. BZAW 254. Berlin: de Gruyter, 1997.

Lauha, Aarre. *Kohelet*. BKAT 19. Neukirchen: Neukirchener, 1978.

———. "Omnia Vanitas: Die Bedeutung von hbl bei Kohelet." In *Glaube und Gerechtigkeit: In Memoriam Rafael Gyllenberg*, edited by Jarmo Kiilunen et al., 19–25. Schriften der Finnichen Exegetischen Gesellschaft 38. Helsinki: Vammalan Kirjapaino Oy, 1983.

Laurent, Françoise. *Les biens pour rien en Qohéleth 5,9–6,6 ou la traverse d'un contraste*. BZAW 323. Berlin: de Gruyter, 2002.

Lavoie, Jean-Jacques. "Bonheur et finitude humaine: etude de Qo 9,7–10." *ScEs* 45 (1993) 313–24.

———. "Vie, mort et finitude humaine en Qo 9,1–6." *ScEs* 47 (1995): 69–80.

Levy, Ludwig. *Das Buch Qoheleth: Ein Beitrag zur Geschichte des Sadduzäismus, kritisch untersucht, übersetzt und erklärt*. Leipzig: Hinrich, 1912.

Lohfink, Norbert. *Kohelet*. NEchtB. Würzburg: Echter, 1980.

———. "Kohelet und die Banken: Zur Übersetzung von Kohelet v 12–16." *VT* 39 (1989) 488–95.

Longman, Tremper, III. *The Book of Ecclesiastes*. NICOT. Grand Rapids: Eerdmans, 1998.

Loretz, Oswald. *Qohelet und der alte Orient: Untersuchungen zu Stil und theologischer Thematik des Buches Qohelet*. Freiburg: Herder, 1964.

McKenna, John E. "The Concept of *Hebel* in the Book of Ecclesiastes." *SJT* 45 (1992) 19–28.

Michel, Diethelm. *Qohelet*. EdF 258. Darmstadt: Wissenschaftliche Buchgesellschaft, 1988.

———. *Untersuchungen zur Eigenart des Buches Qohelet: Mit einem Anhang von Reinhard G. Lehmann Bibliographie zu Qohelet*. BZAW 183. Berlin: de Gruyter, 1989.

Middendorp, Theophil. *Die Stellung Jesu Ben Siras zwischen Judentum und Hellenismus*. Leiden: Brill, 1973.

Miller, Douglas B. "Qohelet's Symbolic Use of הבל." *JBL* 117 (1998) 437–54.

Muilenburg, James. "A Qoheleth Scroll from Qumran." *BASOR* 135 (1954) 20–28.

Murphy, Roland E. *Ecclesiastes*. WBC 23A. Dallas: Word, 1992.

Nebe, G. Wilhelm. "Qumranica I: Zu unveröffentlichten Handschriften aus Höhle 4 von Qumran." *ZAW* 106 (1994) 307–22.

Ogden, Graham. *Qoheleth*. Readings: A New Biblical Commentary. Sheffield: JSOT Press, 1987.

———. "'Vanity' It Certainly Is Not." *BT* 38 (1987) 301–7.

Ploeg, van der, Johannes. *Prediker. De Boeken van het Oude Testament* 8.2. Roermond: Romer & Zonen, 1953.

Podechard, Emmanuel. *L'Ecclésiaste*. EBib. Paris: Gabalda, 1912.

Rudman, Dominic. "A Note on the Dating of Ecclesiastes." *CBQ* 61 (1999) 47–52.

Schoors, Antoon. "Koheleth: A Perspective on Life after Death." *ETL* 61 (1985) 295–303.

———. "(Mis)use of Intertextuality in Qoheleth Exegesis." In *Congress Volume Oslo 1998*, edited by André Lemaire and Magne Sæbø, 45–59. VTSup 80. Leiden: Brill, 2000.
———. *The Preacher Sought to Find Pleasing Words: A Study of the Language of Qoheleth*. 2 vols. OLA 41, 143. Leuven: Peeters, 2004.
———. "Qoheleth: A Book in a Changing Society." *OTE* 9 (1996) 68–87.
———. "The Use of Vowel Letters in Qoheleth." *UF* 20 (1988) 277–86.
Schweizer, R. E. "Body." In *ABD* 1:767–72.
Schwienhorst-Schönberger, Ludger. *"Nicht im Menschen gründet das Glück" (Koh 2,24): Kohelet im Spannungsfeld jüdischer Weisheit und hellenistischer Philosophie*. Herders Biblische Studien 2. Freiburg: Herder, 1994.
———. "Kohelet: Stand und Perspektiven der Forschung." In *Das Buch Kohelet: Studien zur Struktur, Geschichte, Rezeption und Theologie*, edited by Ludger Schwienhorst-Schönberger, 5–31. BZAW 254. Berlin: de Gruyter, 1997.
———. *Kohelet*. HThKAT. Freiburg: Herder, 2004.
Scott, R. B. Y. *Proverbs, Ecclesiastes: Introduction, Translation and Notes*. AB 18. Garden City, NY: Doubleday, 1965.
Seow, Choon-Leong. "Linguistic Evidence and the Dating of Qohelet." *JBL* 115 (1996) 643–66.
———. "The Socioeconomic Context of 'The Preacher's' Hermeneutic." *PSB* 17 (1996) 168–95.
———. *Ecclesiastes: A New Translation with Introduction and Commentary*. AB 18C. New York: Doubleday, 1997.
Seybold, K. "הבל hebhel." In *Theological Dictionary of the Old Testament*, edited by G. H. Botterweck et al., 3:313–20. 15 vols. Translated by D. E. Green. Grand Rapids: Eerdmans, 1974–2006.
Siegfried, Carl. *Prediger und Hoheslied*. Handbuch zum Alten Testament 3.2. Göttingen: Vandenhoeck und Ruprecht, 1898.
Torrey, Charles C. "The Question of the Original Language of Kohelet." *JQR* 39 (1948–49) 151–60.
Tov, Emanuel. *Textual Criticism of the Hebrew Bible*. 2nd rev. ed. Minneapolis: Fortress, 2001.
Tromp, Nicholas J. *Primitive Conceptions of Death and the Nether World in the Old Testament*. BibOr 21. Rome: Pontifical Biblical Institute, 1969.
Ulrich, Eugene. "Ezra and Qoheleth Manuscripts from Qumran (4QEzra and 4QQoh[a,b])." In *Priests, Prophets and Scribes: Essays on the Formation and Heritage of Second Temple Judaism in Honour of Joseph Blenkinsop*, edited by Eugene Ulrich et al., 139–57. JSOTSup 149. Sheffield: JSOT Press, 1992.
Ulrich, Eugene, et al. *Qumran Cave 4, Vol. 11: Psalms to Chronicles*. DJD 16. Oxford: Clarendon, 2000.
Van Hecke, Pierre. "'Wie goed doet, goed ontmoet'... of toch niet? Het daad-gevolgprincipe en zijn tegenstanders." In *Bijbelse wijsheid aan het woord*, edited by Hans Ausloos and Bénédicte Lemmelijn, 47–63. Leuven: VBS-Acco, 2007.
Van Niekerk, M. J. H. "Response to J. A. Loader's 'Different Reactions of Job and Qoheleth to the Doctrine of Retribution.'" *OTE* 4 (1991) 97–105.
Vinel, Françoise. *L'Ecclésiaste*. La Bible D'Alexandrie 18. Paris: CERF, 2002.
Whitley, Charles F. *Koheleth: His Language and Thought*. BZAW 148. Berlin: de Gruyter, 1979.
Whybray, R. N. *Ecclesiastes*. NCB. Grand Rapids: Eerdmans, 1989.

Yeong-Sik Pahk, Johan. "A Syntactical and Contextual Consideration of '*sh* in Qoh IX 9." *VT* 51 (2001) 370–80.

Zimmer, Tilmann. *Zwischen Tod und Lebensglück: Eine Untersuchung zur Anthropologie Kohelets*. BZAW 286. Berlin: de Gruyter, 1999.

Zimmermann, Frank. "The Aramaic Provenance of Qohelet." *JQR* 36 (1945–46) 17–45.

———. "The Question of Hebrew in Qohelet." *JQR* 40 (1949–50) 79–102.

# 4

## Two Jewish American Interpretations of the Book of Job in the Aftermath of the Holocaust

### *A Short Discussion of the Relationship between Job's Modern Reception and Its Ancient Production*

DAVID C. TOLLERTON

University of Bristol

### INTRODUCTION

THE BOOK OF JOB has a rich and complex reception history. For a number of Jewish American religious thinkers responding specifically to the Holocaust, it has, as one of the major treatments of the theme of innocent suffering in biblical literature, often been considered resonant. Yet, for reasons that will be outlined here, the manner in which they understand this biblical text in a post-Holocaust context is neither uniform nor without contention.

This essay is concerned fundamentally with the reception of Job within this specifically modern context of Jewish American thinkers responding to the mass murder of Europe's Jews. Yet the book of Job is a text that originates in the context of the ancient Near East. How do these two geographical and temporal locations relate to one another?

When considering variations between the ways in which Jewish American thinkers read the book of Job in a post-Holocaust context, two things should be considered: what the readers in this context bring with them when they engage with Job, and what the story of Job itself brings with it from its origins in the ancient world. To this end, focus shall be placed upon the post-Holocaust readings of Job presented by two figures: the Holocaust survivor and Nobel Prize-winning writer Elie Wiesel and the Conservative rabbi and theologian Michael Goldberg. On the one hand, the radical differences between the interpretations of Job given by these two thinkers relate, to a very significant degree, to their divergent theological appreciations of the Holocaust. On the other hand, it will be proposed that the differences are also caused by structures within the book of Job that relate to the book's production in the ancient world. However, discussing this relationship between the production and reception of Job is, it will ultimately be asserted, a difficult and risk-prone discourse.

## ELIE WIESEL'S POST-HOLOCAUST READING OF JOB

In terms of levels of influence within collective Holocaust memory in North America, Elie Wiesel is a figure who undoubtedly stands on the highest tier.[1] Alan Berger has written that "Wiesel's writings have become an indispensable starting point for anyone wishing to think seriously about the *Shoah*'s theological and moral implications."[2] This Nobel Prize-winning writer has been spoken of with such reverential epithets as "teacher," "high priest of our generation," and "messenger to all humanity."[3]

Wiesel is not usually described as a theologian because of his frequent utilization of various forms of fiction-based literature rather than any discourse that could be labelled systematic. Indeed he declares himself averse to any sort of systematic consideration of the Holocaust's implications.[4] However, as Berger's comments regarding his significance suggest,

---

1. Some may query this study's alignment of Wiesel with "Jewish American" thought, since he was born in Hungary and writes predominantly in French. He is, however, a U.S. citizen and has been profoundly influential in Jewish American life in recent decades.

2. Berger, "Elie Wiesel," 383.

3. For "teacher of our generation," cf. Berger, "Elie Wiesel," 383. For "high priest of our generation," cf. Berenbaum, *The Vision of the Void*, 5. For "messenger of all humanity," the epithet given to Wiesel by the Nobel committee in 1986, cf. Downing, "Autobiography, Fiction, and Faith," 1441.

4. Note the comments of Berger: "Wiesel's prolific writings assume many forms: cantatas, dialogues, essays, memoirs, plays, and novels . . . Wiesel's thought eludes the systematic tendency of traditional philosophical and theological speculation. His is, instead, a literary or narrative theology that is at its most penetrating when raising rather than answering questions. Wiesel as storyteller can ask, and keep on asking, about those issues

his works have been widely considered to be rich in theological import. Wiesel stands at a point of notable influence for a broad movement that considers the Holocaust to be theologically problematic for Judaism to a profound degree.[5] For thinkers such as Wiesel, this event raises difficult questions regarding how a God within a covenantal relationship with the Jewish people could have allowed their mass extermination.

Because of this, for Wiesel and a number of theologians who, in varying ways, agree with his view that the Holocaust is problematic for Jewish religious thought, the figure of Job has often been considered resonant. To be specific, it is the rebellious Job of the book's poetic dialogues with which they sympathize.[6] Their questioning of providence in modernity may be likened to Job's words regarding God in 9:22–24:

> It is all one: therefore I say, he destroys both the blameless and the wicked. When disaster brings sudden death, he mocks at the calamity of the innocent. The earth is given into the hands of the wicked; he covers the eyes of its judges—if it is not he, who then is it?

It is these defiant sentiments of Job that Wiesel refers to in his most famous work, *Night*, written as a memoir of his experiences during the Holocaust.[7] Discussing his time in the camps, he likens himself to Job because of his theological questioning: "Some talked of God, of his mysterious ways, of the sins of the Jewish people, and their future deliverance.

---

which lie at the core of post-Auschwitz Jewish experience. Referring to the Holocaust, for example, he observes: 'I'm afraid of anyone who comes with a theory, a system, based on that experience. I am suspicious; I don't want theories. I believe the experience was above and beyond theories and systems and philosophies'" (Berger, "Elie Wiesel," 372–73).

5. There are many overviews of such theologies, sometimes described as "Holocaust theology." Cf. Katz, *Post-Holocaust Dialogues*; Morgan, *Beyond Auschwitz*; and Braiterman, *(God) after Auschwitz*.

6. For three such examples of citing Job's rebellion as resonant, cf. Berkovits, *Faith after the Holocaust*, 67–70; Greenberg, "Cloud of Smoke, Pillar of Fire," 34–36; and Blumenthal, *Facing the Abusing God*, 250–56. A notable counter-example is offered by the radical theologian Richard Rubenstein, who strongly asserts that Job's rebellion cannot appropriately be likened to Jewish suffering during the Holocaust. Cf. Rubenstein. "Job and Auschwitz," 421–37.

7. Michael Goldberg has commented that *Night* "may be the best-known Holocaust story penned by a survivor." Goldberg, *Why Should Jews Survive?*, 23.

But I had ceased to pray. How I sympathized with Job! I did not deny God's existence, but I doubted His absolute justice."[8]

It is unsurprising therefore that many have continued referring to Wiesel as a kind of post-Holocaust Job. Dan Cohn-Sherbok, for example, reflects that "Wiesel adopts a Job-like stance. With bitterness he criticises God for allowing the Nazis to destroy the Jewish people. Throughout his novels he expresses outrage that He could have allowed the Jews to endure torture and murder at the hands of the Nazis."[9]

However, Wiesel's relationship with Job in his works after *Night* is not one of uniform empathy. This is because Job's response to suffering is *itself* far from uniform. While Job may be broadly characterized as defiant during the book's poetic dialogues, the Job of the book's opening and closing chapters is seemingly far more accepting of providence. Of particular importance for the present discussion of Wiesel is his ultimately submissive response to God's speeches in 42:1–6:

> Then Job answered the LORD:
> "I know that you can do all things, and that no purpose of yours can be thwarted. 'Who is this that hides counsel without knowledge?'
> Therefore I have uttered what I did not understand, things too wonderful for me, which I did not know. 'Hear, and I will speak; I will question you, and you declare to me.' I had heard of you by the hearing of the ear, but now my eye sees you; therefore I despise myself, and repent in dust and ashes."

After the largely rebellious content of Job's words during the poetic dialogues with his friends, many commentators, such as Robert Gordis, have characterized these lines as "words of submission."[10]

This is an interpretation that Wiesel follows in one of his most sustained discussions of the book of Job after *Night*, a chapter entitled "Job: Our Contemporary" in his 1976 nonfiction work, *Messengers of God: Biblical Portraits and Legends*. Here he again expresses admiration for Job's defiance, but also reflects upon his unease with what he understands to be his repentance in 42:1–6:

---

8. Wiesel, *Night*, 57.
9. Cohn-Sherbok, *God and the Holocaust*, 102.
10. Gordis, *The Book of God and Man*, 120.

> Much as I admired Job's passionate rebellion, I am deeply troubled by his hasty abdication ... I was preoccupied with Job, especially in the early years after the war. In those days, he could be seen on every road of Europe. Wounded, robbed, mutilated. Certainly not happy. Nor resigned. I was offended by his surrender in the text. Job's resignation as man was an insult to man. He should not have given in so easily. He should have continued to protest.[11]

While Job's rebellion in the book's poetic dialogues may appeal to Wiesel, his ultimate capitulation after God's speeches seems unattractive in the aftermath of the Holocaust. Yet in this chapter he finds of a way of redeeming Job, and returning him to the status of attractive theological rebel. He achieves this by suggesting that, despite appearances, Job's repentance was an act of deception:

> Had he remained firm, had he discussed the divine arguments point by point, one would conclude that he had to concede defeat in the face of his interlocutor's rhetorical superiority. But he said yes to God, immediately. He did not hesitate or procrastinate, nor did he point out the slightest contradiction. Therefore we know that in spite or perhaps because of appearances, Job continued to interrogate God. By repenting sins he did not commit, by justifying a sorrow he did not deserve, he communicates to us that he did not believe his own confessions; they were nothing but decoys.[12]

For Wiesel, Job remains the archetypal theological rebel that he admires, even when the surface of the biblical text has him submitting to God.

## MICHAEL GOLDBERG'S POST-HOLOCAUST READING OF JOB

At this point it is worth suspending consideration of Wiesel to examine a quite different post-Holocaust reading of Job. As noted above, the Holocaust, for Wiesel and others, represents a considerable theological problem. However, it would be inaccurate to suggest that this is uniformly

---

11. Wiesel, *Messengers of God*, 234. This disappointment regarding Job's apparent submission mirrors sentiments reflected through the character of the Holocaust survivor, Michael, in Elie Wiesel's earlier 1975 novel *The Town beyond the Wall*: "Michael never ceased resenting Job. That biblical rebel should never have given in. At the last moment he should have reared up, shaken a fist, and with a resounding blow defied that transcendent, inhuman Justice in which suffering has no weight in the balance" (52).

12. Wiesel, *Messengers of God*, 234–35.

the case for Jewish religious thinkers in North America. Note, for example, Jacob Neusner's comments that Jewish identity "based on the Holocaust cannot create a constructive, affirmative, and rational way of being Jewish for more than ten minutes at a time. Jews find in the Holocaust no new definition of Jewish identity because we need none. Nothing has changed. The tradition endures."[13] For Neusner, the suggestion that the Holocaust represents a radical challenge to traditionally conceived Judaism is to be strongly resisted.

A figure who shares this outlook is the Conservative rabbi Michael Goldberg. In his 1995 book, *Why Should Jews Survive? Looking Past the Holocaust toward a Jewish Future*, he reflects that while "through the ages, individual Jewish persons have been brutally persecuted, even murdered, God's promise to sustain the Jewish People has not died. That promise and that People have managed to survive the worst the world could throw at them—including the Holocaust."[14] For Goldberg, as for Neusner, God's covenantal relationship with the Jewish people remains steadfast regardless of the horrors of the Holocaust.

He is consequently unequivocal in his criticism of what he considers to be an overemphasis placed on the Holocaust's significance for American Jews in place of traditional covenantal Judaism. Elie Wiesel, as one of the most significant figures within American Holocaust memory, is a notable focal point for his unease: "In ancient times, the cultic shrine was superintended by priests. Local shrines had local priests while national shrines, for example, the Temple in Jerusalem, had high priests. Without doubt, the Holocaust cult's High Priest is Elie Wiesel. His blessing is sought for every museum and memorial, from the local *bamot* to the central *hechal* in Washington."[15]

Yet for all his radical divergences with a figure he describes as idolatrous, Goldberg, like Wiesel, appeals to Job as a model for post-Holocaust thought. As has been noted above, the figure of Job presents a model of theological anxiety, questioning, and rebellion that some, such as Wiesel, have found noteworthy for post-Holocaust thought. However, Wiesel had

---

13. Neusner, "The Implications of the Holocaust," 308.

14. Goldberg, *Why Should Jews Survive?*, 164.

15. Ibid., 59. Goldberg is specifically critical of what he perceives to be Wiesel's celebrity status, his support of the—in Goldberg's view, overly expensive—United States Holocaust Memorial Museum, and his support for the policies of the state of Israel during conflict with the Palestinians.

to grapple with the fact that Job is not a uniformly rebellious archetype. Indeed, many have noted that throughout the reception history of Job it is his initially submissive acceptance of divine providence that his been dominant. Note, for example, the comments of Robert Gordis:

> [T]here are two radically different Jobs in the biblical masterpiece. One is the hero of the prose tale, whose righteousness is matched by his piety and who retains his faith and patience under the gravest of provocations. The other is the Job of the dialogue, a passionate rebel against the injustice of undeserved suffering, who challenges God Himself. We cannot understand the influence of this powerful and disturbing book on the Western world unless we remember that most of the twenty-five centuries that have elapsed since its composition have been ages of faith. During this long expanse of time it was, by and large, the long-suffering Job of the prologue, and not the passionate and pain-wracked Job of the dialogue, who occupied men's thoughts.[16]

Perhaps one of the best-known lines of the book is Job's (1:21) pious comment after the destruction of his children and wealth that "the LORD gave, and the LORD has taken away; blessed be the name of the LORD." Goldberg makes notable use of Job's pious words to suggest that Jews after the Holocaust should remain steadfast to the ideal of the covenant even if, he acknowledges, it is concluded that God is *ultimately* responsible for suffering:

> [W]hen Job utters those famous words, in light of—and not in spite of—everything that has happened to him, he is acknowledging God as the Lord of everything. . . . In acknowledging God as the ultimate source of even the most horrendous suffering, Job and Jews maintain their integrity by wholeheartedly persisting in speaking the truth. Strikingly, Job only speaks falsely when he presumes (like his "friends") to explain why he suffers.[17]

Here Goldberg has utilized Job as an archetypal figure of piety and acceptance to support his view regarding the need for Jewish religious continuity after the Holocaust. What is notable is that, faced with the archetypal figure of rebellion and questioning that the Job of the poetic dialogues presents, he downplays this in a manner synonymous with Wiesel's downplaying of Job's pious repentance. For Goldberg, Job's questioning in

16. Gordis, *The Book of God and Man*, 219.
17. Goldberg, *Why Should Jews Survive?*, 78–79.

the poetic dialogues represents his notable failure. For Wiesel, Job's piety is his failing, in contrast to his rebellious defiance.

## MODERN AND ANCIENT CONTEXTS
### *The Role of the Readers*

How are we to understand the radical contrast between Wiesel and Goldberg's post-Holocaust readings of Job? There are, it is proposed here, two distinct levels at which this contrast in the book's reception can be understood. The first relates to what the readers, Elie Wiesel and Michael Goldberg, have brought to the text; the second to the structures within the text shaped by its manner of development in the ancient world.

For the moment, focus shall be placed upon the influence of Wiesel and Goldberg's outlooks. It is not difficult to detect where this has taken place. As has been outlined, their readings of Job reflect, to an enormous degree, their respective theological concerns. Thus, since Wiesel is, broadly speaking, committed to an uneasy theological relationship with God by railing against his perceived injustices in the aftermath of the Holocaust, Job's rebellion is emphasized and held up as a model of correct conduct. Conversely, since Goldberg is committed to upholding an untroubled covenantal relationship of trust in God, he empathizes with Job's piety and declares his rebellion to be his a mistake. Clearly, their post-Holocaust theological commitments have shaped their divergent readings of Job.

There are also more subtle considerations that these readers have brought to the text of Job when attempting to render it meaningful for post-Holocaust thought. With regard to Wiesel, a considerable role is played by the interpretive tradition to which he appeals. It is recalled that when faced with the unpalatable nature of Job's repentance, Wiesel declares that Job's words were a deception, and that his rebellion against God continued. How does Wiesel justify such a reading? The answer lies within his appeal in *Messengers of God* to the traditions of rabbinic midrashic interpretation.[18] His comments in the introduction to the book are revealing in this regard: "What is a Jew? Sum, synthesis, vessel. Someone who feels every blow that ever struck his ancestors. He is crushed by their mourning and buoyed by their triumphs . . . All the legends, all the stories retold by the Bible and commented on by the Midrash—and here

---

18. For another post-Holocaust reading of Job that appeals to the traditions of midrashic interpretation, cf. Haar, "Job after Auschwitz."

the term *Midrash* is used in the largest sense: interpretation, illustration, creative imagination—involve us... We have but to reread them to realize that they are surprisingly topical. Job is our contemporary."[19]

Wiesel here refers, on one hand, to Midrash alongside the Bible as a source composed by rabbis in the past, separate from his own writing. Yet on the other hand, by emphasizing the contemporariness of stories such as Job and "the largest sense" of the term *Midrash*, he is clearly situating his own retellings of biblical tales within a broader midrashic tradition of interpretation.

This interpretive tradition has many attributes that are adequately described elsewhere and shall not be discussed any further here.[20] The one attribute that *is* presently important, however, is what has often been recognized as a willingness within Midrash to explore what might be termed "gaps in the biblical narrative." Thus, for example, discussing the story of Cain and Abel in Genesis chapter 4, the rabbinic Midrash *Bereshith Rabbah* speculates a great deal of dialogue between the brothers so as to flesh out Cain's motivations.[21]

Within his reading of Job, Wiesel might be said to similarly explore "gaps in the biblical narrative." By asserting that Job's apparent repentance was false, he is reading far more into the psychology of Job than is provided by the surface of the biblical text. Regardless of how we may feel regarding the plausibility of Wiesel's analysis of Job's words, what is important to note here is that the reading method he has brought to the text has allowed him to redeem Job as a resonant post-Holocaust text by maintaining Job's rebellion even in the face of his apparent submission.

Thus, in this context, both theological outlooks *and* interpretive traditions play a role in shaping engagement with the text. What has been discussed here is undoubtedly not all that can be suggested regarding those considerations that Goldberg and Wiesel have brought to their readings of Job. To a significant degree, the reasons why their interpretations vary relate to the concerns that they carry into their encounter with this biblical text.

---

19. Wiesel, *Messengers of God*, xii–xiii.
20. For a concise introduction to midrash, cf. Neusner, *What Is Midrash?*
21. *Bereshith Rabbah* 22:7. Cf. Handelman, *The Slayers of Moses*, 69.

## The Role of the Ancient

It is proposed here, however, that the book of Job is itself perhaps not entirely passive within its own interpretation. That is to say, there are things which Job brings into modernity from its origins in the ancient world that may play some part in its post-Holocaust reception. Nonetheless, there are notable difficulties in discussing the relationship between the book's production and reception. Firstly, though, attention will be given to what *can* be said regarding this relationship.

Within theoretical consideration of how texts are received, positing such a relationship is not a unanimously acceptable proposition. This is because to refer to something Job brings into modernity is to imply that there are elements of the text that are in some sense "fixed." This is a proposal that the reader-response theorist Stanley Fish rejects in his 1980 work *Is There a Text in This Class? The Authority of Interpretive Communities*. Answering the question of his title, he states,

> There isn't a text in this or any other class if one means by text what E. D. Hirsch and others mean by it, "an entity which always remains the same from one moment to the next." . . . But there is a text in this and every class if one means by text the structure of meanings that is obvious and inescapable from the perspective of whatever interpretive assumptions happen to be in force.[22]

For Fish, what constitutes a text receivable by a reader are not any fixed characteristics of that text, but rather the "interpretive assumptions" the reader brings to it.[23] This paper will agree with Fish only in part. As has been discussed above, the interpretive concerns Wiesel and Goldberg bring to their engagement with the book of Job play a huge role in shaping its meaning for these readers. However, there are elements of this biblical text that *are* fixed, have been fixed since it reached its present form in the ancient world, and have played an important part in shaping the manner in which Wiesel and Goldberg have understood it in modernity.

---

22. Fish, *Is There a Text in This Class?*, vii. Fish quotes from Hirsch, *Validity in Interpretation*, 46.

23. Barton notes the "extreme form of reader-response criticism associated with the name of the American critic Stanley Fish, in which the text almost ceases to have any 'rights' altogether, and the reader takes over the role of the writer entirely. A text, in fact, can be made to mean anything, though this is prevented from lapsing into sheer anarchy by a stress on what Fish calls 'interpretive communities,' groups of readers who share certain aims and styles of interpretation" (Barton, *Reading the Old Testament*, 213).

It is proposed here that what is fixed within the book of Job is not, however, any singular meaning. In fact, what is fixed is the reverse—the *absence* of a singular meaning. This statement requires some explanation.

What is *not* being alluded to here are those strands of modern literary theory that suggest that *all* texts are without singular meanings. John Barton notes that some within biblical studies have appropriated elements of reader-response theory in a manner suggesting that it sheds light only upon how particularly difficult texts are to be dealt with.[24] Theories such as those of Fish are more radical than this and apply to *all* texts, not merely those viewed as obscure. What will be proposed here is something different: that the book of Job has some *specific* structural characteristics that disrupt the notion that it is a text with a singular meaning, characteristics that have ultimately played a role in shaping Wiesel and Goldberg's radically differing post-Holocaust readings.

As has been noted above, the figure of Job presents two significantly different archetypal models: the rebellious Job of the poetic dialogues and the submissive Job of the book's opening and closing sections. Some have argued that this biblical text is an essentially unified work.[25] However, summarizing the views of an array of biblical scholars on the question of Job's dating, David Penchansky, in his 1990 book *The Betrayal of God: Ideological Conflict in Job*, notes that many have argued that these archetypes represent two sources with fundamentally differing attitudes towards how innocent suffering should be responded to. The piety of the prose in which Job declares that "the LORD gave, and the LORD has taken away" is regarded as a pre-exilic faith in divine providence. This was diminished in a *post*-exilic scepticism regarding divine justice, reflected in the depiction of Job railing against providence within the book's poetic sections:

> Various aspects of the frame's theology [the prose of 1–2 and 42:7–17] have been identified as characteristically early. They include a view of retribution that, it is argued, would have more likely pertained before the Israelite experience of exile.[26]
>
> Regarding the theological dating of the center, its rebellious and skeptical note is thought to characterize a profoundly (theologi-

---

24. Ibid., 217–18.
25. For an argument in favor of the book of Job's unity, cf. Habel, *The Book of Job*, 35–39.
26. Penchansky, *The Betrayal of God*, 88.

cally) disillusioned people. . . . Israel had been taken captive and its cultic and political life was destroyed by foreign invaders. These events correspond most closely to the theological picture in the center of Job [the poetry of 3–41:6].[27]

Penchansky rightly notes that this manner of theological dating involves a considerable degree of conjecture. Yet despite the disclaimers necessary, one cannot *wholly* dismiss the possibility that within Job can be seen the impressions of decisively differing attitudes towards the problem of evil.[28] While acceptance of what "the LORD gave, and the LORD has taken away" permeates the book's prose sections, the poetic sections may reflect an authorship less sure of divine justice—or, in its depiction of Job's friends wrongly confident of the protagonist's guilt—certainly more at pains to dismiss any theodicy of rewards and punishments.

This is of significance to discussion of Jewish American post-Holocaust readings of Job. It is not too improper to suggest that one of the decisive factors shaping differences in the readings of Wiesel and Goldberg is the strong possibility that within Job's origins were attitudes—as to whether a God who allowed innocent suffering should be accepted—that differed in ways similar to the views held by Wiesel and Goldberg. Parallels, we can tentatively propose, exist between the contexts of the origins *and* the receptions of the text. These thinkers are able to create radically differing readings of the text not only because of what they have brought to the text, but also because of the ideological ammunition that may have been stored in its ancient origins.

### *The Problematic Relationship between Ancient and Modern*

Immediately, however, concerns arise in the face of this discussion of a relationship between Job's production and reception. The ideal is a relationship in which historical-critical considerations of Job speak freely to discussion of the book's later reception. Yet this ideal is near impossible. This is because it seems unlikely that any contemplation of Job's origins in relation to its reception can avoid looking into the past through a contorting lens.

One might suggest, for example, that Wiesel is able to discover within Job's poetic dialogues the resources for rebellious questioning of

27. Ibid., 89–90.
28. Ibid., 90.

providence because within its origins lies a possibility of similar post-exilic questioning of the divine relationship with the world. It should be questioned, though, whether this consideration of Job's ancient past may not, in truth, have been seriously compromised by the mere suggestion of continuities between the ancient and the modern. For all Job's rebellious defiance in the poetic dialogues, it remains the case that his submissive response to God's final speech is also in the poetic section. One may wish to suggest that his submissive response to God is actually linguistically rather ambiguous—a suggestion that is incidentally not entirely without merit.[29] But the *motivations* for this should be at least queried. This is because the risk would be that one would be merely attempting to rescue Job's defiance for the purpose of retaining some trans-historical link between Job and Wiesel. In considering the origins of this biblical text in relation to its modern reception, charges of anachronism will always remain difficult to ignore.

There is, in summary, the potential for methodological difficulties in mixing consideration of the book of Job's production and its post-Holocaust reception. An illustrative example of this is provided, albeit fleetingly, by a passing comment in David Penchansky's *The Betrayal of God*. It should be stressed, by way of fairness to this scholar, that the following focuses upon only one fairly short paragraph in his book. Examining it closely does however raise some noteworthy questions.

Not uniquely, Penchansky suggests that lying behind the prose sections of the book of Job is a folk story of greater antiquity—a story in which, like the prose sections of the book, Job is presented as a pious figure, accepting of divine providence.[30] More unusually however, Penchansky

---

29. Penchansky notes, "Much controversy remains as to the exact nature of Job's responses to Yahweh's speeches . . . Some have seen them as an abject repentance and recantation of all that had been said previously. Others . . . have noted various degrees of rebellion and rejection in these statements; some even remark at a flat mockery and rejection of Yahweh's authority and majesty. Why the ambiguity? Perhaps there are some linguistic usages inaccessible to modern interpreters. Perhaps the text was damaged or distorted through the process of transmission. Or one might . . . claim that the rebellious meaning is plain, but theologians wish to avoid its implications. At the very least, these statements of Job are intrinsically ambiguous, and because the unusual vocabulary and syntax, they may be read either way. No final adjudication is possible." Penchansky, *The Betrayal of God*, 53–54. Cf. Braiterman, *(God) after Auschwitz*, 37.

30. For another example of discussion of how the prose sections of Job may relate to an older folk story, see Cox, *Man's Anger and God's Silence*, 23–27. This hypothesis that the prose sections rest upon an older folkstory is rejected by Habel, *The Book of Job*, 35–36.

suggests that this folk tale was only pious on its surface. There were within it "seditious elements" and "significant components of irony."[31]

He lists several parts of this reconstructed folk tale that he considers to have been "ironic" and "seditious." For example, while Job's depiction as simultaneously pious and wealthy at the book's opening would tend to support a theodicy of rewards and punishments, that his sufferings are a divine experiment, rather than the result of his iniquities, appears to ironically undercut this theodicy of retribution.[32]

With regard to discussion of Job's post-Holocaust reception, however, it is another of Penchansky's examples of the folk story's "sedition" that is of significance for the present discussion:

> Job's servile obedience [in the folk tale] in the face of such blatant mistreatment is less than admirable. Stephen Mitchell observes "The character called 'The Lord' can do anything to him—have his daughters raped and mutilated, send his sons to Auschwitz—and he will turn the other cheek. This is not a matter of spiritual acquiescence, but of mere capitulation to an unjust, superior force." Is it possible to imagine that ancient people would not also resent such unrealistic piety?[33]

On one level, we could undoubtedly answer Penchansky's question in the positive. Some readers or listeners to the tale of Job's patience in ancient Israel may well have felt that his piety was unrealistic. Indeed, given the extent to which the poetic sections of the book render Job so much less accepting, there were more than likely some who would have found this piety, in the folk story Penchansky reconstructs, deeply unsatisfactory.

Yet the reference to a God who "sends his sons to Auschwitz" (taken from the introduction to Stephen Mitchell's 1989 translation, *The Book of Job*) also raises difficulties.[34] This is because, at least implicitly, Penchansky's argument that the folk story contained a seditious element is, in the above quotation, partly based upon its ancient authors and listeners possessing post-Holocaust sensibilities regarding questions of divine providence. With the notion of a God who "sends his sons to Auschwitz" there come into play the high moral stakes of the aftermath of a peculiarly modern

---

31. Penchansky, *The Betrayal of God*, 36.
32. Ibid., 38.
33. Ibid., 37.
34. Mitchell, *The Book of Job*, vi.

event of mass murder on an industrial scale from a context quite different from that of the ancient Near East. Put simply, it is not clear that what may appear morally abhorrent in a post-Holocaust era would *necessarily* have been the case for the originators of the folk tale.

## CONCLUSIONS

Returning to the primary focus of this chapter—consideration of why two Jewish American thinkers have interpreted Job so differently in the aftermath of the Holocaust—it can be suggested that a tension ultimately remains.

On the one hand, that Wiesel and Goldberg bring much with them to their encounter with Job is clear. It is profoundly doubtful that either would claim that their interpretations are neutral or separate from their considerations of the Holocaust's significance.

On the other hand, the book of Job's origins as a text reflecting ancient differences regarding divine justice is an idea that is difficult to dismiss in its entirety. When facing radically different views of Job, it cannot be discounted that they possess these views in part because Job's production reflects radically differing views regarding the acceptance of divine providence. However, allowing scholarship regarding Job's production to speak to consideration of its reception creates huge demands—demands that, when thinking of the modern, listening to the ancient does not merely dissolve into an anachronistic projection of a post-Holocaust world.

Some may feel this to be an ultimately unsatisfying conclusion. Yet, probably they feel the rub of a problem inherently insoluble by nature. Consideration of a biblical text's reception can never be divorced entirely from questions of the dynamics at play during that text's origins. Any marriage, however, between historical-critical study of the Bible and its later reception must, by necessity, remain an always fractious one if scholarly honesty is to be maintained. Some considering a biblical text's reception history may choose to simply "check out" of the historical-critical conversation, due to an understandable fear that an unpalatable sense of anachronism may irremovably linger behind the scenes. It may be that reception study can get by well enough with reference only to the text "as we now possess it." Yet there remains a tantalizing discourse—if still a distinctly danger-prone one—that suggests that modern conflicts of interpretation may not be unrelated to ideological conflicts in the text's ancient past.

## BIBLIOGRAPHY

Barton, John. *Reading the Old Testament: Method in Biblical Study*. 2nd ed. London: Darton, Longman & Todd, 1996.
Berenbaum, Michael. *The Vision of the Void: Theological Reflections on the Works of Elie Wiesel*. Middletown, CT: Wesleyan University Press, 1979.
Berger, Alan L. "Elie Wiesel." In *Interpreters of Judaism in the Late Twentieth Century*, edited by Steven T. Katz, 369–91. The B'nai B'rith History of the Jewish People. Washington, DC: B'nai B'rith, 1993.
Berkovits, Eliezer. *Faith after the Holocaust*. New York: KTAV, 1973.
Blumenthal, David R. *Facing the Abusing God: A Theology of Protest*. Louisville: Westminster John Knox, 1993.
Braiterman, Zachary. *(God) after Auschwitz: Tradition and Change in Post-Holocaust Jewish Thought*. Princeton: Princeton University Press, 1998.
Cohn-Sherbok, Dan. *God and the Holocaust*. 2nd ed. Leominster, UK: Gracewing, 1996.
Cox, Dermot. *Man's Anger and God's Silence: The Book of Job*. Slough, UK: St. Paul Publications, 1990.
Downing, Fred L. "Autobiography, Fiction, and Faith: Reflections on the Literary and Religious Pilgrimage of Elie Wiesel." In *Remembering for the Future, Working Papers and Addenda*, edited by Yehuda Bauer et al., 2:1441–55. 3 vols. Oxford: Pergamon, 1989.
Fish, Stanley. *Is There a Text in This Class? The Authority of Interpretive Communities*. Cambridge: Harvard University Press, 1980.
Goldberg, Michael. *Why Should Jews Survive? Looking Past the Holocaust toward a Jewish Future*. New York: Oxford University Press, 1995.
Gordis, Robert. *The Book of God and Man: A Study of Job*. Chicago: University of Chicago Press, 1965.
Greenberg, Irving. "Cloud of Smoke, Pillar of Fire: Judaism, Christianity, and Modernity after the Holocaust." In *Auschwitz: Beginning of a New Era? Reflections on the Holocaust*, edited by Eva Fleischner, 7–55. New York: KTAV, 1977.
Haar, Murray J. "Job after Auschwitz." *Interpretation* 53 (1999) 265–75.
Habel, Norman C. *The Book of Job: A Commentary*. London: SCM, 1985.
Handelman, Susan A. *The Slayers of Moses: The Emergence of Rabbinic Interpretation in Modern Literary Theory*. SUNY Series on Modern Jewish Literature and Culture. Albany: State University of New York Press, 1982.
Hirsch, E. D., Jr. *Validity in Interpretation*. New Haven: Yale University Press, 1967.
Katz, Steven T. *Post-Holocaust Dialogues: Critical Studies in Modern Jewish Thought*. New York: New York University Press, 1983.
Mitchell, Stephen, translator. *The Book of Job*. London: Cathie, 1989.
Morgan, Michael L. *Beyond Auschwitz: Post-Holocaust Jewish Thought in North America*. Oxford: Oxford University Press, 2001.
Neusner, Jacob. "The Implications of the Holocaust." *JR* 53 (1973) 293–308.
———. *What Is Midrash?* GBS. Philadelphia: Fortress, 1987.
Penchansky, David. *The Betrayal of God: Ideological Conflict in Job*. Literary Currents in Biblical Interpretation. Louisville: Westminster John Knox, 1990.
Rubenstein, Richard L. "Job and Auschwitz." *USQR* 25 (1970) 421–37.
Wiesel, Elie. *Messengers of God: Biblical Portraits and Legends*. Translated by Marion Wiesel. New York: Simon & Schuster, 2005.
———. *Night*. Translated by Stella Rodway. Hannondsworth, UK: Penguin, 1981.
———. *The Town beyond the Wall*. Translated by Stephen Becker. London: Robson, 1975.

# 5

## Where have all the Female Prophets Gone?
### Women and Prophetic Communication in Mari

JONATHAN STÖKL

Lady Margaret Hall, University of Oxford

### INTRODUCTION

THE CITY OF MARI was discovered on what is now the border between Iraq and Syria on a bend of the river Euphrates.[1] During the excavation, one of the largest archives of Ancient Near Eastern writing ever to be found was discovered, consisting of some 20,000 tablets. These tablets allow us to glance at everyday life in the kingdom of Mari at the time of its king Zimri-Lim in the eighteenth century BCE.[2] We have access to this archive only through the actions of Hammurapi the "Great" of Babylon, who, having joined forces with Zimri-Lim in order to defeat an Elamite invasion into Mesopotamia, betrayed his ally, attacked Mari, and subjugated the kingdom. In the following year, Hammurapi sent his troops back to Mari and razed the city. As part of that process, Babylonian scribes went through the Mariote royal archives and took considerable

---

1. For the archaeology of Mari, cf. Margueron, *Mari, métropole de l'Euphrate*. Good maps can also be found in Margueron, "Mari et le Khabur."

2. I do not wish to go into the question of high, middle, low, and ultra-low chronologies that propose dates that differ considerably from each other. For this discussion, cf. Charpin, "Histoire politique du Proche-Orient Amorrite (2002–1595)," and, more recently, Sassmannshausen, "Zur mesopotamischen Chronologie des 2. Jahrtausends."

amounts of tablets with them to Babylon.³ Our modern day gain spelled doom for the inhabitants of ancient Mari, and for the continued existence of the city as a royal capital. It was inhabited again some time after the razing but only the remains of moderate settlements were discovered by the archaeologists.

Some of the tablets from the royal archives contain evidence for the existence of prophetic activity in the kingdom of Mari. The first letter containing a prophetic oracle was published in 1948, but most have been available only recently in an edition and French translations by Jean-Marie Durand.⁴ In the past few years, three English translations of the corpus have been published: one by J. J. M. Roberts, a second by Martti Nissinen, and the third by Wolfgang Heimpel.⁵ One group of texts, which is important to our topic today, the *correspondance féminine*, was published in cuneiform in the 1960s and translated into German and French in the 1970s.⁶ The prominence of letters by female members of the royal family has been noted⁷—there has even been a doctoral thesis on women at Mari by Bernard Batto—but as I will show below, the results of that study with regard to women in the prophetic process will have to be revised.⁸

I turn to that question here. First, I will critically present a recent anthropological theory on women's agency in prophetic cults. The next step will be a survey of women involved in the prophetic process at Mari.

---

3. On the history and destruction of Mari, cf. Charpin, "Histoire politique," and Heimpel, *Letters to the King of Mari*. For the end of the archive itself, cf. Charpin, "La fin des archives dans le palais de Mari."

4. Cf. Dossin, "Une révélation du dieu Dagan" for the first letter. Durand, *Archives épistolaires de Mari I*; and *Les documents épistolaires du palais de Mari 1, 2, and 3*.

5. Roberts, "The Mari Prophetic Texts in Transliteration and English Translation"; Nissinen, *Prophets and Prophecy in the Ancient Near East*; and Heimpel, *Letters to the King of Mari*. There is also an Italian translation by Cagni, *Le profezie di Mari*.

6. Drawings were published in Dossin, *Archives royales de Mari 10*. The first translation into a Western language of that particular corpus was in Römer, *Frauenbriefe über Religion, Politik und Privatleben in Mari*. A few years later, Dossin published his own translation and commentary: Dossin, *La correspondance féminine*.

7. Römer, *Frauenbriefe*.

8. Batto, *Studies on Women at Mari*. There is, of course, also Sasson, "The Posting of Letters with Divine Messages," which comments that in his category A) "Prophetic Letters Sent from Mari," most letters are written by women and report oracles of female deities. He explains this fact as the result of the men and male deities having temporarily abandoned Mari, leaving the queens and her female staff and the female deities there on their own.

Finally, I will offer my own interpretation of the involvement of women in the prophetic process at Mari.

## WOMEN IN POSSESSIVE CULTS: THE THEORY

Often read as an introduction to the anthropological study of possessive cults around the world, Lewis's *Ecstatic Religion*[9] has had considerable influence on the study of prophecy in Ancient Israel and prophecy in the Hebrew Bible.[10] Thus it forms the basis of Wilson's important study, *Prophecy and Society in Ancient Israel*.[11] With regard to women in possessive cults, Lewis's theory can be summarized thus: Through ecstatic religion, women can alleviate some of the hardships they fall under in traditional patriarchal societies; it functions in a similar way to a safety valve, releasing undue pressure that could destabilize the entire society.[12] However, if the possessive cult is linked to the central religion and its central cult-place, either the mediums tend to be male, or the utterings of a female medium are interpreted by a man.[13] Thus, women are more prevalent in so-called marginal cults, which are not linked to the central ethical system based on the society's religion.

This approach has come under some theoretical criticism by feminist scholars, because it fails to notice the strengths of women in cultures in which possession cults are practiced. Most recently, Keller has offered a different framework for understanding women in possession cults.[14] Coming from a feminist and post-colonial perspective, Keller focuses on the understanding and analysis of power relations. To the standard power axes of race, class, and gender, she adds a fourth axis: the power struggle between possessor and possessed. She argues that the possessing ancestor,

---

9. Lewis, *Ecstatic Religion*.

10. For this often underestimated distinction, cf. Nissinen, "Comparing Prophetic Sources."

11. Wilson, *Prophecy and Society in Ancient Israel*.

12. Lewis does not directly say so, but he implies that this is one of the reasons why possessive cults have a relatively small influence over western society. He regards western societies as much more egalitarian.

13. Cf. for example the importance of the Pythia in ancient Greek and how her oracles needed to be "translated" by male prophets—and, interestingly, it is to that phenomenon that we owe our word *prophet*.

14. Keller, *The Hammer and the Flute*.

spirit, or deity has to be taken into account as an *agentive* force as well.[15] She goes on to say that socio-psychological and other sociologically based theories explaining possession—she calls them "reductionist"—represent a form of academic neo-colonialism.[16]

In her understanding of possession, then, possessed "bodies" are constructed as *instrumental agencies*—possessed bodies do not act out of their own volition, rather it is the deity who acts through them.[17] This concept allows us to interpret possessed women not just as members of the gender which has traditionally been interpreted as the weaker, the one more likely to succumb to possession as a means to protest against her oppression. In fact, using Keller's theory, possessed bodies can be read as themselves possessing a certain strength that allows them to be "used" and "played" by the possessing agent. Taking the possessing deity into account, we can also appreciate why possessed bodies often enjoy high social status themselves, but rarely address the low state in which most women find themselves in these cultures generally (the possessing deity appears not to have much interest in changing the situation of women in general, but is interested instead in realizing its own desires). For theologians, it might be interesting that Keller calls this discursive space—which she creates for the *agency* of supernatural beings—a "theological space."[18]

Keller's theory has been accepted without much criticism, indeed, even embraced by most feminist anthropologists.[19] There are some critical voices, especially Amy Hollywood and Susannah Heschel.[20] In my critical reading, I concur with some of the issues raised by them.

A standard definition of an *agent* is a "subject who acts in the world with intent."[21] In other words, in order for someone to be an *agent*, thus

15. From here on, in the discussion of Keller's theory, *possessing deity* and similar expressions are to be understood as referring to possessing deities, spirits, and ancestors.

16. Said, *Orientalism*. For the field of Near Eastern Studies, cf. Holloway, *Orientalism, Assyriology and the Bible*.

17. I find it interesting that she does not refer to Bynum, *Holy Feast and Holy Fast*. Bynum has a similar theory, but does not use a new understanding of the subjectivity of female ecstatics in the Middle Ages in Europe.

18. Keller, *The Hammer and the Flute*, 83.

19. Cf. the reviews of her book by, Hayes; Klassen; Martin; and Rausch. The only critical review is by Bähre.

20. Hollywood, "Gender, Agency, and the Divine in Religious Historiography"; and Heschel, "Gender and Agency in the Feminist Historiography of Jewish Identity."

21. The philosophical discussion is very much in flux at the moment so that neither the *Routledge Encyclopedia of Philosophy* nor the *Stanford Encyclopedia of Philosophy* of-

possessing *agency*, she has to be a *subject* and act out of her own volition. Here is an example to illustrate the case: by this standard definition, a man who is possessed by a deity who acts through him is no longer an agent—for example, Saul among the prophets.[22] A woman to whom a deity talks, however, and who then decides out of her own volition to go and announce what she has seen or heard, is an *agent* in her own right—and thus creates history.[23]

This latter aspect has been the *Stein des Anstoßes*—or maybe more aptly, the *bone of contention*—for feminist and post-colonial historians. If we define *agency* as we just have, and if we want to take seriously the explanations of the cultures themselves, then possessed women can no longer be described as *agents*. They are, in this interpretation, not involved in making history and possessing power. Instead, *agency* is referred to the gods and spirits who then have to be regarded as *agents* in history. This is why Keller tries to find a new definition of *agency* that allows her to define possessed women as agents, while taking the cultures' own views seriously.

However, by redefining *agency* and applying this newfound category onto the data from other cultures, we are committing precisely the same fallacy as the one that she accuses "Western Scholarship" of: academic colonialism. Thus, Keller claims that she takes the language seriously that is used by most cultures to describe possession. She often uses terms such as *pounced upon* to express that women are being possessed, emulating the languages of these cultures; other such emic terms describe these women as *spiritually weak* or *not vigilant*. This means that the cultures which she cites, Zimbabwe and Malaysia—and one could easily think of further examples—regard possession precisely *not* as a sign of strength, but of at least temporary weakness or lack of vigilance. All she would be able to say, using her interpretive model, and keeping to these cultures' own terminologies, is that the possessed women are—like a good hammer for hammering, or a flute for being played—well-constructed for being non-

---

fers definitions of either *agent* or *agency*. The *Encyclopedia Britannica* only discusses *legal* agency, which is related but not the same. The *Routledge Encyclopedia* does offer a discussion of *moral agency* but only as far as it is different from ordinary agency.

22. 1 Sam 10:9–16 and 19:18–24.

23. The Bible knows of the example of Miriam: Exod 15:20–21. However, while the text calls her הנביאה ("female prophet") it does not indicate when, whether, or how YHWH communicates with her.

vigilant. This is simply not satisfactory. In Keller's interpretation, the position of possessed women is weakened instead of strengthened. By turning around and saying that this non-vigilance is an expression of strength, she flatly contradicts the cultures' own description, and is in turn guilty of the same colonialism of which she accuses others.

Rather than using the image of a hammer or flute, she might have preferred the image of an orchestra musician who, herself an artist, is to some extent wielded by the conductor of the orchestra to produce a piece of art. There are several problems with this imagery, however, with regard to being a good picture for prophecy. While it does show how somebody can be an instrument and still an active agent at the same time, most orchestra musicians perform voluntarily and are not forced by the conductor to perform against their own wills. Further, orchestra musician and conductor are both humans and are, thus, on one existential level, while possessing deities and possessed humans clearly are not. The state of being someone's instrument and an agent at the same time requires free will and equal existential status of both agents.

Keller also "colonizes" other scholars by claiming that they approach possession attracted "by a desire to be in proximity to alterity."[24] I think that this is an impermissible generalization; what I am interested in is how a phenomenon such as prophecy, ostensibly linked to possession but not necessarily the same, works in a number of Ancient Near Eastern societies. In other words, I am interested in how societies, which are long since gone, do or do not deal with aspects of "alterity."[25] With her line of argument, Keller builds up false oppositions and categorizations in order then to criticize them.

I shall finish this critical reading of her work with an aim of hers with which I sympathize greatly: it does not help feminism—and therefore neither men nor women—to describe women only as "exercising the

---

24. Keller, *The Hammer and the Flute*, 103.

25. This means that the societies I look at are by their nature from a very different time than any current society. The term *anachronistic* has assumed a different quality from its traditional meaning of introducing something from a much later time into an earlier setting—for example, a digital watch in a picture of the last supper. In this debate, *anachronistic* refers to scholars portraying—usually other—cultures as on a "lower" level of development. To respect the temporal gap between any currently existing society and societies that ceased to exist a long time ago is a peril when using this term. The failure to realize the distance in time between any modern interpreter of ancient societies and the societies she studies can lead to great distortions in the presentation of these cultures.

agency of the feminine underdog."²⁶ But I do not think Keller manages to achieve the difficult task of describing women's power in situations in which they have often been described only as victims.²⁷

## WOMEN IN MARI PROPHECY: THE EVIDENCE

There are two words used for professional female prophets at Mari: *muḫḫūtum* and *āpiltum*.²⁸ The former is usually understood as a form of ecstatic, who does not control her trances—as Durand puts it, a "fou."²⁹ The latter is often translated as "answerer,"³⁰ even though no *āpil(t)um* is attested as answering a question anywhere.³¹ Recently Paolo Merlo suggested the meaning "translator," adducing a lexical list from twenty-fourth century Ebla, in which *āpilum* is equated with the Sumerian term EME.BAL which means "translator."³² In spite of the pitfalls of relying on etymological relations for the translation of a word,³³ I follow Merlo here, based on three reasons: (1) there were strong links between Early Bronze Age Ebla and Mari,³⁴ (2) the context of *āpil(t)um* contradicts the commonly used meaning, and thus (3) etymology is all we are left with for finding the meaning of the word. Merlo's rendering of *āpil(t)um* as "spokesperson" or "interpreter," however, should be taken *cum grano salis*. I believe that most people in Mari would not have been aware of this Eblaite etymology

26. Keller, *The Hammer and the Flute*, 105.

27. On this, cf. Butler, *Gender Trouble*; idem, *Bodies That Matter*; and idem, *Undoing Gender*.

28. The male forms are *muḫḫûm* and *āpilum* respectively. I will use *āpil(t)um* to refer to both *āpiltum* and *āpilum*, and *muḫḫûm/muḫḫūtum* to refer to both *muḫḫūtum* and *muḫḫûm*. [I no longer support the taxonomy presented here in all details. Rather than understanding the *muḫḫūtum* as a professional female prophet, I classify her and her male counterparts as ecstatic cult functionaries who occasionally prophesy, just as some lay-people occasionally prophesy. For my revised views, see J. Stökl, "Female Prophets in the Ancient Near East."—JS]

29. Cf. Durand, *ARM 26/I*, 386.

30. For the "normal" translation, see Durand, *ARM 26/I*, 386; Nissinen, *Prophets and Prophecy*, 6; and Roberts, "The Mari Prophetic Texts in Transliteration and English Translation," 158–59.

31. Cagni, *Le profezie di Mari*, 21; van der Toorn, "Old Babylonian Prophecy between the Oral and the Written," 59–60; and Nissinen, *Prophets and Prophecy*, 6.

32. Merlo, "*āpilum* of Mari. A Reappraisal."

33. Cf. Barr, *The Semantics of Biblical Language*.

34. Cf. Archi and Giovanna, "A Victory over Mari and the Fall of Ebla," which shows the many, not always amicable, relations between the two cities.

of *āpil(t)um*. They might well have understood it to mean "answerer" even though the *āpil(t)um* never "answered" any questions,[35] and even though the above reconstruction of the etymology is most probably correct.

TABLE 5.1: Professional Female Prophets

| Name | Professional Title | | Texts |
|---|---|---|---|
| anonymous | *muḫḫūtum* | ecstatic/raver | A.994 = ARM 10 50 = ARM 26 237 |
| anonymous | *muḫḫūtum* | ecstatic/raver (pl) | A.1249b+S.142 75+M. (unnumbered) |
| Annu-tabni | *muḫḫūtum* | ecstatic/raver | ARM 22 326 |
| Ḫubatum | *muḫḫūtum* | ecstatic/raver | M.6188 = ARM 26 200 A.368 = ARM 6 45 = ARM 26 201 |
| Innibana | *āpiltum* | interpreter? | A.2264 = ARM 10 81 = ARM 26 204 |

When looking at the prophetic oracles recorded in the letters, the following picture emerges. Among *āpil(t)um*-prophets, men outnumber women by far. While there are nine named, male, *āpilū* and a further six texts that speak of male *āpilū*,[36] there is only one female *āpiltum*, Innibana.[37]

---

35. Much as most Germans today are unaware that etymologically the German word for hammock, *Hängematte*, is derived from a Caribbean word, *hamaca*, which made its way via French and Spanish into northern Europe. That a hammock can indeed be described as a 'hanging mat' probably helped this new understanding of the phonemes of the word *hamaca*. Further examples can easily be found and are often referred to as adulterated loanwords by philologists.

36. The named individuals are 1.) Abiya, *āpilum* of Adad of Aleppo, in A.1968 [published in Durand, *Le culte d'Addu d'Alep*]; 2.) Alpan, *āpilum* of Adad of Kalassu and possibly also of Adad of Aleppo, in A.1121+A.2731 [published in Lafont, "Le roi de Mari"]; 3.) Atamrum, *āpilum* of Šamaš, in ARM 26 414 [published in Charpin, *Archives épistolaires de Mari II*]; 4.) Ili-andulli in ARM 9 22 [published in Birot, *Textes administratifs*]; 5.) Išḫi-Dagan, *āpilum* of Dagan, in T.8 [published in Durand, *ARM 26/I*]; 6.) Isi-Aḫu, *āpilum* of Ḫišamitum, in ARM 26 195; 7.) Lupaḫum, *āpilum* of Dagan, in A.3796, M.11436, and ARM 26 199; 8) Qišatum, *āpilum* of Dagan, in ARM 25 15; and 9) Qišti-Dēritum, *āpilum* of Dēritum, in ARM 26 208. The six texts that mention anonymous *āpilū* are 1) an *āpilum* of an unspecified deity, A.3760; 2) an *āpilum* of Šamaš ARM 26 194, 3) an *āpilum* of Ninḫursag, ARM 26 219; 4.) an *āpilum* of Dagan, ARM 26 223; 5) an *āpilum* of Marduk, ARM 26 371 (published in Charpin, *ARM 26/2*); and 6) an *āplum* [sic] of Dagan of Tuttul, ARM 26 209.

37. ARM 10 81=ARM 26 204.

The only other occurrence of the feminine form is to be found in the text A.1121 + A.2731, in which Nūr-Sîn claims that he transmitted all prophetic messages whether spoken by an by *āpilum*-prophet or an *āpiltum*-prophetess to the king while he lived in Mari and that being abroad he feels even more obliged to do so.[38] In my analysis of the standing of the *āpil(t)um*, I differ only slightly from Durand and describe them as "special agents in prophecy"; they were probably capable of considerable control over their state of trance.[39]

The case of the *muḫḫûm/muḫḫūtum* is different. Of the named individuals, there are four men and two women,[40] Ḫubatum[41] and Annu-tabni.[42] There is also an unnamed *muḫḫūtum*-prophetess in a letter by the queen mother, Addu-Dūrī.[43] Finally, a group of *muḫḫūtum*-prophetesses is mentioned in one of the Rituals of Eštar.[44] There are two different texts, both describing rituals at the end of the month. The text in which the female form occurs is too damaged to understand quite what is happening. However, if they are sufficiently similar, we could take the first text, which is much better preserved, and look at the passage in which the *muḫḫûm*-prophets are mentioned.[45]

38. ³⁴*pānānum inūma ina Māri wašbāku* ³⁵*āpilum u āpiltum mimma awātam* ³⁶*ša iqa[bb]ûnim ana bēliya utār*. "³⁴Earlier, when I lived in Māri, ³⁵whatever an *āpilum*-prophet or an *āpiltum*-prophetess ³⁶sp[ok]e to me, I handed on to my lord."

39. Cf. Durand, *ARM 26/I*, 388–89; Durand, "La religión en Siria durante la época de los reinos amorreos según la documentación de Mari," 326–27; and Charpin, "Le contexte historique et géographique," 22.

40. They are 1) Ea-maṣi, *muḫḫûm* of Itūr-Mēr in ARM 21 333 and ARM 23 446; 2) Ea-mudammiq, *muḫḫûm* of Ninḫursag, in A.4676, ARM 22 167, and ARM 23 446; 3.) Irra-gamil, *muḫḫûm* of Nergal, in M.9717, M.10784, ARM 21 333, ARM 23 446, and ARM 26 222; and 4.) Irra-malik, a *muḫḫûm* of an unspecified deity, in M.9921.

41. She gives an oracle against the Yaminites, as Aḫum, the *šangu*-priest of Anunitum reports to the king, ARM 26 200.

42. She receives a second-rate *utuplum*-garment as part of general distribution of clothing by the royal officials; cf. ARM 22 326.

43. ARM 26 237. This letter also contains a dream by the queen-mother herself.

44. Durand and Guichard, "Les rituels de Mari." See now also Nele Ziegler, *Les Musiciens et la musique*. The second of these two texts is for Eštar of Irradân, a foreign form of the deity, the first is certainly for Eštar, but it remains unclear which form of Ištar is addressed in this ritual.

45. A.1249b+S.142 75+M. (unnumbered) col iii, 4'–7' for the female \**muḫḫātum*, ⁸'*inūm[ma muḫḫātum]* ⁹'*išta[qqalū]* '⁸'Whe[n the *muḫḫātum*-prophetesses] ⁹'remain [in equilibrium]'; and A.3165, ²¹'⁻²³'for the male *muḫḫû*, ²¹'*šumma ina rēš warḫim*] ²²'*muḫḫûm ištaqqa[lma]* ²³'*an[a] maḫḫê[m] ul i[reddû]* '²¹'If at the end of the mon[th] ²²'the *muḫḫûm*-

In that text, the musicians are allowed to leave in case the *muḫḫûm*-prophets remain in a state of equilibrium; if the prophets do go into ecstasy, the musicians have to sing a lament. At the very end of the ritual, a special *meḫsû*-jar is mentioned which is always to be at the disposal of the ecstatics. This jar might or might not contain a liquid which is supposed to help the ecstatics to reach the state of ecstasy that is required. We cannot say anything specific as there is no further information given.[46]

**TABLE 5.2:** Lay Female Prophets

| Name | Title/Description | | Texts |
|---|---|---|---|
| anonymous | *Qammatum* | ?? | A.1047 = ARM 10 80 = ARM 26 197<br>A.925+A.2050 = ARM 26 199<br>A.963 = ARM 26 203 |
| anonymous | *Sinništum* | woman | A.996 = ARM 10 4 = ARM 26 307 |
| anonymous | None | ? | M.13843 = ARM 13 114 = ARM 26 210 |
| anonymous | None | ? | A.671 = ARM 10 8 = ARM 26 214 |
| anonymous | *Sinništum* | Woman | M.8071 = ARM 26 217 |

If we widen our perspective and include non-professionals, this impression is changed. There is a nameless woman described as a *qammatum*-priestess of Dagan of Terqa, a title which suggests a connection to the cult of the god Dagan at the city of Terqa.[47] However, we have no

---

prophet is in equlibriu[m and] ²³'t[o] ravi[ng] he is not [...]', Durand and Guichard, "Les rituels de Mari." Durand and Guichard, followed by Nissinen, *Prophets and Prophecy*, 82, restore the last word in col ii. line ²³'i[reddû] and translate '²¹'Si, à (cette) fin du mois, ²²'l'extatique est en état d'équilibre et ²³'qu'il ne convienne pas à vaticiner....' The number of possible alternatives for the verb at the end of line ²³, while not infinite, is fairly high. The Song in question is the MÀ.E Ú.RE.M[ÉN], which Durand and Guichard, "Les rituels de Mari," 50, identify with the canonical Sumerian lament ME.E UR.RE.M[ÈN].

46. Somewhat surprisingly, Ziegler, *Les Musiciens et la musique*, 61, opts for the interpretation that the music is supposed to lead the ecstatics into a state of ecstasy, even though the musicians are supposed to sing in case the prophets *do* attain a state of trance.

47. She is mentioned in three texts, all probably linked to the same episode: ARM 26 197, 199, 203. Her oracle has also been linked to that of a nameless *muḫḫûm*-prophet, ARM 26 202. Sasson, "Water beneath Straw." Earlier readings of this word as *qabbatum*,

further information of what a *qammatum* does or what her position entails. She simply remains invisible in the entire cuneiform evidence apart from these three texts.

The letter ARM 26 207 by queen Šibtu contains a mysterious episode possibly involving the usage of a liquid to elicit oracles from a man and a woman about *ittātu* "signs."[48] In Durand's understanding, this text, and ARM 26 212 are evidence for the use of intoxicating fluids in helping people reach a state of trance.[49] He understands the word *ittātu* "signs" to refer to the people, as he claims that unlike *šaqûm* ("to give to drink"), *šâlum* ("to ask") cannot be used with two accusatives. Heimpel seems to agree with Durand, in that it is the verb *šaqûm* and not *šâlum* which governs the two accusatives. In his opinion, however, one accusative is the drinker and the other, that which is drunk. Therefore, he thinks that *ittātu* refers to the liquid that "the man and the woman" imbibe.[50] Wilcke points out that according to von Soden's *Akkadisches Wörterbuch*, the Gt-stem of *šâlum* can govern two accusatives especially in Mari. I find Wilcke's solution, which harkens back to Dossin's original translation, the most convincing.[51] In a different letter, Šibtu reports that a servant-girl had gone into trance in the temple of the goddess Anunitum uttering a divine message.[52]

In the letter ARM 26 217 only part of the oracle survives. Furthermore, the part where we would have expected to get an indication as to the title of the speaker is damaged as well. The content that survives certainly does not exclude this possibility. But in all prophetic texts that have all relevant parts extant, the speaker is called with the same title when being presented and in the formula "this is what [NAME/TITLE] spoke." ARM 26 217 has "this woman spoke those words to me,"[53] which makes it more probable

---

as to be found in the CAD, and still linger on in non-specialist literature, are now entirely impossible; Cf. ARM 26 203 ln.12', reading *ša* ⌈*qa*⌉-*am-ma*-[*tim*]; *am* cannot be read *ab*.

48. Understanding this text with Wilcke, "*ittātim ašqi aštāl: Medien in Mari?*" Wilcke thinks that the queen uses alcohol here in a rather conventional way to make people talk more freely.

49. Durand, "In Vino Veritas"; and Durand, *ARM 26/I*, 440–41.

50. Heimpel, *Letters to the King of Mari*, 257.

51. Dossin, *correspondance féminine*, 25–27. Wilcke's translation of this line is "Wegen der Nachricht über den Feldzug, den mein Herr unternehmen will, befragte ich Mann und Weib nach Vorzeichen, während ich (sie mit Wein) bewirtete."

52. ARM 26 214.

53. *sinništum šī annêtim idbubamma*, cf. ARM 26 217:27. On the basis of the "handwriting," Charpin recently identified the sender as Itur-Asdu. Cf. Charpin, "Prophètes et rois," 12 n. 51.

than not that she was a lay person. Consistency in these matters is not, however, of the utmost concern to scribes of cuneiform. In ARM 26 210, Kibri-Dagan mentions a woman who came to him and spoke to him in the name of Dagan.[54]

In Batto's view, the existence of the same word *āpil(t)um* in male and female form points us toward interpreting them as of equal importance.[55] It is true that men and women were involved in all stages of the prophetic process, and I agree with his interpretation of affairs when looking at individual prophets and prophetesses. The level of presence is, however, decidedly different, as we have just seen, with a strong numerical bias towards men among the *āpil(t)um*, the highest-level prophet, and a slight preponderance of men among the *muḫḫûm/muḫḫūtum*. Among lay people who prophesy, women are much more visible. This picture to me suggests almost the opposite of Batto's conclusion, namely that there was a bias against women in professional prophecy and that Mariote society saw a woman's place more in lay prophecy and the transmission of prophecy.

**TABLE 5.3:** Dreamers

| Name | Title/Description | Texts |
|---|---|---|
| Anonymous | | M.9576 = ARM 26 227 |
| Anonymous | | A.1902 = ARM 26 230 |
| Addu-dūri | Queen mother | A.994 = ARM 10 50 = ARM 26 237 |
| Ayala | | A.222 = ARM 26 229 |
| Šimatum | princess | A.2858 = ARM 10 94 = ARM 26 239 |
| Timlu | | A.3424 = ARM 10 117 = ARM 26 240 |
| Zunana | | A.907 = ARM 10 100 = ARM 26 232 |

In her recent study on dreams in the Ancient Near East, Annette Zgoll scrutinizes the Mari-material and identifies 20 texts that have traditionally

---

54. Interestingly, this is one of two texts (the other one is ARM 26 220) in which someone claims to have been sent by a deity. This feature, often seen as one of the constituting factors of Israelite prophecy, clearly did not play that much a part in Mariote prophecy.

55. Batto, *Studies on Women at Mari*, 124–25.

been interpreted as dreams. She goes on to say that one of these texts is a vision and the other 19 are "proper" dreams.[56] Of these 19 dreams, twelve are dreamt by men and seven by women.[57] One anonymous woman in ARM 26 227 saw a dream in which two *muḫḫûm*, who had presumably died, are alive. Another anonymous woman in ARM 26 230 dreams a curious dream in which an old man talks to Itūr-Mēr at the standing stones of Dagan. Queen-mother Addu-dūrī reports one of her own dreams, ARM 26 237, in which she enters the temple of Bēlet Ekallim and laments the departure of all statues in front of the deity, while a voice cries "return Dagan, return Dagan!"[58] In ARM 26 229, Ayala dreams of two women quarrelling about something called *enūtum* which either refers to 'high-priestesshood' or "(temple?) utensils."[59] Princess Šīmatum writes a letter to her father describing a dream, in which someone came to her and told her that Tepāḫum's new-born daughter should be called Tagīd-nawûm.[60] Similarly, in ARM 26 240, Timlû writes to Addu-dūrī and reports a dream in which she was sent by Bēlt Ekallim,[61] presumably to transmit some message which is lost in the broken part of the tablet.

Today, the most common interpretation of the text ARM 26 232 is that Zunana has a dream, which she relates in this tablet. Whether or not

56. Zgoll, *Traum und Welterleben im antiken Mesopotamien*, 552. On the grounds of vocabulary and form, Zgoll interprets ARM 26 236 as a vision (p.164).

57. The men who dreamt are 1) Buzzuran in ARM 26 231; 2) Iddin-ili in ARM 26 238; 3) Malik-Dagan in ARM 26 233; 4.) Nana-lu-til in ARM 26 228; 5) Sammetar in ARM 26 142; 6) Sumu-[. . .] in ARM 26 224; 7) Yasim-Dagan in ARM 26 82; 8) King Zimri-Lim himself in ARM 26 225; and 9) Dagān-naḫmi in Wilcke, "Dagān-nahmis Traum." There are three texts that do not preserve the names of the dreaming men, ARM 26 226, 234 and 235.

58. This text is regarded as the basis for the argument that all the male deities had left Mari.

59. Dossin, "Tablettes de Mari," 28, had translated the word as "fonction de grande prêtresse." Sasson, "Mari Dreams," 291 n. 42, prefers the "utensils" as he does not believe that even in a dream "the high-priest[ess]hood is disposable," and because this meaning of *enūtum* is only attested in Assyrian and Neo-Babylonian, not Old Babylonian. In this interpretation, he is followed by Durand, *ARM 26/I*, 469; Malamat, "Intuitive Prophecy—A General Survey," 77; and Nissinen, *Prophets and Prophecy*, 60.

60. ARM 26 239. Line 7' reads ftur dumu.munus ⸢te*-pa-ḫi-im-m[a*]⸣—the little one (baby), daughter of Tepaḫum. According to Ziegler, *La population*, 73 and Durand, "Trois études sur Mari," 128–29, this means that the child is a daughter of king Zimri-Lim, as Ziegler says, "Le terme de *nârtum* était parfois employé par euphémisme pour désigner des concubines, voire des favorites, du souverain." Ziegler, *Le Harem*, 69.

61. By-form of Bēlet Ekallim.

Dagan's message comes to her as part of that dream or by any other means shall not concern us here. The letter contains a petition to the king about one of her (servant?) girls who has been abducted and whom Zunana wants back.[62]

**TABLE 5.4.1:** Female Senders of Prophetic Letters

| Name | Position | Texts |
|---|---|---|
| Addu-dūrī | Zimri-Līm's mother | A.994 = ARM 10 50 = ARM 26 237<br>A.3420 = ARM 10 53 = ARM 26 195 |
| Inibšina | Zimri-Līm's sister | A.1047 = ARM 10 80 = ARM 26 197<br>A.2264 = ARM 10 81 = ARM 26 204 |

---

62. The lines in question are seven and eight: $^7u$ [D]ag[a]n bēlka uṣall[i]lammad $^8$mam[m]an ul ilputanni, which can be translated either as "$^7$And Dagan, your lord, protected me. $^8$Nobody touched me," or as "$^7$And Dagan, your lord, appeared to me in a dream. $^8$(even though) nobody performed incubation on me." The question can be reduced to the interpretation of uṣall[i]lamma, which is hapax at Mari. Either it is derived from ṣalālu "to sleep," thus, first Ellermeier, *Prophetie in Mari und Israel*, 72–73, but interpreting the D-stem as if it were a Š-stem, in which he is followed by Dossin, *correspondance féminine*, 151, 271. This solution is rendered unlikely by the fact that the suffix should be accusative in that case, and not ventive—*uṣallilanni as opposed to uṣall[i]lamma—as pointed out by Durand, *ARM 26/I*, 471–72. Durand, in turn also derives it from ṣalālu but translates it as "to see in one's sleep," reversing the normal syntax in this case. In this he is followed by Nissinen, *Prophets and Prophecy*, 61–62. Von Soden, "Einige Bemerkungen," 199, and—albeit not explicitly—Römer, *Frauenbriefe*, 63, derive from ṣullulu "to roof" and from there translate "to protect"; P-R. Berger, "Einige Bemerkungen zu Friedrich Ellermeier," 209; and Moran, "New Evidence from Mari on the History of Prophecy," 54, interpret the form as "a denominative of ṣillu 'shade, protection' distinguishing the transitive meaning 'to roof' and the intransitive 'to afford protection.'" Heimpel, *Letters to the King of Mari*, 265 n. 278 follows this interpretation but translates literally, "Dagan, your lord, made a shade for me."

| Šiptu | Queen | A.996 = ARM 10 4 = ARM 26 307 |
| | | A.3178 = ARM 26 211 |
| | | A.671 = ARM 10 8 = ARM 26 214 |
| | | A.3217 = ARM 10 6 = ARM 26 212 |
| | | A.2233 = ARM 10 9 = ARM 26 208 |
| | | A.100 = ARM 10 7 = ARM 26 213 |

TABLE 5.4.2: Female Senders of Letters Reporting Dreams

| Name | Title/Description | Texts |
|---|---|---|
| Addu-dūri | Queen mother | M.9576 = ARM 26 227 |
| | | A.994 = ARM 10 50 = ARM 26 237 |
| | | A.122 = ARM 10 51 = ARM 26 238 |
| Šīmatum | Princess | A.2858 = ARM 10 94 = ARM 26 239 |
| Timlu | | A.3424 = ARM 10 117 = ARM 26 240 |
| Zunana | | A.907 = ARM 10 100 = ARM 26 232 |

If we include the senders of the letters in our review, we get the following structure: letters are either written by court-officials, governors, or female members of the royal family. Of the 63 documents that I know of containing references to prophecy at Mari, 25 were written by men, 28 are from an uncertain background and ten are written by women. Among the letters reporting dreams, nine were written by men, six by women, and four are not identifiable, one of which is an economic text. It is very curious that of the six letters written by women, four report dreams that the writer has had herself.

## WOMEN IN MARI PROPHECY: AN INTERPRETATION

As we have seen, the question of theoretical framework with regard to possessive religion has changed considerably. Post-colonial and feminist perspectives have led to an interpretation of women as more powerful while still realizing that they are caught up in patriarchal systems that controlled most of their lives.

Can these insights help us in the interpretation of women who are involved in prophecy in the Ancient Near East and in the interpretation of the roles women fulfilled in the process of prophetic communication at Mari? I regard a framework that celebrates the strengths of any oppressed people, while still being able to explain their oppression, as positive, but remain reluctant when applying it to ancient cuneiform sources, as our evidence does not permit us to ask all the questions for which we would need answers. Having said that, we can glean some information from the material we have and describe some of the "prophetic" roles that Mariote society assigned to women. And it is no unimportant point that both prophetic professions, the *āpil(t)um* and the *muḫḫûm/muḫḫūtum*, were open to men and to women.[63] Indeed it is this which led Batto and others after him to posit that there was no gender divide among the prophets of Mari.[64]

While most letters containing references to prophecy were written by the various governors, queen Šibtu and the king's mother Addu-dūrī do feature prominently as well, reporting prophecies from both male and female prophets. According to Durand's interpretation of A.1121+A.2731[65] and ARM 26 1, the governors were bound by oath to transmit to the king any divine message that they witnessed.[66] Did the women in the royal household have to swear a similar oath? There is no record of such a stipulation. In their case, Keller's category of *instrumental agency* does not help to explain their role either—neither the queen nor the kings' mothers reports that a deity told her to transmit these messages. I have two explanations for these two women featuring so prominently among the writers of prophetic texts: either they were involved in the cultic life at

---

63. This is fairly unusual. Most positions in relation to temples were only open to one or the other; cf. Fleming, "Prophets and Temple Personnel in the Mari Archives," 51.

64. Batto, *Studies on Women at Mari*, 124–25.

65. Lafont, "prophètes du dieu Adad."

66. Durand, *ARM 26/I*, 13–15.

the temples of the capital, or their function in the palace economy made them more accessible to Mariotes who had had a dream or experienced a prophetic possession.

Alternatively, drawing on Lewis's study of ecstatic religion, we could interpret the fact that there are more men than women in prophecy at Mari as being related to the fact that most of the messages are from the important deities of the respective cities. Further, the archives of Mari are the royal archives, and thus pertain very much to the domain of the central organizing power structure, where, according to Lewis's analysis, we would expect men to dominate.

In summary, all prophetic experiences were open to women at Mari; they are most important in transmitting divine messages from the prophets to the king. Thus they acquire an intermediary (rather than instrumental) quality between the king and the prophet(ess), who themselves are intermediaries—interpreters between humankind and the divine.

## BIBLIOGRAPHY

Archi, Alfonso, and Maria Giovanna. "A Victory over Mari and the Fall of Ebla." *JCS* 55 (2003) 1–44.
Bähre, Erik. Review of *The Hammer and the Flute. Women, Power, and Spirit Possession* by Mary Keller. *Journal of Religion in Africa* 35 (2005) 120–22.
Barr, James. *The Semantics of Biblical Language.* London: Oxford University Press, 1961.
Batto, Bernard Frank. *Studies on Women at Mari.* JHNES 5. Baltimore: Johns Hopkins University Press, 1974.
Berger, P-R. "Einige Bemerkungen zu Friedrich Ellermeier. Prophetie in Mari und Israel (Herzberg 1968)." *UF. Internationales Jahrbuch für die Alter-tumskunde Syrien-Palästinas* 1 (1969) 207–9, 221.
Birot, Maurice. *Textes administratifs de la salle 5 du Palais.* Vol. 1. ARM 9. 2 vols. Paris: Imprimerie nationale, 1960.
Butler, Judith. *Bodies That Matter: On the Discursive Limits of "Sex."* New York: Routledge, 1993.
———. *Gender Trouble: Feminism and the Subversion of Identity.* Thinking Gender. New York: Routledge, 1990.
———. *Undoing Gender.* New York: Routledge, 2004.
Bynum, Caroline Walker. *Holy Feast and Holy Fast: The Religious Significance of Food to Medieval Women.* The New Historicism: Studies in Cultural Poetics. Berkeley: University of California Press, 1987.
Cagni, Luigi. *Le profezie di Mari.* Testi del Vicino Oriente antico 2, Letterature meso-potamiche 2. Brescia: Paideia, 1995.
Charpin, Dominique. *Archives épistolaires de Mari II.* ARM 26/II. Paris: ERC, 1988.
———. "Histoire politique du Proche-Orient Amorrite (2002–1595)." In *Mesopotamien: Die altbabylonische Zeit,* edited by Pascal Attinger et al., 25–480. OBO 160/4. Annäherungen 4. Fribourg: Academic Press, 2004.
———. "La fin des archives dans le palais de Mari." *RA* 89 (1995) 29–40.
———. "Le contexte historique et géographique des prophéties dans les textes retrouvés à Mari." *Bulletin of the Canadian Society for Mesopotamian Studies* 23 (1992) 21–31.
———. "Prophètes et rois dans le Proche-Orient amorrite. Nouvelles données, nouvelles perspectives." In *Recueil d'études à la mémoire d'André Parrot,* edited by Dominique Charpin and Jean-Marie Durand, 7–38. Florilegium Marianum 6. Mémoires de NABU 7. Paris: Société pour l'étude du Proche-orient ancien, 2002.
Dossin, Georges. *La correspondance féminine.* ARM 10. TCL 31. Paris: Geuthner, 1967.
———. *La correspondance féminine.* ARM 10. TCL 31. Paris: Geuthner, 1978.
———. "Tablettes de Mari." *RA* 69 (1975) 23–30.
———. "Une révélation du dieu Dagan." *RA* 42 (1948) 125–34.
Durand, Jean-Marie. *Archives épistolaires de Mari I.* ARM 26/I. Paris: ERC, 1988.
———. "In Vino Veritas." *RA* 76 (1982) 43–50.
———. "La religión en Siria durante la época de los reinos amorreos según la documentación de Mari." In *Mitología y religión del Oriente Antiguo.* Vol. 2/1. *Semitas occidentales,* edited by P. Mander and Jean-Marie Durand, 125–533. Sabadell, Spain: AUSA, 1995.
———. *Le culte d'Addu d'Alep et l'affaire d'Alahtum.* Edited by Jean-Marie Durand. Florilegium Marianum 7. Paris: Société pour l'étude du Proche-orient ancien, 2002.
———. *Les documents épistolaires du palais de Mari 1.* LAPO 16. Paris: CERF, 1997.

———. *Les documents épistolaires du palais de Mari 2*. LAPO 17. Paris: CERF, 1998.

———. *Les documents épistolaires du palais de Mari 3*. LAPO 18. Paris: CERF, 2000.

———. "Trois études sur Mari." *Mari: Annales de recherches interdisciplinaires* 3 (1984) 127–80.

Durand, Jean-Marie, and Michael Guichard. "Les rituels de Mari." In *Recueil d'études à la mémoire de Marie-Thérèse Barrelet*, edited by Dominique Charpin et al., 19–78. Florilegium Marianum 3. Mémoires de NABU 4. Paris: Société pour l'étude du Proche-orient ancien, 1997.

Ellermeier, Friedrich. *Prophetie in Mari und Israel*. Theologische und orientalistische Arbeiten 1. Herzberg a. Harz: Jungfer, 1968.

Fleming, Daniel E. "Prophets and Temple Personnel in the Mari Archives." In *The Priests in the Prophets: The Portrayal of Priests, Prophets, and Other Religious Specialists in the Latter Prophets*, edited by Lester L. Grabbe and Alice Ogden Bellis, 44–64. JSOTSup 408. London: T. & T. Clark, 2004.

Hayes, Kelly E. Review of *The Hammer and the Flute*, by Mary Keller. *JR* 84 (2004) 338–39.

Heimpel, Wolfgang. *Letters to the King of Mari: A New Translation, with Historical Introduction, Notes, and Commentary*. Mesopotamian Civilizations 12. Winona Lake, IN: Eisenbrauns, 2003.

Heschel, Susannah. "Gender and Agency in the Feminist Historiography of Jewish Identity." *JR* 84 (2004) 580–91.

Holloway, Steven W. *Orientalism, Assyriology and the Bible*. Hebrew Bible Monographs 10. Sheffield: Sheffield Phoenix, 2006.

Hollywood, Amy. "Gender, Agency, and the Divine in Religious Historiography." *JR* 84 (2004) 514–28.

Keller, Mary. *The Hammer and the Flute: Women, Power, and Spirit Possession*. Baltimore: Johns Hopkins University Press, 2002.

Klassen, Pamela E. Review of *The Hammer and the Flute. Women, Power, and Spirit Possession*. *HR* 43 (2004) 256–58.

Lafont, Bertrand. "Le roi de Mari et les prophètes du dieu Adad." *RA* 78 (1984) 7–18.

Lewis, I. M. *Ecstatic Religion: A Study of Shamanism and Spirit Possession*. 3rd ed. London: Routledge, 2003.

Malamat, Abraham. "Intuitive Prophecy—A General Survey." In *Mari and the Bible*, edited by Abraham Malamat, 59–82. Studies in the History and Culture of the Ancient Near East 12. Leiden: Brill, 1998.

Margueron, Jean-Claude. "Mari et le Khabur." In *La Djéziré et l'Euphrate syriens: De la protohistoire à la fin du IIe millénaire av. J.-C. Tendances dans l'interprétation historique des données nouvelles*, edited by Olivier Rouault and Markus Wäfler, 99–110. Subartu 7. Brepols: Turnhout, 2000.

———. *Mari, métropole de l'Euphrate au IIIe et au début du IIe millénaire avant J-C*. Paris: Picard, 2004.

Martin, Wendy K. Review of *The Hammer and the Flute. Women, Power, and Spirit Possession*, by Mary Keller, 2002." *Sociology of Religion* 65 (2004) 97–98.

Merlo, Paolo. "*āpilum* of Mari. A Reappraisal." *UF* 36 (2004) 323–32.

Moran, William L. "New Evidence from Mari on the History of Prophecy." *Bib* 50 (1969) 15–56.

Nissinen, Martti. "Comparing Prophetic Sources: Principles and a Text Case," in *Prophets and Prophecy*. Proceedings of the Oxford Old Testament Seminar, edited by J. Day, 3–24. London: T. & T. Clark, 2010.

———. *Prophets and Prophecy in the Ancient Near East*. SBLWAW 12. Atlanta: SBL, 2003.

Rausch, Margaret J. Review of *The Hammer and the Flute*, by Mary Keller. *JAAR* 73 (2005) 1228–31.

Roberts, J. J. M. "The Mari Prophetic Texts in Transliteration and English Translation." In *The Bible and the Ancient Near East: Collected Essays*, 157–253. Winona Lake, IN: Eisenbrauns, 2002.

Römer, Willem H. Ph. *Frauenbriefe über Religion, Politik und Privatleben in Mari. Untersuchungen zu G. Dossin. Archives royales de Mari X (Paris 1967)*. AOAT 12. Kevelaer: Butzon & Bercker, 1971.

Said, Edward W. *Orientalism*. Penguin Classics. London: Penguin, 2003.

Sassmannshausen, Leonhard "Zur mesopotamischen Chronologie des 2. Jahrtausends." *Baghdader Mitteilungen* 37 (2006) 157–77.

Sasson, Jack M. "Mari Dreams." *JAOS* 103 (1983) 283–93.

———. "The Posting of Letters with Divine Messages." In *Recueil d'études à la mémoire de Maurice Birot*, edited by Dominique Charpin and Jean-Marie Durand, 299–316. Mémoires de NABU 3. Paris: Société pour l'étude du Proche-orient ancien, 1994.

———. "Water beneath Straw: Adventures of a Prophetic Phrase in the Mari Archives." In *Solving Riddles and Untying Knots: Biblical, Epigraphic, and Semitic Studies in Honor of Jonas C. Greenfield*, edited by Ziony Zevit, et al., 599–608. Winona Lake, IN: Eisenbrauns, 1995.

Soden, Wolfram von. "Einige Bemerkungen zu den von Fr. Ellermeier in 'Prophetie in Mari und Israel' erstmalig bearbeiteten Briefen aus ARM 10." *UF* 1 (1969) 198–99.

Stökl, Jonathan "Female Prophets in the Ancient Near East." In *Prophets and Prophecy. Proceedings of the Oxford Old Testament Seminar*, edited by John Day, 47–61. London: T. & T. Clark, 2010.

Toorn, Karel van der. "Old Babylonian Prophecy between the Oral and the Written." *JNSL* 24 (1998) 55–70. Reprinted as "From the Oral to the Written: The Case of Old Babylonian Prophecy." In *Writings and Speech in Israelite and Ancient Near Eastern Prophecy*, edited by Ehud Ben Zvi and Michael H. Floyd, 219–34. SBLSymS 10. Atlanta: SBL, 2000.

Wilcke, Claus. "Dagān-na-mis Traum." *Welt des Orients* 17 (1986): 11–16.

———. "*ittātim ašqi aštāl: Medien in Mari?*" *Revue d'assyriologie et d'archéologie orientale* 77 (1983) 93.

Wilson, Robert R. *Prophecy and Society in Ancient Israel*. Philadelphia: Fortress, 1980.

Zgoll, Annette. *Traum und Welterleben im antiken Mesopotamien: Traumtheorie und Traumpraxis im 3. – 1. Jahrtausend v. Chr. als Horizont einer Kulturgeschichte des Träumens*. AOAT 333. Münster: Ugarit-Verlag, 2006.

Ziegler, Nele. *La population féminine des palais d'après les archives royales de Mari: Le Harem de Zimrî-Lîm*. Mémoires de NABU 5. Florilegium Marianum 4. Paris: Société pour l'étude du Proche-orient ancien, 1999.

———. *Les Musiciens et la musique d'après les archives de Mari*. Mémoires de NABU 10. Florilegium Marianum 9. Paris: Société pour l'étude du Proche-orient ancien, 2007.

# 6

# Problems with the Identification of a Synagogue in the Hasmonaean Estate at Jericho

*Archaeological and Historiographical Issues*

LIDIA D. MATASSA

Trinity College Dublin

## INTRODUCTION

DURING THE COURSE OF excavations at the Hasmonaean estate at Jericho in 1998, Ehud Netzer[1] of the Hebrew University at Jerusalem identified one building as a Hasmonaean-period synagogue. This structure had already been partially excavated but not identified during excavations some fifteen years earlier. The reasons Netzer gives for his identification are both interesting and problematic. In the main they comprise the overall shape and construction of the building along with some specific features, all of which lent some initial weight to his claim.[2]

Upon closer examination of the available data, however, it becomes clear that there is no substantial evidence to support that identification, and I am going to show how it is mistaken. I will deal with the ancient sources, the secondary material, and the archaeological remains. I should say at this point that the ancient sources on this subject are scant and

---

1. Netzer is Emeritus Professor of Archaeology at the Institute of Archaeology, Hebrew University of Jerusalem.

2. I will discuss Netzer's claims in some detail below.

deal with dates and balsam produced on the Hasmonaean and Herodian estate and not the occupants of the palaces, much less with the political, economic, social, and/or religious dimensions thereof.

The Hasmonaean-period estate at Jericho is a site about which we know curiously little and about which many assumptions have been made and maintained. The current scholarship is based on the archaeological remains as interpreted by Ehud Netzer. However, we can surmise a little of the history of the area by reference to nearby Tel Jericho.

Tel Jericho is one of the oldest continuously inhabited cities in the world, and the remains of some twenty successive settlements dating back to around 9000 BCE have been excavated on that site. Tel Jericho is just two kilometers north of the Hasmonaean estate excavated by Netzer.

The first archaeological explorations of Tel Jericho were made by Charles Warren of the British Royal Engineers in 1868. Following this, two German archaeologists, Carl Watzinger and Ernest Sellin,[3] conducted excavations from 1907 to 1909 and again in 1911.[4] From 1952 to 1958, the excavations of Kathleen Kenyon[5] provided a flood of useful information derived from her meticulous recording of the site, and she was able to set out a chronology of Tel Jericho through its entire history.[6]

In terms of the local population, we know that Tel Jericho was abandoned after the Babylonian exile, but it is thought that there was a settlement somewhere nearby because, of the people who returned with Ezra to Judaea after the Babylonian exile, three hundred and forty-five men (and their families, servants, slaves, etc.) returned to the Jericho area (Ezra 2:34). By way of tangential support for this, a small Jewish village settlement was excavated at Tel Jericho in 1908–1909 by Sellin and Watzinger.[7] This was dated to the Persian period on the basis of the finds, indicating

---

3. Sellin and Watzinger, *Jericho die Ergebnisse der Ausgrabungen*, 58; Watzinger, "Zur Chronologie der Schichten von Jericho."

4. They excavated at Tell es-Sultan and Tulul Abu el-Alayiq.

5. Kenyon was director of the British School of Archaeology at Jerusalem at that time (now the Kenyon Research Institute in Sheikh Jarrah, in East Jerusalem).

6. Kenyon, *Digging Up Jericho*; Kenyon, *The Bible and Recent Archaeology*; and Kenyon, *Excavations at Jericho*.

7. Sellin and Watzinger, *Jericho die Ergebnisse der Ausgrabungen*, 58; Watzinger, "Zur Chronologie der Schichten von Jericho."

that the Persian period at Tel Jericho extended from the fifth and fourth centuries BCE.[8]

Despite this and the number of other Persian settlements we know of in the land of Israel, there are very few monumental remains dating to this period.[9] This scarcity is sometimes attributed to a widespread destruction at the end of the First Temple Period[10] (although this explanation is by no means universally accepted). In any event, the scarcity of monumental remains may relate to construction methods and materials used (mud brick and wood over field stone foundations), as well as to any destructive event.

There is a gap in our knowledge of the Jericho area in the Hellenistic period, although the area appears to have been fortified (1 Macc 9:50). During the Roman conquest of Judaea and after taking Jerusalem, Pompey the Great undertook to cleanse Judaea of the "haunts of robbers and the treasure-holds of the tyrants," two of which were along the route leading to Jericho (Strabo, *Geographies*, 16.2.40). Under Roman rule, Gabinius made Jericho one of the five administrative centers of Palestine (Josephus, *JW* 1.8.170).

### Tulul Abu el-Alayiq

This site, whose modern Arabic name is *Tulul Abu el-Alayiq*,[11] is the ruin of Hasmonaean and Herodian Jericho. This large agricultural estate at Tulul Abu el-Alayiq may have been constructed as early as 134 BCE.[12] It is located in the western area of the Jericho plain, spanning both sides of the Wadi Qelt not far from its source in the hills to the north. It lies some 7 km west of the River Jordan, 10 km north of the Dead Sea, 1.5 km west of the modern city of Jericho, 2 km south of Tel Jericho (*Tel es-Sultan*), and about 27 km east-northeast of Jerusalem. The site encompasses palatial, residential, administrative, and storage buildings, as well as aqueducts, pools, water installations, balsam and date plantations, and gardens.[13]

---

8. Stern, *Material Culture*, 38.
9. Ibid., 47.
10. Ibid.
11. *Telul* is the Arabic plural of *Tel*. The site comprises two *telul*.
12. *Excavations and Surveys in Israel 1982*, 1:45. Author unattributed in text.
13. I will discuss Netzer's identification below.

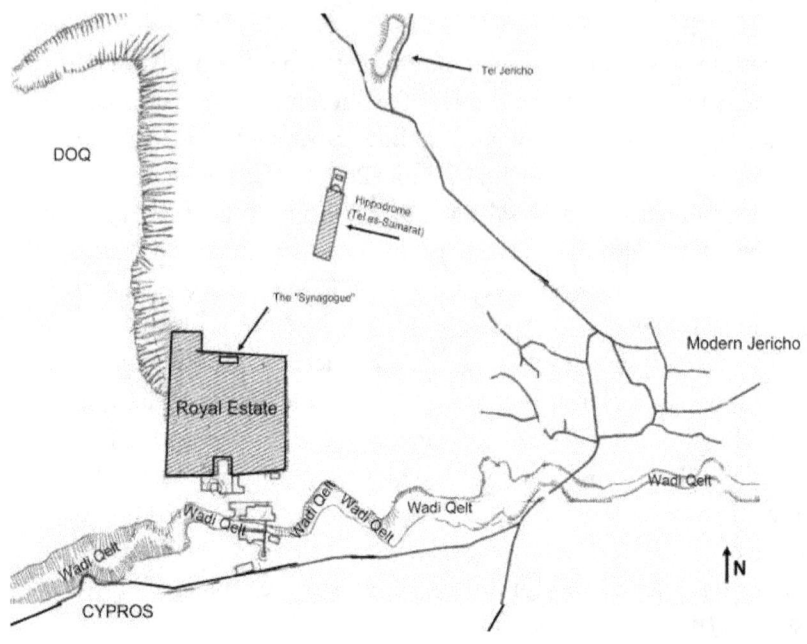

The area of Tulul Abu el-Alayiq / Hasmonaean Jericho (after Netzer 2004)

The estate is situated in a rich agricultural oasis in the Jericho plain, which has a climate of year-round sunny skies and dry air, average summer temperatures of 32–39° C and average winter temperatures of 20–23°.[14] The mean annual precipitation is between 50 mm and 200 mm, falling mainly as rain, almost entirely between October and April and typically falling in short, heavy showers, during which the desert soil can only absorb a limited amount of water,[15] which can result in sudden wadi floods. As a result of the unpredictability of the rain, ancient Jericho (indeed, much of ancient Palestine) relied on aqueducts, cisterns, wells, and springs for its water supply[16] and there was (and still is) a plentiful water supply from the nearby springs at Ain[17] es-Sultan (Elisha's Spring:

---

14. It also has weakened UV radiation and a high oxygen content due to the high barometric pressure.

15. Garbrecht and Peleg, "The Water Supply of the Desert Fortresses in the Jordan Valley."

16. Netzer, *The Architecture of Herod, the Great Builder*, 43.

17. *Ain* is the Arabic word for "spring."

2 Kgs 2:19–22), Ain Duq, Ain Nu'eima, the three springs of Wadi Qelt,[18] and the springs of Auja el-Tahta and Na'aran in the hills northwest of Tulul Abu el-Alayiq.[19]

Unfortunately, there is a large gap between historical references relating to the Hasmonaean estate at Jericho and what constitutes its history according to Ehud Netzer. Therefore, even though this part of Jericho is likely to have been inhabited and cultivated as early as the Persian period, if not earlier, the earliest remains at Tulul Abu el-Alayiq are apparently late Hellenistic.[20]

We do not know precisely which of the Hasmonaeans built the estate, nor precisely when, nor even under what circumstances they were built, although they are tentatively attributed by the excavators of the site to the reigns of Alexander Jannaeus (106–76 BCE) and his widow Alexandra (76–67 BCE).[21]

View to the north / Showing Cypros (top left), Bedouin camp (center left) and Herodian Palace (foreground). Author's photograph.

18. Bromiley et al., *ISBE* 2:995.

19. Stern, *New Encyclopedia of Archaeological Excavations in the Holy Land*, 2:683.

20. *Excavations and Surveys in Israel 1982* (author unattributed), 45: "During our investigations of the Hasmonaean palace and its vicinity, and of the Hasmonaean farm and its water supply systems, it became clear that the palace was built in several stages. Three main stages can be distinguished, the first two tentatively dated to the reign of Alexander Jannaeus (103–76 BCE) and the last to that of his wife, Shlomzion (76–67 BCE)."

21. *Excavations and Surveys in Israel, 1982*, 45.

Because of its location, we can surmise that the estate was built to take advantage of the local climate, the nearby water resources, and other agricultural conditions. And whilst we do not know who ran the estate, we do know that a variety of date palms and balsam were among the produce and that Jericho was a center for the production of balsam. We can assume from the scale of the estate, the variety of dates and the valuable balsam produced there, along with the quality of the architectural decoration of the site as a whole, that it was a place of some importance to both the Hasmonaeans and later to the Herodians.

Adding to these historiographic and archaeological problems, the site itself is difficult to access. It is located in the Palestinian territories, 1.5 km west of the modern town of Jericho. Israelis are not permitted to visit the site, and foreign schools do not excavate there. The site is most definitely not on the tourist trail. Tourists coming into the area are taken to see nearby Tel Jericho and Hisham's Palace, but not Tulul Abu el-Alayiq. The site is not actively protected and a Bedouin family lives there (the same family—though a different generation—as mentioned in Egon Lass's memoir).[22] The Bedouin family does not encourage visitors to the archaeological site, which is surrounded by date plantations. Goats are grazed on and around the site and there are a number of fishponds nearby.[23] The site is directly overlooked by the Israeli military post at Cypros in the hills above the Wadi Qelt (which also makes Cypros difficult to access). All of this makes visiting Tulul Abu el-Alayiq something of an unnerving and not entirely safe experience.[24]

## THE ANCIENT SOURCES

The most informative ancient references available to us are from Strabo, Pliny the Elder, and Josephus, and these relate to the geography and agricultural produce of the area. It is only in marrying the archaeological evidence with the ancient source material that we can build any sort of picture of what the estate of the Hasmonaeans at Jericho might have been

---

22. Lass, *The Seasons of Tulul* is a memoir of the period between January 1974 and April 1976 during which Lass, one of the archaeologists working with Ehud Netzer, lived alongside and befriended a Bedouin family camped at the Wadi Qelt.

23. On my last visit there, one of the fishponds had hundreds of storks circling above, waiting for a chance to get at the fish.

24. I visited the site three times: the first just before the Intifada of 2000, the second in 2004, and most recently in September 2006.

like. However, with so few relevant records, this can only be a speculative process. As I have already stated, the ancient references to Jericho are few and far between, and those that refer specifically to the Hasmonaean estate are even fewer. Following are the main sources.

### Strabo (ca. 64 BCE—ca. 23 CE)

> Hiericus is a plain surrounded by a kind of mountainous country, which, in a way, slopes towards it like a theatre. Here is the Phoenicon,[25] which is mixed also with other kinds of cultivated and fruitful trees, though it consists mostly of palm trees; it is one hundred stadia in length, and is everywhere watered with streams and full of dwellings. Here are also the palace[26] and the balsam park. The balsam is of the shrub kind, resembling Cytisus[27] and terminthus,[28] and has a spicy flavour. The people make incisions in the bark and catch the juice in vessels. This juice is a glutinous, milk-white substance; and when it is put up in small quantities it solidifies; and it is remarkable for its cure of headache and of incipient cataracts and of dimness of sight. Accordingly, it is costly; and also for the reason that it is produced nowhere else. Such is also the case with the Phoenicon, which alone has the caryotic palm,[29] excepting the Babylonian and that beyond Babylonia towards the east. Accordingly, the revenue derived from it is great. And they use the xylobalsam[30] as spice.

Geographies, 16.2.41[31]

---

25. Palm grove.

26. Herod's palace.

27. *Medicago Arborea*. However, while it may have resembled *medicago arborea* in appearance, the Jericho balsam was a plant with a resinous secretion whose effects were healing and/or soothing. We cannot identify the exact plant from which ancient balsam was produced, but we do at least know that Jericho was a center for its production.

28. *Terminthus* is the terebinth tree, *pistacia terebinthus*, from which turpentine is extracted and which also produces small edible nuts.

29. *Palma caryota*, with a walnut-like fruit.

30. *Xylobalsam* is the liquid that oozes from the cut branches of the plant.

31. Translated by Horace Leonard Jones.

### Pliny the Elder (23 CE–79 CE)

Beyond Idumaea and Samaria stretches the wide expanse of Judaea. The part of Judaea adjoining Syria is called Galilee, and that next to Arabia and Egypt, Peraea. Peraea is covered with rugged mountains, and is separated from the other parts of Judaea by the river Jordan. The rest of Judaea is divided into ten Local Government Areas in the following order: the district of Jericho, which has numerous palm-groves and springs of water, and those of Emmaus, Lydda, Joppa, Accrabim, Jufna, Timnath-Serah, Bethlebaoth, the Hills, the district that formerly contained Jerusalem, by far the most famous city of the East and not of Judaea only, and Herodium with the celebrated town of the same name.

*Natural History*, 5.15.70[32]

### Josephus (ca. 37 CE—100 CE)

Now when Pompey had pitched his camp at Jericho (where the palm tree grows), and that balsam which is an ointment of all the most precious, which, upon any incision made in the wood with a sharp stone, distils out thence like a juice) . . .

*JA* 14.4.1(54)[33]

When Cleopatra had obtained thus much, and had accompanied Antony in his expedition to Armenia, as far as Euphrates, she returned back, and came to Apamea and Damascus, and passed on to Judaea; where Herod met her, and farmed of her parts of Arabia, and those revenues that came to her from the region about Jericho. This country bears that balsam, which is the most precious drug that is there, and grows there alone. The place bears also excellent palm trees, both many in number, and those excellent in their kind.

*JA* 15.4.2(96)[34]

---

32. Translated by H. Rackham.
33. Translated by William Whiston.
34. Translated by William Whiston.

*Maccabees*

> Then Bacchides returned to Jerusalem and built strong cities in Judea: the fortress in Jericho, and Emmaus, and Beth-horon, and Bethel, and Timnath, and Pharathon, and Tephon, with high walls and gates and bars.
>
> 1 Macc 9:50[35]

## THE AQUEDUCTS

Excavations conducted from 1973 through 1981 near where Wadi el Qelt flows into the western plains of Jericho found remains of extensive water systems linked with the Hasmonaean estate.[36] Sections of these aqueducts are still visible along the surface near the western edge of the Jericho plain and were first surveyed by the British Survey of Palestine in the 1880s.[37]

The modern excavators found that there were two separate systems drawing water from the springs in the Wadi Qelt and from the springs at Na'aran and Ein el-Auja.[38] These systems brought the water directly from the source to the fields using a system of channels and sluice gates set along the conduits to control flow to different areas.[39] A sluice gate on an ancient aqueduct is normally just a wooden, stone, or metal plate which slides into grooves in the sides of the channel and has to be operated manually. Raising a sluice gate allows water to flow under it. While Netzer found additional stones on either side of some conduit openings to facilitate sluice gates in the Hasmonaean estate, he did not find any built-in grooves for them.[40] This suggests that the sluice gates were a later or even an ad hoc addition to the system as the water systems to the estate were extended and adapted.

There are two main systems of aqueducts in the Wadi Qelt. One runs along the north bank of the wadi, while the other runs along the south

---

35. Translated by John R. Bartlett.
36. Netzer and Garbrecht, "Water Channels," 367.
37. Ibid., n. 3; Wonder and Kitchener, *The Survey of Western Palestine III: Judaea*, 190, 222, 227–28.
38. Netzer and Garbrecht, "Water Channels," 367.
39. Ibid., 377.
40. Ibid.

bank and three additional channels fed by seasonal rains.[41] The estate and its water supply was in constant use from its establishment (in the mid to late second century BCE) until the destruction of the Jerusalem Temple by the Romans in 70 CE.[42] The longest of the aqueducts is the one from the Wadi Qelt to the hill fortress of Cypros, which was also part of the system feeding the plantations of the Hasmonaean estate at Tulul Abu el-Alayiq.[43]

Bearing in mind the tentative nature of the dating of the site, Netzer thought it may have been during the reigns of Alexander Jannaeus (106–76 BCE), or his widow Alexandra (76–67 BCE), that the Na'aran Conduit was built along the mountain ridges and down to the Hasmonaean site.[44] While this aqueduct served many parts of the Hasmonaean estate, its main purpose was to irrigate the plantations on the eastern end of the estate.[45] The addition of this aqueduct allowed for swimming pools, cisterns, ritual baths, and irrigation and drainage systems to be constructed.[46]

The Na'aran and other later aqueducts enabled the production of rich harvests, particularly of balsam[47] and dates. Balsam plants take several years to reach maturity before they can be harvested and processed into perfume oils and various other unguents. Date palms likewise become productive only after a dozen or so years and, according to Josephus, Jericho produced a number of distinct varieties which could be processed into various varieties of food and wine:

> Indeed, this spring [at Jericho] irrigates a larger space of ground than all others, and passes within a plain of seventy furlongs long, and twenty broad; wherein it affords nourishment to those most excellent gardens that are thick set with trees. There are in it may

41. Porath, "Hydraulic Plaster in Aqueducts as a Chronological Indicator," 29.
42. Netzer and Garbrecht, "Water Channels," 377.
43. Amit et al., *The Aqueducts of Israel*, 19 n. 32: "The Hasmonaean-Herodian palace at Jericho got its supply first by the aqueduct from Wadi el-Qelt and then by two additions that brought water from the Na'aran Springs and from Wadi el 'Auja farther to the north. Four outlets attested in the Na'aran branch took water to irrigate the fields and groves of the estates."
44. Porath, "Hydraulic plaster," 31.
45. Netzer, *The Architecture of Herod*, 42.
46. Stern, *The New Encyclopedia of Archaeological Excavations in the Holy Land*, 685.
47. Balsam is a plant resin that is healing and/or soothing in its effect. While we cannot identify the plant from which ancient balsam was produced, we do know that Jericho was a center for its production.

sorts of date palms that are watered by it, different from each other in flavour and name; the better sort of them, when they are pressed under foot, yield an excellent kind of honey, not much inferior in sweetness to that of bees, which are also abundant in this region. Here, too grow the juicy balsam, which is the most precious of all fruits in that place, cypress trees also, and those that bear myrobalanus, so that he who would pronounce this place to be divine would not be mistaken, a spot in which the rarest and the most excellent plants are produced in abundance.

Josephus, *JW* 4.467–69

Given the long-term planning and expense involved in producing balsam and dates, and the horticultural expertise required to maintain productive plantations, it would appear that the estate of the Hasmonaeans at Jericho functioned as an administrative, trade, and agricultural center, and as a pleasant winter resort.

## THE ARCHAEOLOGICAL REMAINS

### Phase 1: The Original Courtyard House

The building Netzer identified as a synagogue is a courtyard house that forms part of a complex of buildings along the eastern end of the Hasmonaean estate between the industrial area and the palace complexes. It is located at the western end of a row of nine residential buildings. At the eastern end of this row of buildings, which stretches some 165 m, is an industrial area. To the southwest of the courtyard house are what Netzer designated as the Twin Palaces. To the west of the courtyard house complex is a large pools complex and a garden. As the courtyard house complex is located between the industrial area and the palace complexes, it may have marked some sort of delineation between the industrial area to the east and the series of phased palace complexes to the west.[48]

---

48. Netzer, *Hasmonaean and Herodian Palaces at Jericho*, 2:159.

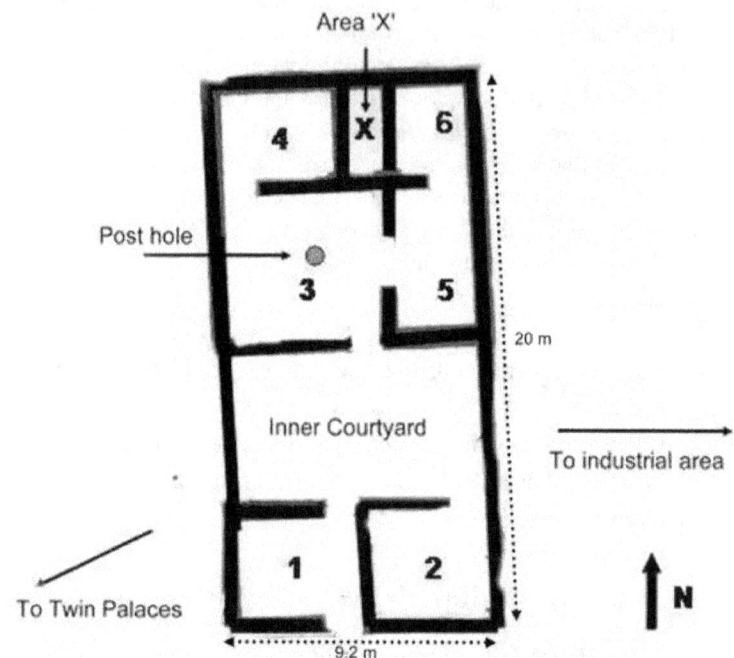

**Phase 1 / The original Courtyard House (after Netzer, 2004)**

The courtyard house was the first phase of this building complex to be constructed. According to Netzer, it was built slightly off-axis to the plan of the neighboring buildings abutting the industrial area to the east. It is rectangular in shape and measures some 20 x 9.2 m. It is comprised of a central courtyard between rooms on the north and south and was built of local materials—that is, mudbrick on top of unworked fieldstone foundations and wadi rubble.[49]

Throughout the entire Hasmonaean estate at Jericho, mudbrick and fieldstones were used and then plastered over so as to look more substantial and costly—a useful economy of scale. This technique was used in many parts of the site, including the original courtyard house referred to here. There is no evidence of painted plaster from the courtyard house, so far as I am aware.

As Netzer rightly argues—in an unpublished article[50] and in a conversation with me in September of 2006—the building he identified as a

---

49. Ibid., 2:160.

50. "A Synagogue in Jericho from the Hasmonaean Period," Unpublished Hebrew article which Prof. Netzer generously e-mailed to me following our conversations in

synagogue would undoubtedly have provoked much more public attention had it been constructed out of basalt ashlars even if it lacked mosaic floors, carved architectural features, and other decorative elements.

In any event, when it was in use, the courtyard house would have looked indistinguishable from buildings constructed of solid masonry. Certainly, it is of a size, quality and complexity to suggest it was used by some member of the Hasmonaean household, be that an official of the estate or a family member, and the courtyard house is common throughout the Mediterranean area in the late Persian, Hellenistic, and early Roman period.[51]

The floor plan of the courtyard house reveals six rooms built around an internal courtyard. The rooms are divided into two rooms to the south and four to the north. The entrance to the courtyard house is at the southern end of the building and leads into the courtyard from between the two southern rooms. Internally, the courtyard leads into the rooms of the northern part of the house. Access to upper floors would have been from outside the building itself via external stairways.

As they are accessed only by one door, the rooms on the north side of the courtyard may have been part of the private quarters of whoever lived and worked in this building. The less private rooms on the south of the courtyard are likely to have been used as reception rooms, office spaces, or for other uses altogether. Indeed, their use need not have been fixed as many elements used in the household would have been portable (desks, chairs, braziers, and cooking equipment, for example). Sleeping quarters would have been on upper floors and on the roof.

Water was easily accessible from water installations nearby, and the main Na'aran conduit runs beside and partly underneath the northernmost wall for the entire width of the building.[52] The importance of this

---

September 2006. The article was very kindly translated for me by Orit Peleg-Barkat of the Institute of Archaeology, Hebrew University of Jerusalem.

51. See, for general examples, residential houses in Hirschfeld, *The Palestinian Dwelling in the Roman-Byzantine Period*; Cahill, *Household and City Organization at Olynthus*, 125, 201, 231; the axonometric reconstruction of the *Mason de la Colline* on Delos and the *Herdraum* house at Ammotopos in Nevett, *House and Society in the Ancient Greek World*, 24–25; the comparisons of courtyard houses in Thorikos in Ault and Nevett, *Ancient Greek Houses and Households*, 86.

52. Netzer, *Hasmonaean and Herodian Palaces at Jericho*, 2:184.

will become clear when we come to look at the Phase 2 water installations and what Netzer has identified as a niche and possible *genizah*.[53]

### The Entrance (Room 1)

The entrance room is located at the southern end of the courtyard house and measures 4.4 m x 3.4 m. A doorway from the outside of the building leads through the entrance room into the central courtyard.[54] The floor of the entrance room was made up of beaten earth above wadi rubble. Underneath the floor of the entry room, in line with the doorway, there is a small water channel[55] that comes from the Na'aran conduit. This channel feeds part of a later water installation (see Phase 2 below).

### Room 2

Room 2 is located directly to the east of the entrance room. It measures some 3.65 m x 3.4 m. This room was accessed via the courtyard on the east side of the building. The floor consisted of the same material as that of the entrance room—that is, beaten earth above wadi fill.[56]

### The Courtyard

The internal courtyard is located in the center of the courtyard house, along its entire width, and situated between Rooms 1 and 2 on the south and Rooms 3 and 5 on the north. It measures 9.2 m x 5.1 m wide and was entered from the south via the entrance between Rooms 1 and 2. A doorway on the north of the courtyard provided access to Room 3, from which the other rooms on the north could be reached.[57] The floor of the courtyard consisted of beaten earth.[58]

### Room 3

Room 3 is the large southwestern room on the northern end of the building and measures 5.45 m x 4. 85 m. The room was accessible from the courtyard on the south via a doorway on its eastern side. There are three

---

53. A *genizah* is a storage archive for sacred and important documents that have gone out of use but cannot be destroyed for religious reasons.

54. Netzer, *Hasmonaean and Herodian Palaces at Jericho*, 2:162.

55. Ibid.

56. Ibid.

57. Ibid.

58. Ibid., 2:163.

other doorways leading from Room 3 to other rooms in the northern part of the courtyard house—one on the east providing access to Rooms 5 and 6, and two on the north, both leading into Room 4 in the northwestern part of the house. Netzer thought this might have been a second courtyard.[59]

The floor was covered with a layer of mudbrick debris which contained Hasmonaean pottery sherds, and was made up of beaten earth over soil. Since the ground surface was not entirely horizontal here, wadi material was piled on top of it to form a level base for the floor. In the center of the room, there is evidence of what might have been a round fireplace or the setting for a wooden column base. It consisted of red burnt clay and ash.[60]

It is safe to assume that this was the location of a column or pillar to support a partially roofed section of the house as the placement of this post hole is directly analogous to the M1 lower city insula in ancient Meiron, where we see a pillar base in more or less the same place as the Jericho courtyard house posthole.[61]

However, the third and second century CE insula at ancient Meiron is not the only analogue to the second century BCE courtyard house at Tulul Abu el-Alayiq. There are many similar buildings, such as the third–second-century BCE house at Beth Yerah, the second-century BCE house at Mount Gerizim, the third–secondnd-century BCE house at Samaria-Sebaste, as well as many others I have not specifically listed here.

---

59. Ibid., 2:164.
60. Ibid.
61. Meyers, et al., *Excavations at Ancient Meiron, Upper Galilee, Israel 1971–72, 1974–75, 1977*, 3:34–35 (the posthole is in the upper left of the plan).

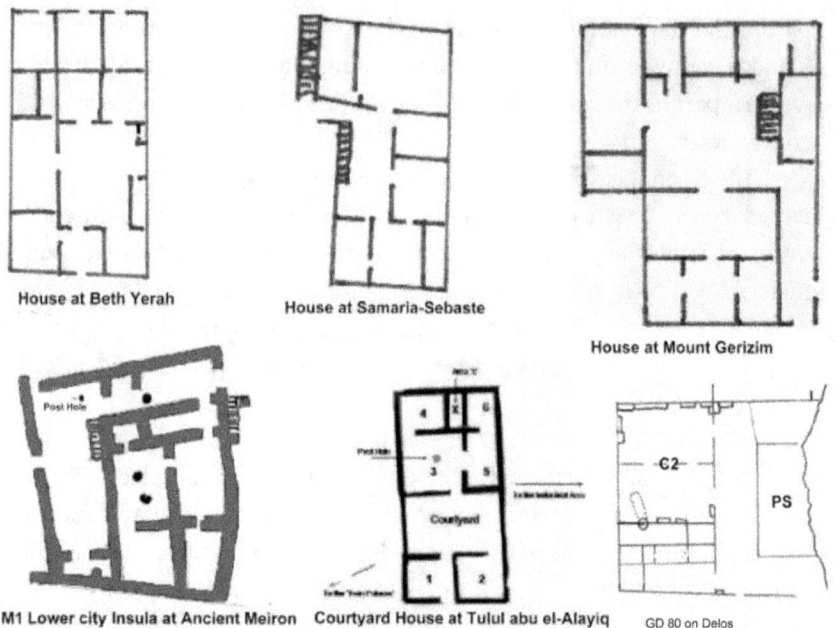

Comparison of courtyard houses

The courtyard house of ancient Israel usually had an internal courtyard that was simply constructed for everyday domestic access. This type of construction was used from as early as the beginning of the second millennium BCE at Ur and can be seen all over the ancient Near East.[62] Because of the temperate climate, domestic chores tended to be conducted in the courtyard and activities needed only be moved indoors during the rainy season.[63]

Room 4

Room 4 of the Tulul courtyard house, located in the northwestern corner of the house, measured 4 m x 3 m. Some mudbrick was preserved on top of the fieldstone foundations of part of the eastern and western walls of this room. The room was originally entered from the south via two doorways,[64] but at some point the eastern door was eliminated. The

62. Hirschfeld, *The Palestinian Dwelling*, 57.
63. Ibid., 272.
64. Netzer, *Hasmonaean and Herodian Palaces at Jericho*, 2:164.

floor consisted of beaten earth over soil. Some lime plaster remains on the south face of the northern wall of this room.[65]

Room 5

Room 5 is located to the east of Room 3 from which it is entered. It measures 4.8 m x 2.75 m. In it, there is an internal doorway leading to another room (Room 6) on the north. The floor consisted of beaten earth over virgin soil and covered with ash, above which was a layer of mudbrick debris which contained Hasmonaean pottery sherds.[66]

Room 6

Room 6 is located in the northeastern corner of the house, and measures 2.8 m x 2.5 m. Some mudbrick is preserved on part of its western wall. Entry to the room was via Room 5. The floor of Room 6 also consisted of beaten earth over virgin soil. A small installation consisting of a quarter-circle formed by a row of pebbles and containing ash was revealed in the northeastern corner of the room. This may have served as a small fixed fireplace or oven.[67]

Space X

Space X, measuring 2.8 m x 1.25 m in size, is located between Rooms 4 and 6. No doorway was found here. Netzer argued that this space (which he calls a "cell") was entered via an opening located at a higher level in one of the walls.[68]

However, it seems more likely that this space represents the base of a stairway that accesses the upper story of the house. This argument is supported by the fact that the floor in this area was some 32 cm higher than that of the other rooms,[69] suggesting it had a compacted floor sufficient to support the base of a stairway. Indeed, a direct parallel to this can be seen in the insula of the lower city of ancient Meiron where a stairway lays along the eastern wall of the internal courtyard and leads to the upper floor of the house.

65. Ibid., 165.
66. Ibid., 164.
67. Ibid., 165.
68. Ibid.
69. Ibid.

In many ways, the insula at ancient Meiron corresponds to the layout of the courtyard house under discussion here. The centermost element of the insula has the same rectangular structure with an entryway, two rooms just inside, a central courtyard, and then rooms leading off to the north, east, and west of the building. In the first phase of the Jericho courtyard house complex, the room marked "3" is similar to the internal courtyard in the insula in ancient Meiron, where there is a column post in the same place as in the corresponding room at Jericho. However, contrary to Netzer's suggestion that the entire internal courtyard at Jericho was covered, it can be seen at Meiron that only a small portion of the courtyard is covered.[70] This makes a great deal of sense in terms of utilization of space and retention of views of the lower parts of the house and the courtyards (both the internal one and the porticoed one).[71]

Moreover, it appears from my personal observations and photographs of the site that the entire courtyard house complex has not been excavated and that, in fact, there are at least two further ground floor rooms on the east side of the original building. Again, this is directly analogous to the M1 lower city insula at ancient Meiron and elsewhere (see examples above) and would suggest that at least the ground floor structure of the Hasmonaean courtyard house and the M1 courtyard house and the other examples given are very similar. It also appears to me that the section of the courtyard house containing Space "X" is in fact a corridor running between the different sections of the house, again as at ancient Meiron (above).

---

70. Meyers et al., *Excavations at Ancient Meiron*, 34–35.
71. Ibid.

Possible additional rooms at the eastern end of the courtyard house adjoining the industrial area. (Author's photos, courtyard house looking southwest and east [respectively].)

Netzer says that the courtyard house is not built along the same axis as the residential row to the east. However, if I am correct about the ground floor layout, then the easternmost wall abuts the residential area precisely, making the shape of the courtyard house rather less than rectangular so as to utilize the available space fully.[72]

*Phase 2*

### The Peristyle Courtyard

In the second phase of the building, what Netzer describes as an "assembly hall" (measuring 16 m x 11.5 m) was added along the western wall of the original courtyard house, with some reconstruction taking place to accommodate those changes. This included opening up two doorways in the western wall of the courtyard house; one leading to the new space, and one leading into the chambers on the south.

The peristyle courtyard is also part of an architectural tradition seen in ancient Israel, reflecting Graeco-Roman influences, albeit on a limited scale.[73] That this particular style is seen in the building programs of the Hasmonaean family is interesting, but should not trouble us overly here.[74]

Netzer argues that this space could not be a second courtyard because other courtyards in the estate had a visual connection with the buildings with which they are connected.[75] In fact, a second, usually larger and more formal, courtyard is a reasonably standard component of a courtyard house of this type in the Hellenistic period.[76] The assembly hall as described by Netzer is quite simply a formal peristyle courtyard.[77]

---

72. See, Nevett, *House and Society*, 24–25; Ault and Nevett, *Ancient Greek Houses*, 86.

73. Hirschfeld, *The Palestinian Dwelling*, 85–86.

74. This is interesting in the context of the ongoing debate about the extent of Hellenistic influences in the land of Israel, a subject I cannot deal with here.

75. Netzer, *Hasmonaean and Herodian Palaces at Jericho*, 2:184.

76. Boardman et al., *Greece and the Hellenistic World*, 388.

77. In Greek and Roman architecture, a peristyle is a columned porch or open colonnade in a building that surrounds a court.

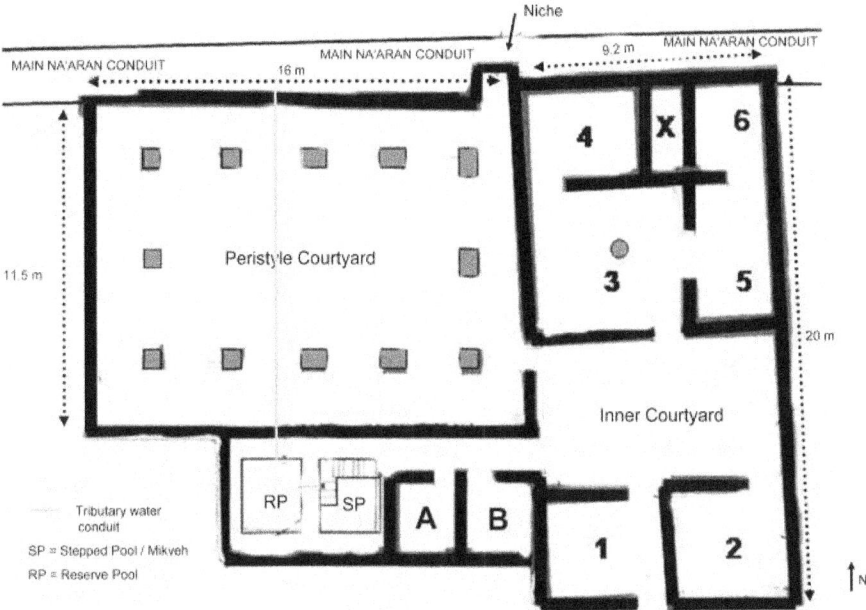

Phase 2 of the courtyard house complex (after Netzer, 2004).

The visual connection Netzer refers to would certainly have existed in the view from the upper floor(s) of the original courtyard house to the peristyle courtyard below. Netzer contradicts his own argument on line-of-sight when he argues that in a later phase of the building one of the columns between the courtyard and the triclinium was moved to provide a line of sight from the triclinium to the courtyard. Thus, there were actually *three* lines of visual connection to this courtyard; the first from the upper floor of the original courtyard house, the second from the triclinium, and the third from the entrance of the original courtyard house into the peristyle courtyard.

Netzer argues that his assembly hall was originally covered because the floor consisted of beaten earth, which is normally used in covered rooms.[78] However, this is not itself an indicator that the courtyard was covered. It was very likely to have been partially or completely paved when in use and treated as a decorative space with plants in pots placed around the space. Moreover, covering the peristyle courtyard would have removed the light source for much of the rest of the ground floor of the

78. Netzer, *Hasmonaean and Herodian Palaces at Jericho*, 2:185.

original courtyard house. It is likely that ground floor rooms looking onto the courtyard(s) would have had windows, so that any light blockage (by roofing the space) would block off that light.[79] In any event, beaten earth (pulverized with hoes and rakes) had another purpose. It reduced moisture evaporation from parched soil and helped drainage so that pooling of rainwater would have been minimized.[80]

Netzer argues that it was the custom to have a peristyle courtyard at a slightly lower level in order to drain rainwater and that therefore his assembly hall could not be a courtyard.[81] However, while in the Hellenistic period double-courtyard houses sometimes had one of the courtyards built at a slightly lower level, this was designed to enhance the entrance into the house proper.[82] The fact that the peristyle courtyard is at the same level as the rest of the complex is irrelevant to drainage in this instance.

Another of Netzer's contentions about his assembly hall is that it was covered and had clerestory windows because, otherwise, there is no explanation for the use of the massive pillars in its construction.[83] The pillars themselves do not survive, however. The *bases* on which they stood are rectangular in shape and vary in diameter, averaging some 85 cm x 70 cm.[84] The pillar bases are built into the stylobate[85] on which they rest, and the best preserved base stands only 50 cm high. The fact that the bases are not of a uniform size lends further credence to the argument that they were not designed to support a roof. The bases are constructed of local field stones bonded with mud.

The upper parts of the pillars that do not survive were most likely mud brick (probably made on-site in the industrial area to the east). They were likely to have been of a narrower diameter or gauge than the bases and would have been plastered and painted to look like solid masonry, as with the rest of the courtyard house complex and other areas of the Hasmonaean estate. Thus, these pillars were by no means massive and were there to support a colonnade which would have been no higher than

---

79. Nevett, *House and Society*, 24–25.
80. Forbes, *Studies in Ancient Technology*, 2:43–44.
81. Netzer, unpublished paper.
82. Boardman and Murray, *Greece and the Hellenistic World*, 388.
83. Netzer, unpublished.
84. Netzer, *Hasmonaean and Herodian Palaces at Jericho*, 2:166–67.
85. A *stylobate* is a step on which column and pillar bases were set.

the external walls of the courtyard. The colonnade was designed to be a decorative feature of such courtyards and to provide some shade in the glaring summer heat and some protection from the winter rain.

Covering a walled courtyard and building clerestory windows (with the consequent bulking out of the courtyard house complex) is highly unlikely. Not only would this have been aesthetically unappealing and wholly out of character with this type of building,[86] but it would also have been unnecessary and, more importantly, would have interfered with light penetration into the ground floor of the house. There would have been no external windows looking out onto the external street, whereas there would have been windows looking onto the courtyard and these would have been thereby rendered obsolete.

Netzer says that the assembly hall is not in proportion to the size of the courtyard house, and that this adds support to his argument that the building is a synagogue, as there is otherwise no reason for the scale of the assembly/reception hall.[87] He also says that his assembly hall is missing a proper residential building which would justify a reception hall on this scale and that the courtyard house itself is not a residence for this hall.[88]

However, as is clear from the parallel examples given, both in Israel and Greece,[89] not only is the courtyard house entirely in proportion to the peristyle courtyard, but was also at least a two-story building. And, as I have already said, there were probably at least another two more rooms on the ground floor of the eastern side of the house, as in the parallels at Meiron and elsewhere. The original courtyard house was therefore wider and more capacious than Netzer suggests. The walls of the very eastern end of the building would then abut, at a slight angle, the residential buildings to the east. There can be no doubt that the courtyard house is the residence attached to the peristyle court. This is an entirely normal

---

86. Cahill, *Household and City Organization at Olynthus*; Nevett, *House and Society in the Ancient Greek World*; Ault and Nevett, *Ancient Greek Houses and Households*; Hirschfeld, *The Palestinian Dwelling*.

87. Netzer, *Hasmonaean and Herodian Palaces at Jericho*, 2:186; Meyers et al., *Excavations at Ancient Meiron*, 1981.

88. Netzer, *Hasmonaean and Herodian Palaces at Jericho*, 2:186 n. 67.

89. Cahill, *Household and City Organization at Olynthus*; Boardman and Murray, *Greece and the Hellenistic World*; Nevett, *House and Society in the Ancient Greek World*; Ault and Nevett, *Ancient Greek Houses and Households*; Meyers, et al., *Excavations at Ancient Meiron*; Hirschfeld, *The Palestinian Dwelling*.

configuration, as is seen from the floor plan and the examples of other courtyard houses given above.

Netzer further describes the peristyle courtyard as a nave surrounded by aisles with square pillars along all four sides. He says that the aisles are situated about 40 cm higher than the nave and that this 40 cm difference enabled the supportive walls that were built between the pillars and separated the nave from the aisles to be used as benches which then allowed about 150 people to sit in the hall.

**Peristyle courtyard looking southeast. (Author's photograph)**

There is, however, no evidence of benches having been in place; there are no visible remains of such.[90] The only raised areas are the platforms on which the pillar bases stand, and this simply circles the courtyard. There is no regular differentiation in floor levels between what Netzer called the nave and the aisles. The few irregular differences in the ground level can be accounted for by soil erosion, earthquake damage and the excavation process itself. This is a peristyle courtyard and is, like the design of the original courtyard house itself, a fairly standard feature of houses of this type.[91]

---

90. Netzer, *Hasmonaean and Herodian Palaces at Jericho*, 2:165–66.
91. Boardman et al., *Greece and the Hellenistic World*, 388.

Of course, even if the structure was a courtyard and not an assembly hall, this would not preclude its use as a synagogue. There is no doubt that the layout of the courtyard could easily have been used for the reading of the Torah to people gathered there. But, equally, any sufficient space—exterior or interior—could serve this purpose.

Finally, Netzer sets up a straw man argument, positing his conclusions against a group of unrealistic alternatives. He asks what the space could possibly have been used for if not as a meeting place and a place for receptions and banquets. He says that it was unlikely to have been used for industrial activity, and unlikely to have been a storage facility or a place for housing animals and that therefore it must have been the assembly hall of a synagogue.[92]

He is obviously correct that this space was not used for industrial activity, or for storage or for animals, but this argument ignores and avoids the conclusion that it *was* a straightforward peristyle courtyard for use by the occupants of and visitors to the courtyard house complex. Here, in this courtyard house complex, a peristyle courtyard is merely a peristyle courtyard.

The Niche

Another reason Netzer identified this building as a synagogue (and the reason he felt was most important) was that he found what he described as a niche in the northeastern corner of the assembly hall (the peristyle courtyard).[93] According to Netzer, its floor was one-half meter lower than the floor of the main assembly space.[94] He argued that the niche contained a wooden cupboard which was later replaced by a cupboard made of fieldstones and mud divided into two compartments, one above the other. The lower one, Netzer argues, could have served as a *genizah*, or storage space for worn-out scrolls and documents. A wooden plate (a sort of a horizontal door) would have covered the lower space of the niche and the upper space could have been accessed more often.[95]

---

92. Netzer, *Hasmonaean and Herodian Palaces at Jericho*, 2:187.
93. Ibid., 168.
94. Ibid., 171.
95. Ibid.

The niche, looking north and burrowing under the Na'aran conduit. (Author's photograph)

Netzer's reconstruction of his niche allows a horizontal 'door' to be raised or lowered to allow access to the internal compartments, one above the other. According to him, the lower compartment may have been used to store sacred scrolls and other important documents.

Netzer says that what was initially a wooden interior to the niche was eventually replaced with stone, transforming the space into a two-tiered compartment[96] and that the wooden structure was replaced because of fire destruction.[97] He says that because the niche (both the upper and lower tier) was entirely coated with lime plaster, it was used for the storage of sacred scrolls and was, in fact, a *genizah*.[98]

There are obvious problems with Netzer's understanding of this space. One is that the back of the lower part of the niche lies directly *beneath* the main Na'aran conduit. The solution here is to understand the niche as a small overflow tank designed to regulate water flow in the main

96. Ibid., 168.
97. Ibid., 171.
98. Ibid.

channel some 8 meters after it branches off into a tributary channel flowing down the peristyle courtyard to the water installations at the south of the building complex.

The branching off into a smaller south-flowing channel would have disrupted the flow of water, and the sluice gate system to the tributary channel leading south could only work if there was some diversion or overflow available to the still oncoming east-flowing water. Without this mechanism, the water would have simply risen higher and flowed over the top of the sluicegate, flooding the surrounding area, wasting valuable water and damaging the property.[99]

There are a number of points leading to and within the courtyard house building where the flow of water along the main conduit and its tributaries is controlled by sluice gates. If sluice gates are suddenly opened or closed, water in transit can transmit a shockwave backwards and forwards along the conduit (this is known as *water hammer* and it can destroy the conduit or pipe through which it flows).[100] The overflow tank (Netzer's niche), makes certain that any water shockwave can be safely contained. The tank can then be accessed for maintenance (and water collection) from the upper compartment.[101]

Netzer's reconstruction is, however, correct in almost all other respects. The placing and removal of a horizontal door between the two compartments is precisely how the overflow mechanism would have functioned. The horizontal door would have been able to stay in place as long as the flow along the main Na'aran conduit was slow and regular. If the water was moving faster or deeper than usual, the upper compartment could have been opened to extend containment.

Nonetheless, it would be eccentric, to say the least, to use such a mechanism in such a location for the safekeeping of sacred or valuable objects. Netzer's assembly hall is a peristyle courtyard and the niche or *genizah* is a simple overflow tank—an integral part of the water system in this building.

---

99. Hodge, *Roman Aqueducts and Water Supply*, 233.
100. Ibid.,154.
101. An overflow for a water conduit, in much the same position as at Jericho, can be seen at the fountain house of Theagenes: Hodge, *Roman Aqueducts*, 26.

### The Water Installations

Also belonging to the second phase of the building are the three rooms south of the peristyle courtyard, the largest of which contains a substantial water installation. This installation consists of two pools, one with steps for access and the other a reserve tank of equal size, but without the stepped access. Netzer identified the water installation as a *miqveh* with a reserve or *otzar*, and argued that the other two small rooms in this row of three rooms were probably for changing. There were two smashed storage jars in the bottom of the stepped pool and a number of smashed vessels in the overflow pool.[102]

A small channel connects the reserve to the immersion pool and that reserve pool is connected to the small tributary channel of the Na'aran conduit which runs under the floor of the peristyle courtyard some 8 meters west of the overflow tank. Two channels emerge from the corridor above Rooms A and B and then follow a line towards the entranceway to the original courtyard house, leaving the building to the south. There is what appears to be another small sluice mechanism just along the wall of Room 1 on the courtyard side, controlling the flow of water out of the building and further down the north-south incline.[103]

In the event that this building is not a synagogue and that the water installations represent the totality of the water supply to the household, it would appear that this is not a miqveh complex, although, of course, it could be a miqveh without being part of a synagogue complex. However, it appears to me that the water installations are rather too deep and too steep to be used for ritual purposes. The stepped pool is 2.25 m x 2.25 m in size, is 3.65 m deep, and has ten steps, of unequal height. The reserve pool is 2.65 m x 2.4 m in size and is 3.78 m deep.[104]

With a water supply and sufficient space so readily available, it would have been more than possible to build a shallower and wider-stepped *miqveh* here specifically for ritual purposes. It would seem that this may not be a purpose-built miqveh, but rather a cistern and reserve for the provision of water to this household.

---

102. Netzer, *Hasmonaean and Herodian Palaces at Jericho*, 2:180.
103. Ibid., 163.
104. Ibid., 178–79.

## Phase 3

### The Triclinium[105]

In the third phase of the building, a triclinium was added to the assembly hall and this is another of Netzer's reasons for believing that this building was a synagogue, again based on similarity with other sites, such as the synagogue with triclinium at Herodium.[106] The reconstruction involved in this latter phase involved a wall being dismantled, and one corner of the building being completely eliminated. In order to add the triclinium, changes were made in the courtyard.

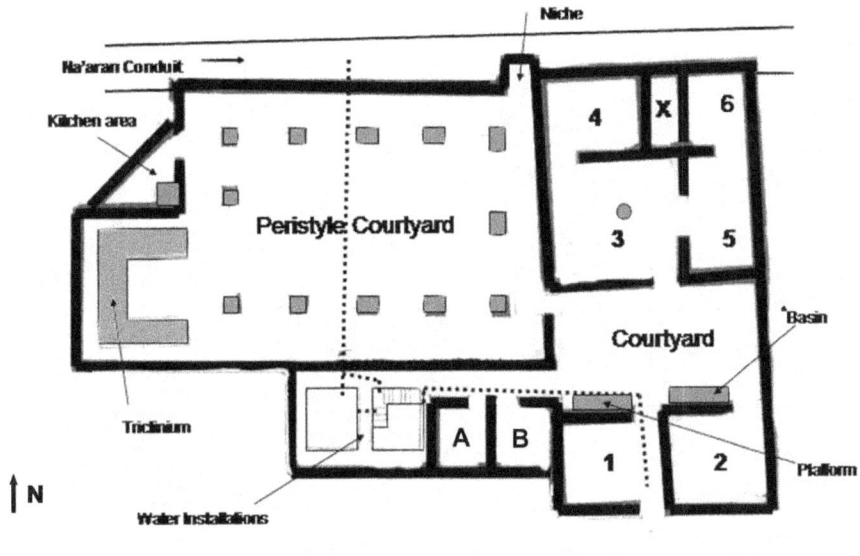

Phase 3 / The triclinium. (after Netzer, 2004)

Part of the western wall was dismantled and one of the pillars (directly outside the triclinium) was moved about two meters to the north, apparently so that there was a direct line of sight between the triclinium and the peristyle courtyard. Netzer argued that this was so that people dining in the triclinium could see the rest of the synagogue assembly during meals. It seems far more likely that the line of sight was altered so that

---

105. The *triclinium* is a U-shaped platform for reclining on while dining, usually seen in the Roman world.

106. Netzer, Kalman, and Laureys, "A Synagogue from the Hasmonean Period," 217; Netzer, "The Hasmonaean and Herodian Winter Palaces at Jericho," 95.

diners could enjoy the decorative space and pleasant evening temperature outside.

### The Kitchen

Adjacent to the triclinium is a triangular room that Netzer says was probably a kitchen. A podium in the right-angled corner bears evidence of fire and suggests that it may once have supported a stove. I have no argument with this interpretation.

The triclinium (bottom right) and kitchen (bottom center) looking southwest. (Western edge of the peristyle is in left center.) Author's photograph.

## THE SCHOLARSHIP ON HASMONAEAN JERICHO

### *Shanks*[107]

Herschel Shanks, responding to Netzer's identification of the "synagogue" in Hasmonaean Jericho, takes the view that the building complex is important because of its architecture, but questions whether it is a synagogue on the basis that there is no clear archaeological evidence— that is, no architectural indicators, no epigraphy, and no donor plaques.[108]

---

107. Hershel Shanks, "Is It or Isn't It—A Synagogue?"
108. Ibid.

He goes on to list the clues that led Netzer to consider the building complex a synagogue, and says that the first clue is the immersion pool and its reserve. Shanks also accepts this pool as a mikveh because it is a stepped pool with a supply coming from the Na'aran Conduit and because it complies with the prescriptions for a mikveh. He concurs with Netzer that the other rooms along this section of the complex were probably dressing rooms.[109]

Shanks repeats Netzer's assertion about the triclinium being the second clue to the building complex's identification as a synagogue and goes on to say that triclinia are well-known in the Roman world, but rare in Palestine.

He comes to the third clue, the niche, and has apparently accepted Netzer's contention as to its construction and use. Shanks asks if all these clues are sufficient to identify the Jericho building as a synagogue and cites Netzer's claim that the most important basis for his conclusion is its similarity to the Gamla synagogue. He leaves acceptance or rejection of Netzer's thesis to the reader, but applies no scrutiny to Netzer's claims.

However, in his acceptance of Netzer's interpretation of the construction of the building, he necessarily leans towards agreement rather than otherwise. There is nothing in Shanks's brief discussion that adds anything to the debate; it is a recitation of Netzer's findings and conclusions.

## Rapuano[110]

Rapuano approaches Netzer's identification from a different angle. He looks at what the purpose of a synagogue might have been in the Hasmonaean period, when the earliest part of the courtyard house complex was built. He does not question Netzer's interpretation of the architecture of the building, nor of the uses to which it could have been put.[111] He questions whether the eastern part of the Jericho complex could have been used for the convening of a small core of original members or leaders, while the pillared hall, added at a later stage, was designated for larger assemblies.[112]

---

109. Ibid.

110. Rapuano, "The Hasmonaean Period 'Synagogue' at Jericho and the 'Council Chamber' at Qumran."

111. Ibid., 54 n. 16; Netzer, "A Synagogue in Jericho from the Hasmonaean Period," 216.

112. Rapuano, "The Hasmonaean Period 'Synagogue' at Jericho," 55.

This however does not seem particularly realistic to me, as the original phase of the courtyard house points towards its having been a residence, as I have already shown.

### Schwarzer and Japp

Of the scholars who have looked at Netzer's identification, Schwarzer and Japp have looked the most closely and have offered various explanations for how the courtyard house complex might have developed throughout its three-phased existence until its destruction in 31 BCE. Because of the general lack of evidence to prove his case, they do not accept Netzer's argument that the structure was a synagogue or that any part of it was designed as a synagogue.[113]

While they do not reject Netzer's interpretation and reconstruction of the niche out of hand, they do say that its function is unknown[114] and, further, that while it is clear that the niche at the synagogue at Gamla was used to store something valuable, this is not the case for the Jericho niche.[115] While Schwarzer and Japp were unable to correctly identify the niche as what it actually is (an overflow tank—one of the components of the courtyard house complex's water supply directly linked into the main Na'aran Conduit), they were at least able to note that it may not have functioned as a genizah as had been suggested by Netzer.

### Stacey

Stacey, who worked on the excavations at Tulul Abu el-Alayiq, takes a similar approach to Netzer's identification of a synagogue at Hasmonaean Jericho, asking whether, if a building served primarily for the secular administration of an estate and any religious activities held in it only served a very small part of the community, it could really be called a synagogue.[116]

---

113. Schwarzer and Japp, "Synagoge, Banketthaus oder Wohngebäude," 280.
114. Ibid., 279.
115. Ibid.
116. Stacey, "Was There a Synagogue in Hasmonaean Jericho?"

### Inge Nielsen

Nielsen rejects arguments that compare the courtyard house complex to other buildings.[117] She says that one must take the surroundings and the cultural context into consideration. She accepts Netzer's interpretation of the remains, including a *miqveh* and a *genizah* and, having accepted his explanation, accepts the identification of a synagogue.[118]

### Lee I. Levine

Levine acknowledges that if Netzer's identification were found to be correct, then this site would be the earliest known synagogue in the land of Israel but that "when all is said and done, there is very little hard evidence on which to base such a conclusion." Levine says that there is no known synagogue parallel to the Jericho building, no evidence to suggest that the niche was ever used to store scrolls, and more differences than commonalities between Jericho and the comparator Netzer used, Gamla. Moreover, he says that the location of this building is curious (as whom could it possibly serve?), and that it is indeed similar to many Hellenistic and Roman villas.[119] Levine says that future excavations on the site may clarify the situation further.[120] These further excavations would seem to me to be rather unlikely as now the site lies within the Palestinian territories.

## CONCLUSIONS

Of the building at Tulul Abu el-Alayiq which he identified as a synagogue, Ehud Netzer said that it was "an important contribution to a clearer picture of the appearance and functioning of synagogues from the Hasmonaean period (if not earlier), at least until the destruction of the Second Temple."[121] As it is my contention that his identification is incorrect, it follows that his conclusions should not be added to the current body of material on early synagogues, as they obscure the material record.

It is clear that the contemporary historical record provides little in terms of our understanding of the Hasmonaean estate at Jericho. What

---

117. Nielsen, "Synagogue (synagogé) and Prayerhouse (proseuché)," 75.
118. Ibid., 75.
119. Levine, *The Ancient Synagogue*, 73.
120. Ibid., 74.
121. Netzer, Kalman, and Laureys, "A Synagogue from the Hasmonaean Period," 221.

we do have comes to us almost wholesale from Ehud Netzer, relying on the excavations and his interpretation thereof. Given that there are so few textual references to this estate, there is no meaningful way in which we can assign ownership of particular areas of the site to any one group or person and so even Netzer himself has only tentatively dated the site.

Curiously, Netzer does not consider his synagogue to have been part of the palace and thinks it is not necessary that the palace had a synagogue. He believes that this was a synagogue designed for and built by workers. He argues that he does not think that there can be any reasonable alternative explanation for the function of the building, other than its being used as a place of assembly.[122] However, as I have shown, there are very obvious alternative explanations and there is no evidence whatsoever in any shape or form for the existence of a workers' synagogue—either at Tulul Abu el-Alayiq or elsewhere—in this period.

Netzer's identification is also flawed in saying that this "prototype" of the synagogue fulfilled the requirement for assembly. This building is unlike any identified synagogue, and did not survive even into the reign of Herod, but was destroyed in the earthquake of 31 BCE and built over by Herod's second palace some 5 years later.

More oblique support is lent to my argument in that Netzer's interpretation of other areas of the estate is equally speculative. He argues that the Hasmonaeans' stimulus to build in Jericho was the pursuit of pleasure. He says that the main purpose of the lavish and splendid pools complex was for entertainment and leisure, and that the gardens were areas of tranquillity.[123] As has been already stated above, Netzer is erroneously extrapolating backwards from Herod (and his particularly lavish building program), to the Hasmonaeans.[124]

All things considered, it would appear that this building complex, from its first phase as a courtyard house, through its second and third enlarging phases, was the dwelling of an official of the estate or even a member of the Hasmonaean household. It is wedged between the industrial estate to the east and the more luxurious elements of the estate to the west, and its use would therefore appear to be related to its location.

---

122. Ibid., 221; Levine, "The Development of Synagogue Liturgy in Late Antiquity," 124–59.

123. Netzer, *Hasmonaean and Herodian Palaces at Jericho*, 1:335.

124. Stacey, "Was There a Synagogue in Hasmonaean Jericho?"

Finally, adding to the delicate framework of the chronological development of the synagogue requires a great deal of care and attention, and I would argue that more evidence is required before a building could or should be identified as being of religious significance. In the particular case of the courtyard house complex at Tulul Abu el-Alayiq, there is no reason to do so.

## BIBLIOGRAPHY

Amit, David et al., editors. *The Aqueducts of Israel.* Journal of Roman Archaeology, Supplementary Series 46. Portsmouth, RI: Journal of Roman Archaeology, 2002.

Ault, B. A., and L. C. Nevett, editors. *Ancient Greek Houses and Households.* Philadelphia: University of Pennsylvania Press, 2005.

Bar-Nathan, Rachel. *Hasmonaean and Herodian Palaces at Jericho: Final Reports of the 1973–1987 Excavations.* Vol. 3, *The Pottery.* Jerusalem: Israel Exploration Society, Institute of Archaeology, Hebrew University, 2002.

Bartlett, John R. *1 Maccabees.* Guides to Apocrypha and Pseudepigrapha. Sheffield, UK: Sheffield Academic, 1998.

———. *Jericho.* Cities of the Biblical World. Guildford, UK: Lutterworth, 1982.

Boardman, John et al., editors. *The Oxford History of Greece and the Hellenistic World.* Oxford: Oxford University Press, 1988.

Bromiley, Geoffrey W., et al. editors. *The International Standard Bible Encyclopedia.* Vol. 2. Exeter: Paternoster, 1982.

Cahill, Nicholas. *Household and City Organization at Olynthus.* New Haven: Yale University Press, 2002.

Conder, C. R., and H. H. Kitchener. *The Survey of Western Palestine.* Vol. 3, *Judaea.* 1883. Reprint, Tel-Aviv: Kedem, 1970.

*Excavations and Surveys in Israel 1982*, Vol. 1, English Edition of *Hadashot Arkheologiyot*, Archaeological Newsletter of the Israel Department of Antiquities and Museums, Numbers 78–81, Jerusalem, 1982.

*Excavations and Surveys in Israel 1983*, Vol. 2, English Edition of *Hadashot Arkheologiyot*, Archaeological Newsletter of the Israel Department of Antiquities and Museums, Numbers 82–83, Jerusalem, 1983.

*Excavations and Surveys in Israel 1984*, Vol. 3, English Edition of *Hadashot Arkheologiyot*, Archaeological Newsletter of the Israel Department of Antiquities and Museums, Numbers 84–85, Jerusalem, 1984.

Forbes, R. J. *Studies in Ancient Technology.* Vol. 1. 2nd ed. Leiden: Brill, 1964.

———. *Studies in Ancient Technology.* Vol. 2. 2nd ed. Leiden: Brill, 1965.

Garbrecht, Günter, and Yehuda Peleg. "The Water Supply of the Desert Fortresses in the Jordan Valley." *BA* 57 (1994) 161–62.

Gibson, Shimon. "The Pool of Bethesda in Jerusalem and Jewish Purification Practices of the Second Temple Period." *Proche-Orient Chrétien* 55 (2005) 270–93.

Goldstein, Jonathan A. *1 Maccabees.* AB 41. Garden City, NY: Doubleday, 1976.

Goodenough, Erwin. *Jewish Symbols in the Greco-Roman Period.* Bollingen Series. Princeton: Princeton University Press, 1988.

Hirschfeld, Yizhar. *The Palestinian Dwelling in the Roman-Byzantine Period.* Studium Biblicum Franciscanum, Collectio Minor 34. Jerusalem: Franciscan, 1995.

Hodge, A. Trevor. *Roman Aqueducts & Water Supply.* 2nd ed. London: Duckworth, 2002.

Hoss, Stephanie. *Baths and Bathing: The Culture of Bathing and the Baths and Thermae in Palestine from the Hasmonaeans to the Moslem Conquest.* British Archaeological Reports International Series 1346. Oxford: Archaeopress, 2005.

Josephus. *The Works of Josephus.* Translated by William Whiston. 1980. Reprint, Whitefish, MT: Kessinger, 2003.

Kee, Howard Clark, and Lynn H. Cohick, editors. *Evolution of the Synagogue: Problems and Progress.* Harrisburg, PA: Trinity, 1999.

Kenyon, Kathleen. *The Bible and Recent Archaeology*. Rev. ed. by P. R. S. Moorey. Atlanta: John Knox, 1987.

———. *Excavations at Jericho*. 5 vols. London: British School of Archaeology in Jerusalem, 1960–1983.

———. *Digging Up Jericho*. London: Benn, 1957.

Lass, Egon H. E. *The Seasons of Tulul*. Xlibris, 2005.

Lawrence, A. W. *Greek Architecture*. Revised by R. A. Tomlinson. 5th ed. Yale University Press Pelican History of Art. New Haven: Yale University Press, 1996.

Levine, Lee I., editor. *Ancient Synagogues Revealed*. Jerusalem: Israel Exploration Society, 1982.

———. "Ancient Synagogues: A Historical Introduction," in *Ancient Synagogues Revealed*, edited by Lee I. Levine, 1–10. Jerusalem: Israel Exploration Society, 1982.

———. *The Ancient Synagogue: The First Thousand Years*. 2nd ed. New Haven: Yale University Press, 2005.

———. "The Development of Synagogue Liturgy in Late Antiquity." In *Galilee through the Centuries: Confluence of Cultures*, edited by Eric M. Meyers, 123–44. Duke Judaic Studies Series. Winona Lake, IN: Eisenbrauns, 1999.

———. "The Revolutionary Effects of Archaeology on the Study of Jewish History: The Case of the Ancient Synagogue." In *The Archaeology of Israel: Constructing the Past, Interpreting the Present*, edited by Neil Asher Silberman and David B. Small, 166–89. JSOTSup 237. Sheffield, UK: Sheffield Academic Press, 1997.

Meyers, Eric M. et al. *Excavations at Ancient Meiron, Upper Galilee, Israel 1971–72, 1974–75, 1977*. Meiron Excavation Project 3. Cambridge, MA: American Schools of Oriental Research, 1981.

Netzer, Ehud. "Architecture in Palaestina prior to and during the Days of Herod the Great." In *Akten Des XIII Internationalen Kongresses für Klassische Archäologie*, by Deutsches archäologisches Institut, 37–50. Mainz: Zabern, 1990.

———. *The Architecture of Herod, the Great Builder*. TSAJ 117. Tübingen: Mohr/Siebeck, 2006.

———. *Hasmonaean and Herodian Palaces at Jericho: Final Reports of the 1973–1987 Excavations*. Vol. 1. Jerusalem: Israel Exploration Society, Institute of Archaeology, Hebrew University of Jerusalem, 2001.

———. *Hasmonaean and Herodian Palaces at Jericho: Final Reports of the 1973–1987 Excavations*. Vol. 2, *Stratigraphy and Architecture*. Jerusalem: Israel Exploration Society, Institute of Archaeology, Hebrew University of Jerusalem, 2004.

———. "The Hasmonaean and Herodian Winter Palaces at Jericho." *IEJ* 25 (1975) 89–100.

———. "Jericho." In *ABD* 3:723–40.

———. "A Synagogue in Jericho from the Hasmonaean Period." Unpublished Hebrew article. Translated by Orit Peleg-Barkat. 2006.

Netzer, Ehud, and Gunter Garbrecht. "Water Channels and a Royal Estate of the Late Hellenistic Period in Jericho's Western Plains." In *The Aqueducts of Israel*, edited by David Amit et al., 366–79. Journal of Roman Archaeology Supplementary Series 46. Portsmouth, RI: Journal of Roman Archaeology, 2002.

———, Ya'akov Kalman, and Rachel Laureys. "A Synagogue from the Hasmonean Period Recently Exposed in the Western Plain of Jericho." *IEJ* 49 (1999) 203–21.

Nevett, L. C. *House and Society in the Ancient Greek World*. New Studies in Archaeology. Cambridge: Cambridge University Press: 1999.

Nielsen, Inge. "Issues of Current Interest. Synagogue (*synagoge*) and Prayerhouse (*proseuche*): The Relationship between Jewish Religious Architecture in Palestine and the Diaspora." *Hephaistos* 13 (2005) 63–111.

Pliny, the Elder. *Natural History*. Vol. 2. Translated by H. Rackham. LCL. Cambridge: Harvard University Press, 1969.

Porath, Yosef. "Hydraulic Plaster in Aqueducts as a Chronological Indicator." In *The Aqueducts of Israel*, edited by David Amit et al., 25–36. Journal of Roman Archaeology Supplementary Series 46. Portsmouth, RI: Journal of Roman Archaeology, 2002.

Rapuano, Yehudah. "The Hasmonaean Period 'Synagogue' at Jericho and the 'Council Chamber' at Qumran." *Israel Exploration Journal* 51 (2001) 48–56.

Reich, Ronny. "The Hot Bath-House (Balneum), the Miqweh, and the Jewish Community in the Second Temple Period." *JJS* 39 (1988) 102–7.

Runesson, Anders. *The Origins of the Synagogue: A Socio-Historical Study*. ConBNT 37. Stockholm: Almqvist & Wiksell, 2001.

Schwarzer, Holger, and Sarah Japp. "Synagoge, Banketthaus oder Wohngebäude." *Antike Welt* 3 (2002) 277–88.

Sellin, Ernst, and Carl Watzinger. *Jericho die Ergebnisse der Ausgrabungen*. Osnabrück: Zeller, 1973.

Shanks, Herschel, *Judaism in Stone: The Archaeology of Ancient Synagogues*. New York: Harper & Row, 1979.

———. "Is It or Isn't It—A Synagogue? Archaeologists Disagree over Buildings at Jericho and Migdal." *BAR* 27 (2001) 51–57.

Stern, Ephraim. *Material Culture of the Land of the Bible in the Persian Period 538–332 B.C.* Warminster, UK: Aris & Phillips, 1982.

———, editor. *The New Encyclopedia of Archaeological Excavations in the Holy Land*. Vol. 2, *Emmaus–Jerusalem*. Jerusalem: The Israel Exploration Society, 1993.

———, editor. *The New Encyclopedia of Archaeological Excavations in the Holy Land*. Vol. 3, *Jokneam–Pella*. Jerusalem: The Israel Exploration Society, 1993

Strabon. *The Geography of Strabon*. Translated by Horace Leonard Jones. LCL 241. London: Heinemann, 1930.

Stacey, David. "Was There a Synagogue in Hasmonaean Jericho?" *The Bible and Interpretation*. Online: http://www.bibleinterp.com/articles/Hasmonean_Jericho.htm/.

Watzinger, Carl. "Zur Chronologie der Schichten von Jericho." *ZDMG* 70 (1926) 131–36.

# 7

# Iranian-Judaean Interaction in the Achaemenid Period

JASON M. SILVERMAN

Trinity College Dublin

## INTRODUCTION

WHILE DISCUSSING THE QUESTION of the influence of Persian ideas on Judaism in the Achaemenid period, scholars have often been sidetracked by looking for textual influences and ignoring the physical, social interactions of peoples in the empire. In any culture, but particularly in a primarily oral culture, personal interactions can be more formative than textual ones. Before examining textual evidence, then, the opportunities and contexts for social interaction need to be explored. Social interaction can happen on a variety of levels, either in the course of official business and administration or in the course of daily economic and social activities. The aim of this paper is to evaluate the evidence for various situations where Judaeans and/or Israelites[1] would have interacted with Persian and Iranian peoples[2] in the normal course of daily experience.

---

1. In this chapter *Judaeans* are understood to be the descendants of the citizens of the old Judaean kingdom and *Israelites* to be the descendants of the old Northern Israelite kingdom. *Yahwists* is used as a term to encompass both communities. The question of the relation of Yahwism to Judaism cannot be discussed here.

2. There were a variety of Iranian peoples in the Achaemenid Empire, the Persians

When all the different potential locations for interaction at formal and informal levels are considered, it is sociologically more likely than not that Judaeans would have come into contact with Iranians. The question then remains whether interacting populations would also interact intellectually with at least some of each other's ideas—be the ideas political, cultural, or religious. Due to the complexity of the issue, the *content* of the ideas cannot be discussed here, only the *contexts* for interaction.

*Interaction* is a deliberately broad term in this paper; it encompasses a variety of types of intercourse, from superficial to significant, and represents the social-situational phenomenon of the meetings of cultures as well as the "intellectual" side. The intellectual side of interaction is generally referred to as *influence* or *dialogue*, but these terms are inconsistently used. Hinnells offers a suggestive discussion of the types of influence possible between communities, and his ideas are worth keeping in mind through this paper's investigations, even if they cannot be brought to bear in detail.

Hinnells notes two basic types of influence, each with their own variations.[3] The first type is the conscious imitation or borrowing of elements from another tradition. This can be either positive (i.e., accepting ideas that are accepted in another tradition) or negative (i.e., rejecting ideas that are rejected in another tradition). The second type of influence is the conscious rejection of another tradition.

The rejection of another tradition, however, can still affect the rejector's own tradition in two ways. It can result in the rejection of aspects of the held tradition that are seen to conform too closely to the rejected one. It can also result in the adoption of the modes of discourse of the rejected tradition in order to combat or argue with it. Hinnells notes that borrowing or imitation will often occur consciously while rejection will often occur subconsciously, although either can simultaneously function consciously and subconsciously.[4] Both of these types of influence are possible—even likely—even in situations *without* external coercion (such as a state-mandated reform program).

---

being only one of them. The term *Iran* derives from the word *Arya*, and was already recognized in antiquity to include the Persians, the Medes, the Caspians, the Bactrians, the Scythians, and others speaking Iranian languages. For an overview see Fortson, *Indo-European Language and Culture*, chapter 11.

3. See Hinnells, "Zoroastrian Influence on the Judeo-Christian Tradition," 9–11.
4. Ibid., 10.

It is not the purpose of this paper to discuss examples of influence per se. Rather, it is to suggest that, whatever the likelihood of a minority group being influenced by a dominant culture, the likelihood is much increased when the two cultures in question *also* can be demonstrated to have interacted on a personal level. This personal level includes administrative scenarios as well as scenarios from the course of everyday life. Another related question, which cannot, unfortunately, be discussed here, is the role of women in interaction between two (ancient) cultures. Women, of course, played important roles in society including intermarriage, child-rearing, and economic activities. A full examination of the position and role of women in Judaean-Iranian interaction deserves attention.[5]

There were many opportunities for Judaeans and other Yahwists to come in contact with Persians and other Iranian peoples, both within the land of Palestine and in the diaspora. The exact locations where Judaeans might have been influenced by Persian ideas cannot be proved—indeed they were probably absorbed over time and in a variety of locations—but opportunities for absorption can be amply demonstrated.

As the entirety of the Yahwistic world lived under Achaemenid rule for roughly two hundred years, there are too many scenarios to discuss each in detail.[6] Five broad geographical areas (Babylonia, Media and Iranian lands, Asia Minor, Egypt, and Palestine) serve to suggest the kind of situations where Persian presence and Judaean or Israelite presence can be demonstrated. These locations can then offer more concrete suggestions for the kind and type of interaction which occurred.

Historians and biblical scholars have sometimes contented themselves with exploiting the relatively sparse archaeological record of the Persian period as evidence of Persian laissez faire and/or nonpresence.[7] But the vagaries of retrieval, well-known to archaeology, warn against this "arguing from silence." Instead of focusing on the gaps, discussion of

---

5. Brosius, *Women in Ancient Persia (559–331 BC)* discusses evidence available on women in the Achaemenid Empire, but her discussion is largely focused on royal women. Her discussion of women in the Persepolis tablets (146–82) notes the important role women played in the economy, at least at Persepolis.

6. This fact is put well in Olmstead, *History of the Persian Empire: Achaemenid Period*, 465: "In the case of the Jews, the whole oriental world, throughout which they were even now so widely scattered, recognized a common master. The importance of this factor in the religious evolution of the Jews cannot be overestimated."

7. See the excellent article on this issue (particularly in reference to Asia Minor): Root, "From the Heart: Powerful Persianisms in the Art of the Western Empire," 1–29.

some of the positive evidence available suggests the likelihood of multiple Persian-Judaean contacts throughout the Achaemenid period and even into the Hellenistic period.[8]

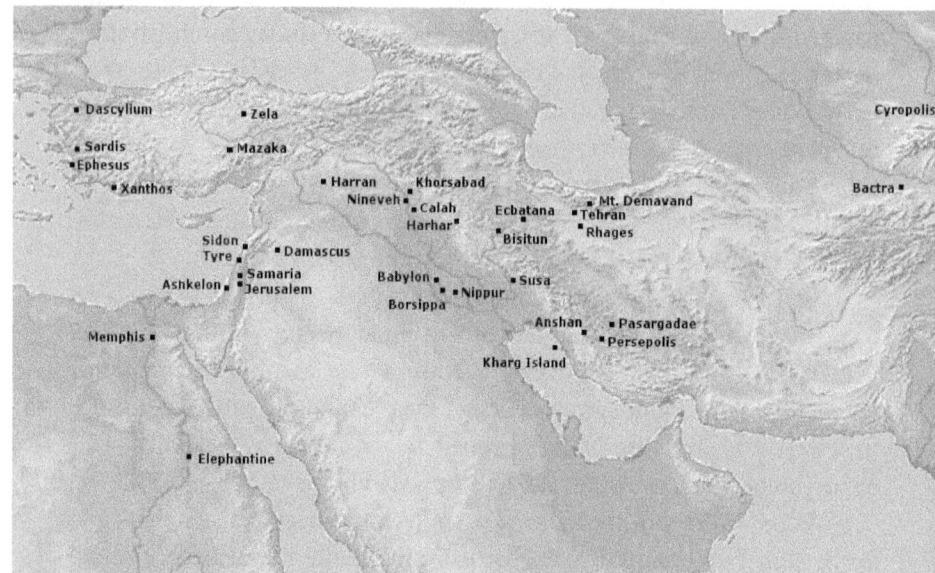

## BABYLONIA

Nebuchadnezzar deported Judaean exiles to the region of Nippur, on the Chebar River/Canal (Tel Abib) (Ezek 1:1, 3; 3:15; 10:15, 20, 22). From the conquest of Cyrus—or at the latest, Darius I—estates of Persian nobles and Iranian colonies existed around Nippur. These estates included the lands of Prince Achaemenes, his son Phradates, and the Egyptian satrap Aršam, who held a manor near Nippur.[9] Indeed, Dandamaev notes that entire districts around Nippur were held by Persian nobles.[10] Beyond official estate colonies, the Neo-Babylonian and Achaemenid periods saw increasing immigration into Babylonia from the Iranian Plateau.[11] This

---

8. For ease of reader reference, when possible primary sources are cited according to the published versions used.

9. On Achaemenes see Dandamaev, "The Domain-Lands," 123–27. For Aršam, see Zadok, *On West Semites in Babylonia*, 13. See also Bickerman, "The Babylonian Captivity," 344–45

10. Dandamaev, "The Domain-Lands," See esp. 127.

11. Zadok, "On the Connections between Iran and Babylonia in the Sixth Century B.C.," 67 directly states this but gives no evidence. Later (72), his notes show a variety of

could partially be explained by Dandamaev's suggestion that Nippur's importance increased under the Achaemenids, particularly following the supposed suppression of the city of Babylon by Xerxes.[12]

Since the suppression of Babylon is doubtful, it is better to attribute the colonization to military concerns (such as horse- and bow-fiefs) and economic activities. Akkadian tablets mention at least one settlement of Magi among these settlements;[13] this detail is suggestive, although the exact implications are difficult to elucidate as the exact nature of the Magi is unclear. Since they certainly functioned as priests, the most obvious explanation would attribute the Magian settlement to the religious needs of the Iranian settlers, although an entire settlement would not (presumably) be needed to fulfill those needs. If the Magi operated as propagandists and scholars, as some suggest (see below), then perhaps their presence is more understandable.[14]

The Judaean community at Nippur is partially illuminated by the Murašu Archive. While making ethnic or religious identifications based solely on names is problematic, they can be used as a source for some general probabilities. Zadok opines that the scribes of the Murašu Archive were more familiar with *YHW* as a deity than were other Babylonian scribes, obliquely indicating the important presence of YHWHists in the region.[15] According to Daiches, at least 70 Jews can be identified in

---

Iranian settlements in the region of Nippur (nn. 124, 125, 126, 128, 130); Coogan, *West Semitic Personal Names in the Murašu Documents*, 1.

12. See Dandamaev, *A Political History of the Achaemenid Empire*, 186. Modern research, however has debated the idea that Xerxes harshly treated Babylon after its revolt. See Kuhrt and Sherwin-White, "Xerxes' Destruction of Babylonian Temples."

13. See the mention in Oppenheim, "The Babylonian Evidence of Achaemenian Rule in Mesopotamia," 579; Zadok, "Iranians and Individuals Bearing Iranian Names in Achaemenid Babylonia," 113.

14. The Magi appear in the Persepolis Tablets performing the mysterious *lan* ritual; Hallock, *Persepolis Fortification Tablets*, Oriental Institute Publications 92 (Chicago: Chicago Univ Press, 1969), 227–29 (PF 757–59, 769, 772); Cf. the discussions in Handley-Schachler, "The *Lan* Ritual in the Persepolis Fortification Texts," 195–204; Razmjou, "The *Lan* Ceremony and Other Ritual Ceremonies in the Achaemenid Period," 103–17. For excellent reviews of the scholarship on the Magi, see de Jong, *Traditions of the Magi: Zoroastrianism in Greek and Latin Literature*, 387–403; and de Jong, "The Contribution of the Magi." Cf. Boyce, *The Early Period*, 10–11; Boyce, *Under the Achaemenians*, 84–85.

15. Zadok, *The Jews in Babylonia during the Chaldean and Achaemenian Periods*, 49–53.

the records, two of whom had Persian names;[16] Zadok counts 64 with YHWHistic names, but allows for up to 100 persons represented in the archive in total.[17] Some of these Judaeans served as servants to Persians, some as royal officials, including one who was "over the birds of the king."[18] One Judaean, with the Persian name Gu-uk-ka-', was a servant of a Persian and son of an interpreter-scribe.[19] There is also evidence that Judaeans owned horse- and bow-fiefs.[20] The Judaean community quite naturally represented all social strata, many of which required interaction with the local Persian officials. In particular, it is likely that the royal officials and the owners of military estates would have had regular administrative and military interaction.

Several names in the archive indicate at least the beginnings of Persian borrowing: Judaeans borrowed the Persian word *tiri* for the formation of several non-Iranian names.[21] Since the Persian language was largely spoken only among Persians,[22] this is evidence of some co-mingling. Indeed, the occupation of interpreter-scribe for the Persian authorities was held by at least three or four Judaeans in the Nippur region.[23] The position of interpreter-scribe is ideally positioned for exposure to Persian ideas and ideologies; these officials were essential for the functioning of the Persian administration and were present at all official communications.

Old Persian was primarily a spoken language confined to use among the Persians, Aramaic was the language of the administration throughout the empire, and local languages were still used locally. Interpreter-scribes received oral commands in Persian and wrote them in Aramaic, or received written communications and read them out in Persian or the local

---

16. Daiches, *The Jews in Babylon*, 27–70. Cf. Zadok, *Jews in Babylonia*, 33–34.

17. Zadok, *Jews in Babylonia*, 14, 79.

18. Daiches, *The Jews in Babylon*, 29. This role may have been related to the Achaemenid noble's fondness for falconry. See Oppenheim, "Babylonian Evidence," 550.

19. Zadok, *Jews in Babylonia*, 65.

20. Ibid., 66–68.

21. Daiches, *The Jews in Babylon*, 16–17; cf. a different name using *tiri* in 1 Chr 4:16 (תיריא); Coogan, *West Semitic*, 86. Daiches cites *tiri* as meaning "power," but that does not appear to be correct—rather it is a name of a deity. The word does not seem to appear in either Avestan or Old Persian (Cf. Kent, *Old Persian: Grammar, Texts, Lexicon*; and Bartholomae, *Altiranisches Wörterbuch*, neither of which list *tiri*), except as the name of an obscure deity who received a day name in the Zoroastrian Calendar.

22. Briant, *From Cyrus to Alexander*, 77.

23. Zadok, *Jews in Babylonia*, 69.

language.²⁴ Only scribes working with Persian officials would have had exposure to the Old Persian language; scribes working on the local level would have worked between their local language and Imperial Aramaic. While certain Persian words were borrowed into Imperial Aramaic, such as *data*, a specific knowledge of Old Persian implies direct contact with the Persian administration. The use of an Iranian word to create a non-Iranian name (such as *Tiriyah*), then, implies at least one Judaean scribe had direct, regular contact with Persian officials. This regular contact further implies familiarity with the system of administration as well as various Persian ideologies.

The potential significance of Judaean interpreter-scribes working for Persian officials is very high. Considering the small percentage of the population as a whole who could write, it is very likely that even a few scribes would represent a significant percentage of the total number of Judaean scribes; it is also possible that they would know their fellow scribal colleagues working elsewhere and, perhaps, even be in dialogue with them. If Ezra did in fact bring a written Torah to Palestine, it is likely that some of this Torah was codified by Judaean scribes also working for the Persian administration. Regardless of the official authorization of the contents,²⁵ this implies that the Judaean authors/redactors of parts of the Hebrew Bible were in personal interaction with the Persian administration. Without official inspection of the contents of particular documents, some general influence could be expected in such situations. If the administration in fact did take active interest in the contents, then even more influence could be expected. Of course, all of these interactions are only interactions among a literate elite, which, at least initially, may have had very little impact on the oral majority.

New tablets (so-called TAYN tablets) have recently been discovered which reveal the presence of other Judaean Communities in Babylon—at ālu ša Našar and āl-Yāhūdu, both probably near Borsippa.²⁶ Pearce considers that these new tablets provide evidence of what she refers to as an

---

24. Olmstead, *History of the Persian Empire: Achaemenid Period*, 177. See also Briant, *From Cyrus to Alexander*, 507–10; Gershevitch, "Old Iranian Literature," 5; Cf. Greenfield, "Aramaic II: Iranian Loanwords in Early Aramaic," 257; Greenfield thinks loanwords entered Hebrew via Aramaic.

25. Cf. the discussions in J. W. Watts, *Persia and Torah*.

26. Pearce, "New Evidence for Judeans in Babylonia," 403.

"administrative fiscal district" composed largely of Judaeans.[27] She bases this on the appearance of the term *šušānû*, the official in charge of a fiscal district (*hatru*).[28] If this is true, such a community would likely have had at least periodic contact with Persian officials, even if the tablets so far only evidence two Persian names.[29] Unfortunately, collections of receipts and contracts are unable to provide much information towards the exact nature or level of Persian administrative interaction with particular economic ventures, beyond certain types of labor.[30] While the Treasury Tablets show that the Great King was heavily involved in detailed decisions, at least in the imperial heartland, it is difficult to know how heavily controlled other areas of the empire were.[31]

If Pearce's understanding that the new communities represent "administrative fiscal districts" is correct, it would be reasonable to expect at least a periodic interaction with Persian officials even if they were not dictating managerial concerns. At least the upper echelons of the district would be expected to have a familiarity with the mechanisms and fiscal ideologies of the administration which they served. If significant trading occurred, opportunities for unofficial interaction would have existed at the most basic level of trading experience. It is impossible to reconstruct this situation/scenario in any detail, but it is reasonable that the many ethnicities in each location would have come into contact while buying and selling their wares, whether these were locally produced goods, imports, or local imitations of imperial models.

Ezra 8:15–20 records that Ezra was able to identify distinct communities of Levites and temple servants still intact at Casiphia, an unknown location presumably different from the communities around Nippur.[32] Even without further information, Ezra's report and the TAYN tablets indicate that the Judaean exiles were not exclusive to Nippur. They

---

27. Ibid., 405.

28. Ibid., 406.

29. Ibid., 404.

30. Cf. the comments in Briant, *From Cyrus to Alexander*, 805–06; Pearce, "New Evidence," 407–8.

31. Cameron, *Persepolis Treasury Tablets*, 12–13.

32. There is an interesting suggestion that the use of המקום (as well as the reference to Levites) in Ezra 8:17 indicates the presence of a temple or sanctuary here, but there seems to be no evidence for it. See the suggestion in Brockington, *Ezra, Nehemiah and Esther*, 100. Cf. Blenkinsopp, "Temple and Society in Achaemenid Judah," 52–53.

could have come into contact with Persians throughout the Satrapy of Babylonia, where there were many Persian-confiscated lands.[33]

Smith posits the presence of pro-Cyrus propagandists in Babylonia prior to its fall.[34] Indeed, he argues that the propagandists' Persian ideology is particularly evident in Second Isaiah. Regardless of the presence of Persian agents or the ideology of Second Isaiah, it is clear that Cyrus (II) was known before his advance in 539. Much has been written on the dubious historicity of the Nabonidus Chronicle and the Cyrus Cylinder,[35] but it is reasonably clear that Cyrus was known (and perhaps anticipated) in Babylon from his battles with Astyages, King of Media (550 BCE).[36] The prophecy in Jer 51 seems to confirm some form of this expectation among some of the Judaean exiles.[37] Perhaps the enigma of "Darius the Mede" in Dan 5:31 also reflects this situation in an oblique manner.[38] Even if there was no pre-emptive use of propaganda by the Persians, Cyrus certainly made use of typical ideological propaganda after his acquisition of Babylon. The Judaean exiles certainly would have heard some of this propaganda, and it may have played a role in Second Isaiah's discourse. Kingsley suggests that Plutarch's description of an eschatological one-world government (μίαν πολιτείαν) implies that a religio-political ideol-

33. Cf. Dandamaev, "The Domain-Lands," 123.

34. Smith, "II Isaiah and the Persians."

35. While Olmstead, *History of the Persian Empire: Achaemenid Period*, 36–55, largely accepts the documents as historical, Kuhrt, "Nabonidus and the Babylonian Priesthood," discounts their validity. Cf. the discussion in Vanderhooft, "Cyrus II, Liberator or Conqueror? Ancient Historiography concerning Cyrus in Babylon."

36. Glassner, *Mesopotamian Chronicles*, 235–37.

37. Cf. Vanderhooft, "Cyrus II, Liberator of Conqueror?" 365; Holladay, considers the Jeremiah references to be glosses, but glosses which predate the Cyrus invasion. See Holladay, *Jeremiah 2*, 397, 398, 405, 407, 427; Cf. Levine, "Prelude to Monarchy," 43.

38. To the non-Iranian world, Cyrus's defeat of Astyages was viewed more as an internal coup than the rise of a new empire; Greeks continued long afterwards to confuse the distinction between Mede and Persian. Darius I appears to be the first to declare himself specially Persian rather than Median. (See Graf, "Medism"; Dandamaev, *A Political History of the Achaemenid Empire*, 19. Cf. Gershevitch, *The Cambridge History of Iran* 2:147.) Perhaps the designation of Darius as "the Mede" simply reflects earlier premonitions in Babylon. While the final redactional reason for the designation "Mede" in the book of Daniel may be to fit the four-empire scheme, the historical confusion between Media and Persia certainly did not hinder such use, as Collins admits, and it may be part of the reason. See the comments in Collins, *Daniel*, 30–31. In any case, the possibility for knowledge of Persian ideas among the Babylonian exiles exists from at least the fall of Babylon, if not before.

ogy was propagated by Xerxes prior to his crossing of the Hellespont.[39] Was Xerxes following a precedent set by Cyrus in his previous campaigns? If propaganda was deliberately disseminated, it seems likely that the Judaeans living in Babylonia would have heard it second-hand via word-of-mouth as well as from any official propagandists.

Judaean exiles in Babylon had several opportunities for interacting with Persians and Persian ideology. They could have come in contact with them in private and official economic affairs, in official administrative interactions, and by way of official propaganda either before, during, or after Cyrus's conquest.

## MEDIA AND IRANIAN LANDS

There is also evidence of Judaeans and Israelites living in Iranian lands during the Achaemenid period. According to 2 Kgs 17:6, 18:11, Assyria exiled Israelites to unnamed cities in Media (721 BCE). Diakonoff, citing the letters of Mannu-kī-Ninua,[40] suggests these cities may have been Harhar and Kišessu, in the former Kingdom of Ellipi. Younger concurs, claiming that these two cities are the only Median cities over which Sargon had sufficient control to be able to repopulate.[41] The Book of Tobit, if it reflects its setting at all historically,[42] seems to indicate that some of the Northern exiles kept their identity and religion—implying that there were Israelite communities around the Median cities of Ecbatana and Rages, both of which feature in Tobit's narrative. (Ecbatana is about fifty miles from Harhar.) The mention of Rages (Raga) may be significant; it is likely the point of entry for Zoroastrianism to the west.[43] Indeed, the appearance in

---

39. Kingsley, "Meetings with Magi," 193; see Plutarch, *Isis and Osiris*, §370, (114–15).
40. See Diakonoff, "Media," 82.
41. Younger, "The Deportations of the Israelites," 223.
42. On Tobit as written for Iranian Jews, see Boyce and Grenet, *Zoroastrianism under Macedonian and Roman Rule*, 414; Moulton, *Early Zoroastrianism*, 246–53. On the dubiousness of historical information in Tobit, see Grabbe, "Israel's Historical Reality after the Exile," 13.
43. See Boyce, "Persian Religion in the Achemenid Age," 281. Cf. Boyce, *Under the Achaemenians*, 7–8; Moulton, *Early Zoroastrianism*, 247. Zaehner, *The Dawn and Twilight of Zoroastrianism*, 33, places Zarathuštra himself in Rhages (sic), although this is impossible from a linguistic perspective.

Tobit of Asmodeus the demon (from *Aešma*-daeva, the only demon in the *Gathas*) is one of the few generally acknowledged Iranian borrowings.[44]

It is worth remembering that Israelites were deported by the Assyrians more than once, both to the Assyrian "core" not far from Khorsabad as well as to outlying (Median) locations.[45] Not only Israelites were exiled by Assyria; a significant number of Judaeans from Lachish and other towns were deported by Sennacherib and presumably settled elsewhere in the Assyrian Empire (701 BCE).[46] When the Empire of Assyria was itself conquered (Nineveh was conquered by the Medes and Babylonians in 612 BCE),[47] the lands were divided between the Medes and the Babylonians, opening a possibility that the exiles in Assyria also could have been in contact with other exiles either in Media or Babylonia. These observations, taken together with the previous evidence of migration from Iran to the alluvial plains, suggest the possibility that these former exiles were in contact with their Babylonian counterparts. Zadok even suggests that several of the clans which are recorded in Ezra-Nehemiah are descendants of the deportees to Media.[48] The relationship between Judaeans, Israelites, and emerging Judaism is difficult to elucidate, but these hints suggest that the groups related to the biblical traditions were broadly dispersed and in contact with each other, even in the sixth century.

The book of Nehemiah (1:11) preserves the tradition of Nehemiah serving as a cup-bearer to the king in Susa. The position of cup-bearer was extremely high and important, as it represented the king at his most vulnerable.[49] Even if the accuracy of this title is doubted, Nehemiah's

---

44. Schwarz, "Religion of Achaemenian Iran," 682; Boyce and Grenet, *Zoroastrianism under Macedonian and Roman Rule*, 414; Moulton, *Early Zoroastrianism*, 250; cf. Yarshater, "Iranian Common Beliefs and Worldview," 348. However, Ginzberg, *Legends of the Jews*, VI, 299 (nn. 83–85) rejects this for an Aramaic origin.

45. Younger, "The Deportations of the Israelites," 215, 221–22.

46. Sennacherib claims to have exiled 200,150 Judaeans, but does not mention to where he exiled them. See Hallo, *The Context of Scripture*, 2:303. The taking of Lachish is also represented by Sennacherib in Nineveh in his palace reliefs. See figure 117 and figure 180 in Collon, *Ancient Near Eastern Art*, 142–44 and 215, respectively.

47. Glassner, *Mesopotamian Chronicles*, 221–23.

48. See Zadok, *Jews in Babylonia*, 41–44. Bickerman, "Babylonian Captivity," makes no mention of these. From a different perspective, Gordon, "North Israelite Influence on Postexilic Hebrew," argues that Israelite-Judaean interaction is evidenced by the occurrence of Ugaritic parallels in Late Biblical Hebrew, but his arguments seem dubious at best.

49. Briant, *From Cyrus to Alexander*, 264.

position must have been sufficiently high to merit two appointments to govern Yehud. Does such a high position of a Judaean in Susa, one of the imperial capitals, suggest the presence at least of a small community in the area?

Nehemiah's memoir (1:2) records the arrival of his brother, Hanani (חנני), and "certain men from Judah." Myers suggests this may have been an official delegation from the leaders of Jerusalem to the king, but if this were the case, one wonders why they only spoke to Nehemiah and not to the king.[50] Perhaps, instead, the kinship of Nehemiah and Hanani suggests that Hanani was already involved in administrative duties and had originally set out from Susa previously on official business. Briant suggests that Hanani may even be the same official as the Hanni (*sic*) (חנניה) mentioned in correspondence of the Elephantine community.[51] If this connection can be made, it suggests a tradition of at least one family serving in the Persian "civil service," but this is uncertain.

The book of Esther implies there was a Jewish community around Susa, which Zadok tentatively identifies with the clan known as 'Elam.[52] Dandamaev seems to think there was a large Jewish community in Susa,[53] and Kessler also intimates that Elam was a "major centre" of a Yahwistic population, but neither gives reasons for these opinions.[54] In any case, if no one else, Nehemiah himself had frequent and intimate contact with his Persian lords. Boyce argues that this contact would have not only familiarized Nehemiah with Zoroastrian purity laws, but would have required his observance of them.[55] She points out in this connection that one of the major themes in his memoirs is the observation of religious purity. Whether or not it is wise to go that far, one would expect that Nehemiah's position would have required detailed knowledge of royal ideology and policy and have acquainted him with the culture of the Persian elites.

50. Myers, *Ezra Nehemiah: Introduction, Translation, and Notes*, 94–95.

51. Referring to the "Passover Papyri," Briant, *From Cyrus to Alexander*, 586; the reconstructed Aramaic text may be found in Porten, *Archives from Elephantine*, 311, and in English reconstruction (with discussion on the identification of Hananiah), 128–33; as well as in Porten, *The Elephantine Papyri in English*, 125–26. Hanani also appears in Cowley, *Aramaic Papyri of the Fifth Century B.C.*, 135–36 (Papyrus no. 38).

52. Zadok, *Jews in Babylonia*, 43.

53. Dandamaev and Lukonin, *The Culture and Social Institutions of Ancient Iran*, 298.

54. Kessler, "Persia's Loyal Yahwists," 95. He cites no evidence, however.

55. See Boyce, *Under the Achaemenians*, 189.

Nehemiah's position as cup-bearer would certainly have involved a degree of interaction with the Persians and their world view which was much higher than that of other Judaeans or Israelites in the empire. Consequently, his role in the formation of a new polity in Palestine makes his involvement in the Persian hierarchy significant for the question of interaction and influence. Especially in his official role governing Yehud, he would have been required to ensure that official propaganda and ideology were disseminated in the region, and he likely interacted with his superiors in *Abar Nahara*.

There is also some evidence from the Persepolis tablets of Judaeans working in the Persian heartland itself, although the evidence is limited to a few names. Lipinski claims to find evidence for five, possibly six, individuals with Jewish names in the Persepolis tablets.[56] He lists the names as Abijah, Zachariah, Hezekiah, Nathaniel, Shabbatai, and possibly Samson.[57] These individuals worked as storekeepers, clerks, and messengers. As the Persians utilized a wide variety of ethnicities to work on the extensive building projects of the kings, it would not be surprising to find evidence of at least a few Judaean workers among them.[58] However, the existence or non-existence of a full community is impossible to ascertain from a few isolated names in tablets. While inconclusive, this evidence suggests a broader horizon for interaction among the Diaspora than what is described in the biblical texts.

The sources presented so far evidence at least a minimal presence of Judaeans and Israelites in three major centers of Achaemenid Iran: Ecbatana, Susa, and Persepolis. This is significant for the question of Judaean-Persian interaction, even if the size of these groups was relatively small. It should be remembered in this context that the authors of the received text of the traditions were also probably a relatively small group. But whatever the size of the groups in this period, some Judaeans did remain in Iranian lands into the Roman period and beyond (Cf. Acts 2:9)—perhaps partly descended from the communities hinted at here.

---

56. Lipinski, "Western Semites in Persepolis."

57. The names are here normalized to typical English spellings. They appear on 102, 106, 107, 107–8, and 110–11, respectively.

58. On the use of multi-ethnic workers, see the Susa foundation tablets (DSaa, DSf, DSz); a brief translation is available in Briant, *From Cyrus to Alexander*, 172–73. Cf. Kent, *Old Persian*, 142–44.

The possibility that Judaeans and/or Israelites lived in Iranian lands would be extremely important for interaction if confirmed, even though for now the evidence remains tantalizingly sparse. Because a higher percentage of the populations in these regions can be expected to be Iranian, it follows that anyone living in them would interact with more Iranians more often than in other areas of the Empire. What impact these communities had on other communities in the Diaspora is difficult to assess; do the Books of Tobit and Esther represent a memory of real communities' locations, or are they merely "amusing" romances?[59] In any case, Nehemiah—and, perhaps, also his brother—is an example of at least one Judaean whose interaction would have occurred in the Persian heartland.

## ASIA MINOR/ ANATOLIA

The large area of Asia Minor, with its many imperial and cultural traditions, is too large to deal with in detail here. The brief account here points to hints of extended Persian presence in various areas and their relative proximity to known Judaean communities. In general, the Persian presence in Asia Minor, both in terms of ethnic Iranians and cultural influences, was significant well into the Hellenistic and even the Roman period.[60] The evidence available from Greek texts and archaeology[61] indicates significant Iranian populations in various regions, although the exact details are difficult to reconstruct. Perhaps most significant from the perspective of this study is the continued presence of an Iranian "diaspora" in Asia Minor long after the fall of the Achaemenid Empire.

As late as 562 CE, the Sasanian emperor felt it necessary to negotiate with the Byzantine emperor to prevent the persecution of Zoroastrians in

---

59. Gruen, *Diaspora*, 147–48, 156, sees no necessary connection with diaspora communities.

60. The evidence for the extent of Persian influence has sometimes been obscured by Western pro-Greek bias. This bias can be noted perusing the public explanations of the Lycian displays at the British Museum—nowhere is it indicated that these monuments were produced in the Persian Empire or that any of the motifs could have any relation at all to the Persians. Cf. the comment in Root, "From the Heart,"14 (and the article in general).

61. For more detailed discussions see Raditsa, "Iranians in Asia Minor"; Kaptan, "A Glance at Northwestern Asia Minor during the Achaemenid Period"; Boyce and Grenet, *Zoroastrianism under Macedonian and Roman Rule*, 197–308.

Asia Minor.[62] These Zoroastrians must be largely descendants of Persian colonists who moved to Asia Minor. Satrapal-military colonies began in Anatolia as early as Cyrus's campaign.[63] Greek authors show that Persian landholders were part of the defense structure of the empire;[64] Xenophon even regarded colonists to be *essential* to Cyrus's organization of the empire.[65] Sekunda suggests seven types of Persian residence were possible in Anatolia, mostly of a military nature.[66] Thus, Anatolian residents—including any Judaeans—had many centuries to come into contact with Persians and their ideas. Jones even thinks that Persian influence was most likely in the Hellenistic Period, when both diasporas spoke Greek.[67]

Josephus claims that Antiochus the Great moved two thousand Judaean families from Babylon to Lydia and Phrygia (*JA* 12.147–53), and later he records that some participated in the Senate of Sardis (*JA* 14.259–61). While it is not known if this was the first arrival of the Judaeans in Asia Minor, they seem to have been a fairly populous and prosperous minority, particularly in Sardis, where a large synagogue with at least thirty donors was discovered.[68] This building is quite late, but some suggest that Obad 1:20 indicates that Judaeans were in Sardis in the Persian period.[69] Trebilco thinks that the Jewish community dates to at least 200 BCE, even though the synagogue itself is much newer.[70] If the early Christian communities in Asia Minor reflect Judaean communities, as Feldman suggests, then a large percentage of these (Ephesus, Tralles,

---

62. Apparently Sasanian emperors twice interceded on behalf of co-religionists, in 464 and 562. See Boyce and Grenet, *A History of Zoroastrianism*, III, 239 and 257.

63. See Briant, *From Cyrus to Alexander*, 66, 704.

64. Ibid., 500–501. He cites Plutarch, Thucydides, and Xenophon.

65. Xenophon, *Cyropaedia*, 8.6.10–12 (pp. 413–15). See also Sekunda, "Achaemenid Settlement," 83.

66. Sekunda, "Achaemenid Settlement," 83–84.

67. Jones, "An Examination of the Influence of Zoroastrianism," 54–60.

68. Feldman, *Jew and Gentile in the Ancient World*, 73; on the synagogue, with references, see Levine, *The Ancient Synagogue*, 85; Boyce and Grenet, *Zoroastrianism under Macedonian and Roman Rule*, 224.

69. Obadiah 1:20 mentions Jews from Sepharad (ספרד). The Persian name in Aramaic for Sardis was also ספרד. Lipinski, "Obadiah 20," 370; Cf. Seager, "The Synagogue at Sardis," 178; Watts, *The Books of Joel, Obadiah, Jonah, Nahum, Habakkuk, and Zephaniah*, 68, considers Sepharad to be Hesperides in North Africa; Raabe, *Obadiah*, 266–68, considers a location near either Harhar or Sardis to be the most likely identifications.

70. Trebilco, *Jewish Communities in Asia Minor*, 57.

Laodicea, Colossae, Miletus) had Persian colonists during and following the Achaemenid period. Ephesus in particular—and Lydia generally—were accused by Greeks of being too heavily Persianized.[71]

Lydia—and Sardis in particular—was likely home to large numbers of Iranians. Sardis was the seat of the Satrap Tissaphernes and his successors;[72] imitation of Persian styles can be seen in Sardis's pottery from shortly after Cyrus's conquest.[73] According to Strabo (13.4.13),[74] the Hyrcanian Plain to the west of Sardis was named after Iranian colonists from Hyrcania. He also mentions a "Plain of Cyrus" but does not indicate where it is. An inscription to "Zeus Baradates" (365 BCE) or "law-giving Zeus," found in Sardis, has been interpreted as referring to Ahura Mazda,[75] and has been compared to an inscription to "Zeus of the Persians" from Nakoleia.[76] Pausanias, *Description of Greece* 5.27, lists Persians and Persian cults in the Lydian cities of Hierocaesarea and Hypaipa, and the cult of Anaitis existed until at least the reign of Augustus in Sardis.[77] Tralles seems to have been the site of the *oikos* of Tissaphernes as well as a garrison.[78] Josephus mentions Judaeans in Halicarnassus (*Ant* 14.258), also a place of Persian settlement.[79] Dascylium was a satrapal seat, and may have housed a Judaean community in the early fifth century BCE.[80]

As an example of the likelihood of Persian presence and influence within Asia Minor during the Achaemenid Period, it is worth noting Lycia. Lycia and its capital, Xanthos, exhibit the presence of significant "Persianizing" and Persian presence. Shahbazi refers to Lycia as a "hardcore Achaemenid colony,"[81] although Sekunda thinks it is more likely the local

---

71. Cf: Plutarch, *Lysander*, 3.2 (pp. 238–41); Briant, *From Cyrus to Alexander*, 701.

72. Cf. Xenophon, *Anabasis*, 1.1.6–7 (p. 49).

73. Dusinberre, "Satrapal Sardis:," 100–101.

74. Strabo, *Geography*, 6, 185.

75. Boyce and Grenet, *Zoroastrianism under Macedonian and Roman Rule*, 205; Burn, "Persia and the Greeks," 341.

76. Sekunda, "Achaemenid Settlement," 131.

77. Pausanias, *Description of Greece*, 547; Boyce and Grenet, *Zoroastrianism under Macedonian and Roman Rule*, 224, 235–36.

78. Sekunda, "Achaemenid Settlement," 92, 96–97.

79. Ibid., 96.

80. Lipinski, "Obadiah 20," 368–69.

81. Shahbazi, "The Irano-Lycian Monuments," 2.

dynasts remained in power underneath the satrap until Artaxerxes III.[82] Even if this is the case, these dynasts themselves appear to have had been "Persianized." Shahbazi identifies clear signs of Persian motifs and styles on the famous "Harpy Tomb," "Xanthos Stele," and "Nereid Monument," even suggesting that the Nereids are actually representing the Ahuranis, consorts of Ahuramazda.[83]

In 545, Xanthos was apparently rebuilt with colonists, including Iranians.[84] Burials in the region evidence both embalming and exposure, being examples of Persian noble and Magian practice respectively.[85] Even if much acculturation in the region is due to intermarriage, as Sekunda suggests, this implies the presence of individual Persians for the locals to intermarry.[86] In any case, heavy Persian influence existed in this region at least throughout the Achaemenid Period.[87] Lycia certainly was not the only former kingdom to have hosted Iranian colonists in Asia Minor. How long this influence remained is uncertain, however, and it may have faded by the time a Judaean community arrived in the area.[88]

Perhaps the most strongly attested presence of Persians outside of Iran is in Cappadocia, which was under Median control from the time of Cyaxares.[89] Darius III's ability to use troops raised from Phrygia and Cappadocia at the Battle of Gaugamela implies that those troops were from Iranian colonies there;[90] Alexander's troops would have prevented

---

82. Sekunda, "Achaemenid Settlement," 87.

83. Shahbazi, "The Irano-Lycian Monuments," 156. On the Harpy Tomb see pp. 21–71; on the Xanthos Stele, pp. 72–103; on the Nereid Monument, pp. 104–32. Cf: Sekunda, "Achaemenid Settlement," 97.

84. Shahbazi, "The Irano-Lycian Monuments," 60; Cf. Briant, *From Cyrus to Alexander*, 503–5, which concurs.

85. Shahbazi, "The Irano-Lycian Monuments," 174–89.

86. Sekunda, "Achaemenid Settlement," 105; cf. 100.

87. Zahle, "Achaemenid Influences in Lycia," particularly 153. See also Briant, *From Cyrus to Alexander*, 503–5.

88. Appealing to 1 Macc 15:16–23, Trebilco lists Lycia as containing a Jewish community by 138 BCE. See Trebilco, *Jewish Communities in Asia Minor*, 6–7.

89. Diakonoff, "Media," 125–26. At the moment, there appears to be little archaeological evidence of this, however. Although Summers once suggested that there was a Median Imperial capital in Cappadocia (see Summers, "The Median Empire Reconsidered," 55–73), new research seems to have invalidated this theory. See Summers, "Aspects of Material Culture."

90. Sekunda, "Achaemenid Settlement," 110–11.

the recruitment of new, non-Iranian troops. Former Persian satraps and their descendants managed to establish independent kingdoms in Pontus and Cappadocia, quite often successfully resisting Macedonian and Roman rule. And, unlike the evidence of Persian presence in other areas, direct evidence of their worship is available: a sanctuary with an altar to "Omanus" (Vohu Manah) has been found in Zela, and an altar with a man in "Median" dress holding the *baresman* (sacred bundle of twigs) was found near Bünyan.[91] Strabo (11.8.4; 12.3.37) also describes a temple to Anaitis, Omanus, and Anadatus in Zela, which was "governed as a sacred precinct of the Persian gods" (ὡς ἱερὸν διῴκουν τῶν Περσικῶν θεῶν).[92] In 15.3.15 he claims that Magi known as "fire-kindlers" (Πύραιθοι) have several fire temples (Πυραιθεῖα) in this region.[93]

Bishop Basil of Cappadocia, in a letter dated to 377 CE, claims that "Magusaeans" (Μαγουσαίων) are found throughout the region.[94] When the Magus Kirder passed through Cappadocia, he claimed to find many Zoroastrians living there.[95] As mentioned above, Trebilco believes that 1 Macc 15:16–23 implies that there were Judaeans in Cappadocia (as well as Caria and Lycia) by 139–38 BCE,[96] perhaps ancestors of the communities in Acts 2.[97] Interestingly, Trebilco posits the possibility of a Judaean-Persian syncretistic cult in Cappadocia in the fourth century CE.[98] If this is correct, it certainly points to interaction between Judaeans and Persians in this area, even if it occurred well after the Achaemenid period.

As can be seen from the diverse evidence mentioned above, the presence of Persians outside of Iran proper was certainly not an insignificant phenomenon.[99] Any community in these regions had ample opportunity

---

91. Boyce and Grenet, *Zoroastrianism under Macedonian and Roman Rule*, 264–65; cites Bittel, "Ein persischer Feueralter aus Kappadokien."

92. Strabo, *Geography*, 5, 263, 441.

93. Strabo, *Geography*, 7, 177.

94. Basil, *The Letters*, 44–47 (Letter 258); although the note in the Loeb edition considers these to be imports from Magusa in Arabia, Boyce and Grenet, *Zoroastrianism under Macedonian and Roman Rule*, 277, considers them to be Zoroastrian Magi.

95. Boyce and Grenet, *Zoroastrianism under Macedonian and Roman Rule*, 277.

96. Trebilco, *Jewish Communities in Asia Minor*, 6–7.

97. Ibid., 25.

98. Ibid., 164.

99. For a fuller discussion of the evidence in Asia Minor, see Boyce and Grenet, *Zoroastrianism under Macedonian and Roman Rule*, 197–308.

for contact with Iranians and their culture and ideas. It seems that several areas in which Judaean presence is probable, at least in the Hellenistic period, also show evidence of some Iranian colonization. While the evidence is piecemeal for the Persian period proper, the information is interesting in the overall context of interaction and suggests a longer incubation period than the two hundred years of direct Persian rule.

The date of Yahwistic communities in Asia Minor is uncertain, so it is impossible to know whether it represents another region for interaction during the Achaemenid Empire. The significant point to note here, however, is that the descendants of Iranian colonists remained in the region into the Hellenistic-Roman periods, when Judaean communities do begin to appear. With this in mind, Hinnells, Jones, and Widengren consider the Hellenistic communities in Asia Minor to be the most important locus for Judaean-Iranian interaction.[100] While interesting, such an investigation is beyond the scope of this paper.

## EGYPT

The Yahwistic military colony at Elephantine has drawn considerable attention due to the archives found there.[101] The colonists served the Persians but claimed to pre-date the invasion of Cambyses.[102] The papyri show a remarkable level of governmental intervention in the affairs—including religious affairs—of the garrison. As Porten notes, Bagavahya's endorsement of the reconstruction of the Elephantine temple only addresses Persian officials;[103] he even claims that all the leading positions around Elephantine were held by Persians.[104] It is telling that the Yahwists of Elephantine write to the governors of Judah and Samaria; they appear to assume that these governors have some form of jurisdiction or

---

100. Hinnells, "Zoroastrian Influence on the Judeo-Christian Tradition," 14–17; Jones, "An Examination of the Influence," 54–60; Widengren, *Iranisch-semitische Kulturbegegnung in parthischer Zeit, in toto*, which focuses on the Parthians and their contacts in the Ancient Near East.

101. See in particular the history of the colony in Porten, *Archives from Elephantine*, 278–98. The colonists are called "Yahwistic" as their provenance is unclear, whether from Israel or Judah.

102. Cowley, *Aramaic Papyri*, no. 30–32 (pp. 107–24); cf. Porten, *Papyri*, 139–49.

103. Cowley, *Aramaic Papyri*, no. 32 (pp. 122–24); cf. Porten, *Papyri*, 148–49.

104. Porten, "Persian Names in Aramaic Documents from Ancient Egypt," 175.

influence regarding their affairs.[105] Thus, not only does it seem that the various groups were in contact with the Persian administration, but that they were in contact with each other. Indeed, an apparent Judaean was sent by the government to regulate Passover.[106] Thus, while the Persian administration did involve itself in local religious affairs, they appear (at least in this case) to have done so through the mechanisms of the relevant community (Yehud and/or Samaria).

The political complexities of the empire are nicely demonstrated by the correspondence over the destruction of the colonists' temple in 410 BCE. Several levels of local, Persian, and kinsmen authorities (Judaean, Samaritan) are involved in the decisions and petitions. It is worth noting as well that the island of Elephantine is across the Nile from Syene, a town which housed the *fratarak* of Upper Egypt.[107] Persian officials are frequently referred to in many capacities in the papyri, which is consonant with being near an administrative center. One of the papyri confirms that the Persians brought their religion with them by mentioning the presence of a "Mazdayasna" (מזדיזן) official,[108] whatever that term implies.[109] The satrapy, particularly around Elephantine, seems to have hosted a large mix of Iranians of various descriptions besides Persians proper as well.[110] It is clear from these papyri that this particular community had ample contact with the Persians as well as other Judaean and Israelite communities. It is even possible that Hananiah's bringing of the Passover regulations marked the beginning of increased contact between the Yahwistic communities.

Besides the Yahwistic colony at Elephantine, the Hebrew Bible indicates the presence of Judaeans in Egypt in a variety of places, from several periods and for varying reasons. Isa 11:11 expects a recall of Judaeans from Egypt, Pathros, and Nubia (מצרים פתרוס, כוש), and Jeremiah prophesies to the Judaeans in Migdol, Tahphanhes, Noph, and Pathros (מגדל,

105. Cowley, *Aramaic Papyri*, no. 30–32 (pp. 107–24); cf. Porten, *Papyri*, 139–49.
106. See discussion above on Hananiah.
107. Bresciani, "Egypt, Persian Satrapy," 364–65.
108. Cowley, *Aramaic Papyri*, no. 37 (pp. 132–35); cf. Porten, *Papyri*, 127–28.

109 . *Mazdayasna* means "worshipper of (Ahura) Mazda." This term certainly is consonant with Zoroastrianism but does not necessarily require it. The term adequately describes the religion of the Old Persian inscriptions (which prominently mention Ahura Mazda), whether one wishes to view the kings as Zoroastrian or not. For the word, see Bartholomae, *Altiranisches Wörterbuch*, 1160–61. Benveniste, "Le terme iranien *mazdayasna*," 5–9 views it as a personal name rather than an office.

110. Porten, "Persian Names in Aramaic Documents from Ancient Egypt," 176–77.

ארץ פתרוס ,נף ,תחפנחס). These passages imply at least nominal Judaean groups throughout Egypt. Jeremiah curses the Judaeans of Egypt (24:8; 44), but was himself taken to Egypt with fleeing Judaeans (43).[111] At least one of these locations definitely had a Persian presence—Memphis, the seat of the Egyptian satrapy.

Even during rebellions, the Persian presence in Egypt was not entirely eliminated. In one of the extant papyri, Aršam commands his servants to protect his holdings from the insurgents.[112] The presence of Persians therefore cannot be excluded even during the interruptions of Persian rule. It is also possible that Persians remained behind in Egypt after Alexander, just as they did in Asia Minor; the term *Mtj* (either Mede or Persian), at any rate, remained in use in Egypt into the third century BCE.[113]

The fate of the Yahwists at Elephantine is unknown, although the community probably did not survive the Persian Empire, given the local hostility towards it in the papyri. However, Judaean communities remained in Egypt in other locations up through at least the Roman Period, notably at Alexandria. Thus Egypt offered another location for Yahwists to interact with Persians on various levels in the Achaemenid Period, and possibly into the Hellenistic.

## PALESTINE

Within the land of Palestine, there were several opportunities for contact with Persians. The coast was heavily fortified and provisioned.[114] Gaza had a garrison large and loyal enough to thoroughly resist Alexander (although Arrian attributes the resistance to Arab mercenaries: *Anabasis* 2.25.4—26.7).[115] Even in the areas outside direct Satrapal control, such as Sinai and the Negev, permanent Persian garrisons are attested (Beersheba, Arad, Khirbet Ritmah).[116] Briant notes that ostraca from Beersheba and

---

111. Cf. Porten, "The Jews in Egypt," 375.
112. Driver, *Aramaic Documents of the Fifth Century B.C.*, (Doc. 7), 23–25.
113. Bresciani, "Egypt, Persian Satrapy," 372.
114. Stern, "New Evidence," 222.
115. Briant, *From Cyrus to Alexander*, 716; Arrian, *Anabasis Alexandri, Books 1–4*, 213–19.
116. Stern, "New Evidence," 223; Stern, *Material Culture of the Land of the Bible in the Persian Period 538–332 B.C.*, 45; Cf. Lipschits, "Achaemenid Imperial Policy," 26.

Arad attest to a "very thorough mingling" of populations, including Persians and Judaeans.[117] Yehud itself seems to have had at least several forts (Horvat Zimri, Khirbet Abu et-Twein, Har Adar).[118] In addition to military installations,[119] the Persian king likely held crown lands in Yehud (as in other provinces), perhaps what was previously held by the Davidic monarchy. Ackroyd thinks the "king's forest" (literally "paradise"- הפרדס אשר למלך) in Neh 2:8 refers to these lands.[120] In this respect, it may be significant that the governor of Judah, to whom the Elephantine colonists wrote, had the Persian name Bagavahya (בגוהי), perhaps a Persian or a Judaean official with a Persian name.[121] Either possibility offers a Persian connection—either a Persian official in Jerusalem, or a Judaean with a Persian affiliation.

The use of the term *bira* (בירה) in Neh 2:8, 7:2 indicates that Nehemiah turned Jerusalem into an administrative center, complete with a fortified garrison.[122] Indeed, a cognate of בירה is used of Persepolis as well.[123] Nehemiah's arrival into Jerusalem (2:9) implies that he brought (additional?) troops to Palestine with him.[124] While the Achaemenids used foreign and mercenary troops in their army, like empires before it, it is unlikely that no Iranians would have been in such a contingent, especially as Nehemiah was coming directly from Iran with cavalry (פרשים). Nehemiah's efforts to populate the city (Neh 11)—in direct contact with the citadel—ensured that at least some Judaeans would have come in contact with the garrisoned troops. Considering the size of the city, it would be remarkable for the Jerusalem residents and troops to remain aloof from each other.[125]

Excavations at Ashkelon have revealed an extraordinary number of dog burials, the vast majority from the Persian period; every site at

---

117. Briant, *From Cyrus to Alexander*, 717; cf. the notes on p. 1017.
118. Carter, *The Emergence of Yehud in the Persian Period*, 133, 166–69.
119. Ibid., 284, offers a map of suggested forts and administrative centres in Yehud.
120. Ackroyd, "The Written Evidence for Palestine," 215.
121. Cowley, *Aramaic Papyri*, no. 30 (pp. 108–19); Porten, *Papyri*, 139.
122. Lipschits, "Achaemenid Imperial Policy," 26; Hoglund, *Achaemenid Imperial Administration*, 210; Carter, *The Emergence of Yehud*, 44–45.
123. Cameron, *Persepolis Treasury Tablets*, 140–41 (tablet 36, line 2).
124. Knauf, "Bethel," 304 suggests Nehemiah brought a battalion.
125. Carter, *The Emergence of Yehud*, 147–48.

Ashkelon attesting Persian presence attests dog burials.[126] Dog burials have also been found in several other sites in Persian-period Palestine (Ashdod, Tell el-Hesi, Arad, Dor), albeit not in such spectacular numbers.[127] These finds are provocative, especially as regional attitudes towards the dog were generally negative or, at best, ambivalent; the biblical text generally supports a culturally negative view (Deut 23:19; Prov 26:11, 17; Qoh 9:4; Matt 7:6). The exceptions were Egypt and Persia, where dogs were esteemed.[128] Due to Egypt's long history in the coastal region, one would suppose the likelihood of Egyptian influence, especially as dog burials and mummification are found in Egypt. No such burials are attested in Ashkelon, however, for any of the periods of Egyptian control.[129]

It seems significant that all the parallel Palestinian dog burials listed by Wapnish and Hesse are in the Persian period. Thus, dog burial appears to be a wholly Persian-period phenomenon, at least in Palestine. While Wapnish and Hesse acknowledge a solitary dog burial in Achaemenid Iran in what may be a fire temple, they dismiss the relevance of Iranian veneration for dogs due to Sasanian-period scruples over the burial of bodies.[130] They fail to note several important points, however. First, canine-veneration is Indo-Iranian and so can be confidently dated to the Achaemenid period, and, second, the development of exposure is a relatively late phenomenon: burials are attested at Persepolis.[131] That the Achaemenids had a policy towards the treatment of dogs may be implied by Justinus, but the passage is dubious historically.[132] In any case, Iran appears to be the most likely source for such treatment of dogs. As Ashkelon

---

126. Wapnish and Hesse, "Pampered Pooches or Plain Pariahs?," 60.

127. Ibid.," 67–69. One of the other sites includes Arad, a location known to have been a site of a station of the Royal Road (on the Royal Road, see below.) See Israel Eph'al, "Changes in Palestine," 177.

128. Collins, *A History of the Animal World*, 292, 301–3; Collins also mentions the Ashkelon burials: 41920; Wapnish and Hesse, "Pampered Pooches or Plain Pariahs?," 71–73.

129. Wapnish and Hesse, "Pampered Pooches or Plain Pariahs?," 71.

130. Ibid. For the Iranian burial, ibid., 70; for Zoroastrian custom, ibid., 72.

131. On dogs in Iran, see Boyce, *The Early Period*, 163, 302–3; on the Persepolis burials, see Schmidt, *Contents of the Treasury and Other Discoveries*, 117–23; Cf. Grenet, "Burial II," 559.

132. The passage in question (*Historiae Philippicae* 19.1.10) is available online: Justinus, *Historiae Philippicae*.

possibly housed the Persian governor of the Ashdod province,[133] it seems most likely that the dog burials evidence either significant Persian residency or high acculturation during the Persian period.

In the province of Samaria, there is some evidence of Persian presence. According to Stern, the Persian period strata of the city of Samaria was nearly obliterated, so not much evidence has been found in the city itself.[134] However, the finds at Wâdī ed-Dâliyeh have produced some Persian seals similar to those in other areas of the empire.[135] The papyri also revealed an interesting name—יהובגה.[136] This is another example of the use of a Persian word to create a new, Yahwistic name (using Persian *baga*, "god"). In addition, an imported Achaemenid vase and a bronze throne leg in clear Achaemenid style have been found near Samaria.[137] The metalware was also copied by local pottery makers.[138] Three clearly Achaemenid objects have also been found at Khirbet Ibsan; Amiran even sees echoes of the winged disk motif on one,[139] ultimately positing the "significant role" of Achaemenid elements in the culture of Palestine and the empire as a whole.[140]

Although meagre, this evidence confirms that the province of Samaria was not isolated from the rest of the empire. Stern suggests that tombs near Shechem indicate the possibility of Iranian colonists.[141] Uehlinger also suggests the possible presence of Persian colonists in Samaria, based on a higher number of "powerful Persianisms" on Samarian coins.[142] The

---

133. Stern, "New Evidence," 222.

134. Stern, *Material Culture*, 29.

135. Available in Winn Leith, *Wadi Daliyeh I: The Wadi Daliyeh Seal Impressions*, particularly 191, 193, 199, 204, and 209–31 and associated plates. Cf. Cross, "The Papyri and Their Historical Implications," 17–29, as well as plates 62 and 63.

136. Gropp et al., *Wadi Daliyeh II: The Samaria Papyri from Wadi Daliyeh and Qumran Cave 4 XXVIII*, WDSP 7, 7 and 7, 10 (pp. 80–81); Cf. Knoppers, "Revisiting the Samarian Question," 276.

137. Stern, *Material Culture*, 142 (vase—although Stern denies the significance); 143–44 (bronze throne leg). Cf. the mention in Lipschits, "Achaemenid Imperial Policy," 31. Originally published in Tadmor, "Fragments from an Achaemenid Throne from Samaria."

138. Stern, *Material Culture*, 146–48, 231.

139. Amiran, "Achaemenian Bronze Objects," 135–38.

140. Amiran, "The Persian-Achaemenid Impact on Palestine."

141. Stern, "Achaemenian Tombs from Shechem."

142. Uehlinger, "'Powerful Persianisms' in Glyptic Iconography of Persian Period Palestine," particularly 178–79.

throne leg fragment and metalware items are clearly prestige items and signaled the owners' desire to identify with the imperial culture. The throne leg probably belonged to the governor, but the other items could have been owned by local elites. That the Achaemenid-style metalware was copied by local potters indicates that at least a modicum of non-elite interest in Achaemenid culture existed as well.[143]

If there were Iranians or Iranian influences in Samaria, it is likely they reached Yehud as well. Whatever the details of the ethnicities of the Shechem tomb-builders, Knoppers argues convincingly that the break between Samari(t)ans and Judaeans was not decisive until well after the Persian period, despite the attitude of Nehemiah, and that their mutual contacts may have been significant. He considers the separation between them a matter more of administration/politics than of religion or culture.[144] In fact, Ezra-Nehemiah seems to confirm close relations between the two communities, despite attempts to prevent them (particularly Neh 6:17–19; 13:1–9; see also Neh 2:19; 3:33–35; 4; 10:31 and Ezra 4:1–5; 9:1—10:44). While a level of rivalry may have existed between the local administrative units, all of the Palestinian *medinahs* were still ultimately under Persian hegemony and unlikely to have been able to prevent interaction between each other.[145] Yehud clearly was not exempt from interactions with its northern *medinah* and that *medinah*'s influences.

It is often noted that Palestine lies in a strategic location between Mesopotamia and Egypt, and that Jerusalem in particular lies on an important trade route.[146] Any group travelling between the two of necessity would pass through the land. The history of the Achaemenid Empire contains several large-scale operations which brought armies and baggage trains through Palestine. Cambyses conquered Egypt in 525, and it is likely that preparations for the invasion began in the reign of Cyrus.[147] Revolts and reconquests required repeated military incursions into Egypt

---

143. Cf. the comments to this effect in Dusinberre, "Satrapal Sardis," 97. On local pottery, see Stern, *Material Culture*, 231.

144. Knoppers, "Revisiting the Samarian Question," 278–79. Cf. Cross, "Aspects of Samaritan and Jewish History," 201–11; Cross, "The Papyri and Their Historical Implications" put forth similar arguments.

145. Carter, *The Emergence of Yehud*, 294.

146. Cf. Knauf, "Bethel," 304–5.

147. Briant, *From Cyrus to Alexander*, 49.

(486–84, 460–54; revolt in 405 which was followed by unsuccessful attacks in 373, 350, and reconquest in 342).

Prior to, during, and after these campaigns, the various *medinahs* along the route to Egypt must have often hosted Persian officials and troops. Indeed, the Great King himself sometimes participated in the campaigns (Cambyses, ca.525; Xerxes I, ca.484; Artaxerxes III, ca.345–42). Wherever the king went, including into battle, the entirety of his court—with the associated pomp, courtiers, and Magi—followed.[148] This appears to be a significant point which is often overlooked in the discussion. The residents of Palestine could hardly have remained oblivious to or aloof from the masses of people involved in these campaigns. It is also highly improbable that the Great King would not have used the opportunity of his presence for promoting royal ideology, both in person and via his officials. If the architecture of Persepolis—or, indeed, the accounts of Xerxes's campaign against Greece—are any indication, the Great Kings were well aware of the propagandistic opportunities of ritual and procession.[149] It seems, then, that each campaign against Egypt afforded opportunities for interaction with Iranians above and beyond the situational norm of locally stationed officials and military units.

However the administration of Yehud is understood, it is unlikely that it would have been left to its own devices.[150] In this regard, it is worth noting that even during the periods of Egyptian independence, ostraca show Persian control reaching into Idumaea and the Negev.[151] Yehud would certainly have been required to facilitate the logistic and provisional needs of Persian troops operating in the region. Even if one considers Persian control over Yehud's administration as very indirect, it is clear there were Iranian troops, officials, and perhaps traders travelling

---

148. Ibid., 186–89.

149. Persepolis is certainly designed to impress, if not necessarily for the "Nowruz" festival. Cf. Cool Root, *The King and Kingship in Achaemenid Art: Essays on the Creation of an Iconography of Empire*, 279 (on Nowruz). On Xerxes's pomp, cf: Herodotus VII.40–41, 54–55 (*The Persian Wars V–VII*, 354–57, 368–71).

150. Some various opinions are available in Berquist, *Judaism in Persia's Shadow*, particularly 233–37; Hoglund, *Achaemenid Imperial Administration*, 244; Grabbe, *A History of the Jews and Judaism in the Second Temple Period, Vol I*, 132–55; Lipschits, "Achaemenid Imperial Policy," 19–52.

151. Graf, "The Persian Royal Road System," 183–84; Cf. Eph'al, "Changes in Palestine," 109–17.

in the region. Judaeans had ample opportunity to come into contact with Persians within Palestine.

## THE ROYAL ROAD AND ROYAL MAIL

In this discussion of potential locations for Persian contact, one final point remains—one which properly involves all the regions so far discussed. Herodotus describes a complex network known as the Royal Road from Sardis to Susa (*Hist* 5.52-3; 5.35; 8.98).[152] He describes this massive distance as provided with fortresses, hostelries, and riding-posts (ἀγγαρήϊον) positioned at a day's journey between each set of stations. This system included rapid royal couriers (ἄγγελοι or *pirradaziš*), escorts for travels on official business,[153] and even fire-signals.[154]

Yet the royal road and mail were not limited to the route between the central capital and the Greek-inhabited lands of primary interest to Herodotus; the entire empire was connected by it. Indeed, one part of it ran through Palestine to Memphis. Use of this road required a "passport" or *miyatukkaš*, just as in Neh 2:7.[155] A papyrus from 'Aršam, Satrap of Egypt, records an order for the precise provisioning of one on official business, indicating the duty of the local provincial leaders for the upkeep of the stations within their jurisdiction.[156] The administrators, be they local dynasts or external Persian appointees, were thus required to maintain regular contact with the couriers, escorts, and officials passing through on official business. Such a complex system, able to provision various quantities of grain, wine, beer, and sheep, as well as provisions for the horses (presumably including blacksmiths), implies a substantial local involvement in the provisioning of these hostels and ἀγγαρήϊον.[157] That there was considerable interest and effort in this system is shown by the Persepolis archives.[158] It is likely that many of the officials using this system were Iranians, and that both Ezra and Nehemiah also used it while travel-

---

152. Herodotus, *The Persian Wars*, Books V–VII, 57–61, 39; Books VIII–IX, 97.
153. Gershevitch, *The Cambridge History of Iran*, 2:402–3. Cf. Ezra 8:21–23; Neh 1:9.
154. Graf, "The Persian Royal Road System," 168.
155. Briant, *From Cyrus to Alexander*, 357–70. On "passport," ibid., 364; Cf. Graf, "The Persian Royal Road System," 168–69.
156. Driver, *Aramaic Documents*, Document 6 (pp. 20–23).
157. Cf. Graf, "The Persian Royal Road System," 188.
158. Cf. the travel rations in Hallock, *Persepolis Fortification Tablets*, 365–440.

ling. Thus this network provides one more locus where populations and groups—including Judaeans, Israelites, and Iranians—could interact.

What kind of interaction can be expected from this complex system? Most obviously, and directly, it would have involved the communication of official policy and orders. But on a more human, personal level, it is to be expected that the hostelries would have frequently provided an unofficial forum for discussion and interaction between fellow-travellers and perhaps their local suppliers. It would be unusual, given the human desire for companionship and the extraordinary distances covered by the network, that messengers and officials would remain sequestered from social interaction with their hostel-keepers, tavern-keepers, and providers. While the travellers were certainly not modern tourists, it is hard to see how such a long, complicated, and heavily used system could not have facilitated interaction over its two-hundred-year history. Certainly, folktales, anecdotes, proverbs, and so on would have been frequently transmitted along this system—in addition to the official memoranda.

## CONCLUSION

All of the foregoing shows nothing conclusive; it does, however, show how possible it was for Judaeans and Israelites and Persians/Iranians to come physically into contact with each other throughout the Achaemenid Empire during the reign of the Achaemenids and even well into the Hellenistic period. This remains true regardless of the decisions taken on each possible settlement. This paper focused on instances and situations where actual, physical interactions were likely or possible. The scholar must also consider—in addition to these practical factors—the less physical dynamics of *zeitgeist* and word-of-mouth transmission of ideas. Since political, religious, and culture influences are more often a matter of prolonged contact and of unconscious absorption and/or reaction, it is highly probable that any instances of influence happened gradually and differently in various Yahwistic communities. As debate grew and continued on what it meant to be Judaean, Israelite, or Jewish, with various communities holding their own interpretations of their traditions—it behooves the scholar to ask which is more likely—that this process was in dialogue with the Persian elements in the political, cultural, and religious context, or that it was completely segregated from them?

In the context of cultural-religious interaction and influences, it is not necessary to find a single, definitive location. Indeed, considering the complexities of the Jewish Diaspora and the "Yahwism to Judaism" question, such an answer is unlikely and unconvincing. The discussion above suggests that any interactions would have necessarily been gradual, widespread, and sporadic. This context implies multiple locations for a variety of levels of interaction, from superficial to extensive. These interactions would have been official as well as accidental—both administrative and socio-economic. All this needs to be taken into account when discussing possible contexts for textual questions in Biblical Studies.

## BIBLIOGRAPHY

Ackroyd, Peter R. "The Written Evidence for Palestine." In *Achaemenid History IV: Centre and Periphery*, edited by Heleen Sancisi-Weerdenburg and Amélie Kuhrt, 207–20. Proceedings of the Groningen 1986 Achaemenid History Workshop. Leiden: Nederlands Institute voor het Nabije Oosten, 1990.

Amiran, Ruth. "Achaemenian Bronze Objects from a Tomb at Kh. Ibsan in Lower Galilee." *Levant* 4 (1972) 135–38.

———. "The Persian-Achaemenid Impact on Palestine." In *A Survey of Persian Art*, edited by Arthur Upham Pope, 14:3017–23. London: Oxford University Press, 1967.

Arrian. *Anabasis Alexandri, Books I–IV*. Translated by P. A. Brunt. Cambridge: Harvard University Press, 1976.

Bartholomae, Christian. *Altiranisches Wörterbuch*. Strassburg: Trübner, 1904.

Basil, Saint. *The Letters*. Vol. 4. Translated by Roy J. Deferrari. LCL. Cambridge: Harvard University Press, 1934.

Benveniste, Emile. "Le terme iranien *mazdayasna*." *Bulletin of the School of Oriental and African Studies* 33 (1970) 5–9.

Berquist, Jon L. *Judaism in Persia's Shadow*. Minneapolis: Fortress, 1995.

Bickerman, Elias J. "The Babylonian Captivity." In *The Cambridge History of Judaism*, edited by W. D. Davies and Louis Finkelstein, 1:342–57. 4 vols. Cambridge: Cambridge University Press, 1984.

Bittel, K. "Ein persischer Feueraltar aus Kappadokien." In *Satura: Früchte aus der antiken Welt*, edited by Otto Weinrich, 15–29. Baden: Kunst und Wissenschaft, 1952.

Blenkinsopp, Joseph. "Temple and Society in Achaemenid Judah." In *Second Temple Studies I: The Persian Period*, edited by Philip R. Davies, 22–53. JSOTSup 117. Sheffield, UK: JSOT Press, 1991.

Boyce, Mary. *A History of Zoroastrianism*. Vol. 1, *The Early Period*. Handbuch der Orientalistik VIII.1.2.2A.1. Leiden: Brill, 1975.

———. *A History of Zoroastrianism*: Vol. 2, *Under the Achaemenians*. Handbuch der Orientalistik VIII.1.2.2A.2. Leiden: Brill, 1982.

———. "Persian Religion in the Achemenid Age." In *The Cambridge History of Judaism*, edited by W. D. Davies and L. Finkelstein, 1:279–307. Cambridge: Cambridge University Press, 2000.

Boyce, Mary, and Frantz Grenet. *A History of Zoroastrianism*. Vol. 3, *Zoroastrianism under Macedonian and Roman Rule*. Vol. III. Handbuch der Orientalistik VIII.1.2.2.3. Leiden: Brill, 1991.

Bresciani, Edda. "Egypt, Persian Satrapy." In *The Cambridge History of Judaism*, edited by W. D. Davies and Louis Finkelstein, 1:358–72. 4 vols. Cambridge: Cambridge University Press, 1984.

Briant, Pierre. *From Cyrus to Alexander: A History of the Persian Empire*. Translated by Peter T. Daniels. Winona Lake: Eisenbrauns, 2002.

Brockington, L. H. *Ezra, Nehemiah and Esther*. The Century Bible. London: Nelson, 1969.

Brosius, Maria. *Women in Ancient Persia (559–331 BC)*. Oxford Classical Monographs. Oxford: Clarendon, 1998.

Burn, Andrew R. "Persia and the Greeks." In *The Cambridge History of Iran*, edited by Ilya Gershevitch, 2:292–391. 7 vols. in 8 bks. Cambridge: Cambridge University Press, 1985.

Cameron, George G. *Persepolis Treasury Tablets.* OIP 65. Chicago: University of Chicago Press, 1948.
Carter, Charles E. *The Emergence of Yehud in the Persian Period: A Social and Demographic Study.* JSOTSup 294. Sheffield: Sheffield Academic Press, 1999.
Collins, Billie Jean, editor. *A History of the Animal World in the Ancient Near East.* Handbuch der Orientalistik I.64. Leiden: Brill, 2002.
Collins, John J. *Daniel.* Hermeneia. Minneapolis: Fortress, 1993.
Collon, Dominique. *Ancient Near Eastern Art.* London: British Museum, 1995.
Coogan, Michael David. *West Semitic Personal Names in the Murašû Documents.* HSM 7. Missoula: Scholars, 1976.
Cowley, A. *Aramaic Papyri of the Fifth Century B.C.* 1923. Osnabrück: Zeller, 1967.
Cross, Frank Moore, Jr. "Aspects of Samaritan and Jewish History in Late Persian and Hellenistic Times." *HTR* 59 (1966) 201–11.
———. "The Papyri and Their Historical Implications." In *Discoveries in the Wâdī Ed-Dâliyeh,* edited by Paul W. Lapp and Nancy L. Lapp, 17–29. Annual of the American Schools of Oriental Research 41. Cambridge, MA: American Schools of Oriental Research, 1974.
Daiches, Samuel. *The Jews in Babylon in the Time of Ezra and Nehemiah according to Babylonian Inscriptions.* Jews' College Publication 2. London: Jews' College, 1910.
Dandamaev, Muhammad A. "The Domain-Lands of Achaemenes in Babylonia." *Schriften zur Geschichte und Kultur des Alten Orients* 11 (1974) 123–27.
———. *A Political History of the Achaemenid Empire.* Translated by W. J. Vogelsang. Leiden: Brill, 1989.
Dandamaev, Muhammad A., and Vladimir Lukonin. *The Culture and Social Institutions of Ancient Iran.* Translated by Philip L. Kohl. Cambridge: Cambridge University Press, 1989.
Davies, W. D., and L. Finkelstein, editors. *The Cambridge History of Judaism.* Vol. 1, *The Persian Period.* Cambridge: Cambridge University Press, 1984.
Diakonoff, I. "Media." In *The Cambridge History of Iran,* edited by Ilya Gershevitch, 2:36–148. 7 vols. in 8 bks. Cambridge: Cambridge University Press, 1985.
Driver, G. R. *Aramaic Documents of the Fifth Century B.C.* Oxford: Clarendon, 1954.
Dusinberre, Elspeth R. M. "Satrapal Sardis: Achaemenid Bowls in an Achaemenid Capital." *AJA* 103 (1999) 73–102.
Eph'al, Israel. "Changes in Palestine during the Persian Period in Light of Epigraphic Sources." *IEJ* 48 (1998) 106–19.
Feldman, Louis H. *Jew and Gentile in the Ancient World: Attitudes and Interactions from Alexander to Justinian.* Princeton: Princeton University Press, 1993.
Fortson, Benjamin W., IV. *Indo-European Language and Culture: An Introduction.* Oxford: Blackwell, 2004.
Gershevitch, Ilya, editor. *The Cambridge History of Iran.* Vol. 2, *The Median and Achaemenian Periods.* Cambridge: Cambridge University Press, 1985.
———. "Old Iranian Literature." In *Iranistik: Literatur,* 1–31. Handbuch der Orientalistik I.IV.2.1. Leiden: Brill, 1968.
Ginzberg, Louis. *Legends of the Jews.* Translated by Henrietta Szold. 7 vols. Baltimore: Johns Hopkins University Press, 1998.
Glassner, Jean-Jacques. *Mesopotamian Chronicles.* SBLWAW 19. Leiden: Brill, 2004.
Gordon, Cyrus H. "North Israelite Influence on Postexilic Hebrew." *IEJ* 5 (1955) 85–88.

Grabbe, Lester L. *A History of the Jews and Judaism in the Second Temple Period.* Vol 1, *Yehud: A History of the Persian Province of Judah.* Library of Second Temple Studies 47. London: T. & T. Clark, 2004.

———. "Israel's Historical Reality after the Exile." In *The Crisis of Israelite Religion: Transformation of Religious Tradition in Exilic and Post-Exilic Times,* edited by Bob Becking and Marjo C. A. Korpel, 9–32. OtSt 42. Leiden: Brill, 1999.

Graf, David F. "Medism: The Origin and Significance of the Term." *JHS* 104 (1984) 15–30.

———. "The Persian Royal Road System." In *Achaemenid History VIII: Continuity and Change,* edited by Heleen Sancisi-Weerdenburg et al., 167–89. Proceedings of the Last Achaemenid History Workshop, Ann Arbor, Michigan. Leiden: Nederlands Institute voor het Nabije Oosten, 1994.

Greenfield, Jonas C. "Aramaic II: Iranian Loanwords in Early Aramaic." *Encyclopaedia Iranica* 2 (1986) 256–59.

Grenet, Frantz. "Burial II: Remnants of Burial Practices in Ancient Iran." *Encyclopaedia Iranica* 4 (1990) 559–61.

Gropp, Douglas M. et al. *Wadi Daliyeh II: The Samaria Papyri from Wadi Daliyeh and Qumran Cave 4 XXVIII.* DJD 28. Oxford: Clarendon, 2001.

Gruen, Erich S. *Diaspora: Jews amidst Greeks and Romans.* Cambridge: Harvard University Press, 2002.

Hallo, William W., editor. *The Context of Scripture.* Vol. 2, *Monumental Inscriptions from the Biblical World.* Leiden: Brill, 2000.

Hallock, Richard T. *Persepolis Fortification Tablets.* OIP 92. Chicago: University of Chicago Press, 1969.

Handley-Schachler, Morrison. "The *Lan* Ritual in the Persepolis Fortification Texts." In *Studies in Persian History, Essays in Memory of David M. Lewis,* edited by Maria Brosius and Amélie Kuhrt, 195–204. Achaemenid History 11. Leiden: Nederlands Institute voor het Nabije Oosten, 1998.

Herodotus. *The Persian Wars, Books III–IV.* Translated by A. D. Godley. LCL. 1921. Cambridge: Harvard University Press, 2000.

———. *The Persian Wars, Books V–VII.* Translated by A. D. Godley. LCL. 1922. Cambridge: Harvard University Press, 2006.

———. *The Persian Wars, Books VIII–IX.* Translated by A. D. Godley. LCL. 1925. Cambridge: Harvard University Press, 2001.

Hinnells, John R. "Zoroastrian Influence on the Judeo-Christian Tradition." *Journal of the K. R. Cama Oriental Institute* 45 (1976) 1–23.

Hoglund, Kenneth G. *Achaemenid Imperial Administration in Syria-Palestine and the Missions of Ezra and Nehemiah.* SBLDS 125. Atlanta: Scholars, 1992.

Holladay, William L. *Jeremiah 2: A Commentary on the Book of the Prophet Jeremiah Chapters 26–52.* Hermeneia. Minneapolis: Fortress, 1989.

Jones, Elaine Marie. "An Examination of the Influence of Zoroastrianism on the Development of Belief in Resurrection of the Dead in Judaism." Master's thesis, University of Wales, 1989.

Jong, Albert de. "The Contribution of the Magi." In *Birth of the Persian Empire,* edited by Vesta Sarkhosh Curtis and Sarah Stewart, 85–99. The Idea of Iran 1. London: Tauris, 2005.

———. *Traditions of the Magi: Zoroastrianism in Greek and Latin Literature.* Religions in the Greco-Roman World 133. Leiden: Brill, 1997.

Justinus, Marcus. *Historiae Philippicae*. (*Epitome of the Philippic History of Pompeius Trogus*). Translated by John Shelby Watson.. London: Bohn, 1853. Online: http://www.forumromanum.org/literature/justin/english/index.html/.

Kaptan, Deniz. "A Glance at Northwestern Asia Minor during the Achaemenid Period." In *A Persian Perspective: Essays in Memory of Heleen Sancisi-Weerdenburg*, edited by Wouter Henkelman and Amélie Kuhrt, 189–202. Achaemenid History 13. Leiden: Nederlands Institute voor het Nabije Oosten, 2003.

Kent, Roland Grubb. *Old Persian: Grammar, Texts, Lexicon*. 2nd ed. New Haven: American Oriental Society, 1961.

Kessler, John. "Persia's Loyal Yahwists: Power Identity and Ethnicity in Achaemenid Yehud." In *Judah and the Judeans in the Persian Period*, edited by Oded Lipschits and Manfred Oeming, 91–122. Winona Lake: Eisenbrauns, 2006.

Kingsley, Peter. "Meetings with Magi: Iranian Themes among the Greeks, from Xanthus of Lydia to Plato's Academy." *JRAS* 5 (1995) 173–209.

Knauf, Ernst A. "Bethel: The Israelite Impact on Judean Language and Literature." In *Judah and the Judeans in the Persian Period*, edited by Oded Lipschits and Manfred Oeming, 291–350. Winona Lake: Eisenbrauns, 2006.

Knoppers, Gary N. "Revisiting the Samarian Question in the Persian Period." In *Judah and the Judeans in the Persian Period*, edited by Oded Lipschits and Manfred Oeming, 265–90. Winona Lake: Eisenbrauns, 2006.

Kuhrt, Amélie. "Nabonidus and the Babylonian Priesthood." In *Pagan Priests: Religion and Power in the Ancient World*, edited by Mary Beard and John North, 117–56. London: Duckworth, 1990.

Kuhrt, Amélie, and Susan Sherwin-White. "Xerxes' Destruction of Babylonian Temples." In *Achaemenid History II: Greek Sources*, edited by Heleen Sancisi-Weerdenburg and Amélie Kuhrt, 69–78. Proceedings of the Groningen 1984 Achaemenid History Workshop. Leiden: Nederlands Institute voor het Nabije Oosten, 1987.

Lapp, Paul W., and Nancy L. Lapp, editors. *Discoveries in the Wâdī Ed-Dâliyeh*. Annual of the American Schools of Oriental Research 41. Cambridge, MA: American Schools of Oreintal Research, 1974.

Levine, Lee I. *The Ancient Synagogue: The First Thousand Years*. New Haven: Yale University Press, 2000.

Levine, Louis D. "Prelude to Monarchy: Iran and the Neo-Assyrian Empire." In *Iranian Civilization and Culture: Essays in Honour of the 2,500th Anniversary of the Founding of the Persian Empire*, edited by Charles J. Adams, 39–46. Montreal: McGill University Institute of Islamic Studies, 1972.

Lipinski, E. "Obadiah 20." *VT* 23 (1973) 368–70.

———. "Western Semites in Persepolis." *Acta Antiqua Academiae Scientarum Hungaricae* 25 (1977) 101–12.

Lipschits, Oded. "Achaemenid Imperial Policy, Settlement Processes in Palestine, and the Status of Jerusalem in the Middle of the Fifth Century B.C.E." In *Judah and the Judeans in the Persian Period*, edited by Oded Lipschits and Manfred Oeming, 19–52. Winona Lake, IN: Eisenbrauns, 2006.

Lipschits, Oded, and Manfred Oeming, editors. *Judah and the Judeans in the Persian Period*. Winona Lake, IN: Eisenbrauns, 2006.

Moulton, James H. *Early Zoroastrianism: The Origins, the Prophet, the Magi*. 1913. Hibbert Lectures 1912. Amsterdam: Philo, 1972.

Myers, Jacob M. *Ezra Nehemiah: Introduction, Translation, and Notes.* AB 14. Garden City, NY: Doubleday, 1965.

Olmstead, A.T. *History of the Persian Empire: Achaemenid Period.* Chicago: University of Chicago Press, 1948.

Oppenheim, A. Leo. "The Babylonian Evidence of Achaemenian Rule in Mesopotamia." In *The Cambridge History of Iran*, edited by Ilya Gershevitch, 2:529–87. 7 vols. in 8 bks. Cambridge: Cambridge University Press, 1985.

Pausanias. *Description of Greece, Books 3–5.* Translated by W. H. S. Jones and H. A. Ormerod. LCL. Cambridge: Harvard University Press, 1977.

Pearce, Laurie E. "New Evidence for Judeans in Babylonia." In *Judah and the Judeans in the Persian Period*, edited by Oded Lipschits and Manfred Oeming, 399–412. Winona Lake: Eisenbrauns, 2006.

Plutarch. *Isis and Osiris.* In *Moralia*, vol. 5, 351c–438e, translated by F. C. Babbitt, 6–191. LCL Cambridge: Harvard University Press, 1935.

———. *Lysander and Sulla.* In *Plutarch's Lives*, vol. 4, translated by Bernadotte Perrin, 233–321. LCL 80. London: Heinemann, 1986.

Porten, Bezalel. *Archives from Elephantine: The Life of an Ancient Jewish Military Colony.* Berkeley: University of California Press, 1968.

———. *The Elephantine Papyri in English: Three Millennia of Cross-Cultural Continuity and Change.* DMOA 22. Leiden: Brill, 1996.

———. "The Jews in Egypt." In *Cambridge History of Judaism*, edited by W. D. Davies and Louis Finkelstein, 1:372–400. 4 vols. Cambridge: Cambridge University Press, 1984.

———. "Persian Names in Aramaic Documents from Ancient Egypt." In *Irano-Judaica V: Studies relating to Jewish Contacts with Persian Culture throughout the Ages*, edited by Shaul Shaked and Amnon Netzer, 165–86. Jerusalem: Ben Zvi Institute, 2003.

Raabe, Paul R. *Obadiah: A New Translation with Introduction and Commentary.* AB 24D. New York: Doubleday, 1996.

Raditsa, Leo. "Iranians in Asia Minor." In *The Cambridge History of Iran*, edited by Ehsan Yarshater, 3.1:100–15. 7 vols. in 8 bks. Cambridge: Cambridge University Press, 1983.

Razmjou, Shahrokh. "The *Lan* Ceremony and Other Ritual Ceremonies in the Achaemenid Period: The Persepolis Fortification Tablets." *Iran* 42 (2004) 103–17.

Root, Margaret Cool. "From the Heart: Powerful Persianisms in the Art of the Western Empire." In *Achaemenid History VI: Asia Minor and Egypt; Old Cultures in a New Empire*, edited by Heleen Sancisi-Weerdenburg and Amélie Kuhrt, 1–29. Proceedings of the Groningen 1988 Achaemenid History Workshop. Leiden: Nederlands Institute voor het Nabije Oosten, 1991.

———. *The King and Kingship in Achaemenid Art: Essays on the Creation of an Iconography of Empire.* Acta Iranica 19. Leiden: Brill, 1979.

Schmidt, Erich F. *Contents of the Treasury and Other Discoveries.* OIP 69. Chicago: University of Chicago Press, 1957.

Schwarz, M. "Religion of Achaemenian Iran." In *The Cambridge History of Iran*, edited by Ilya Gershevitch, 2:664–97. 7 vols. in 8 bks. Cambridge: Cambridge University Press, 1985.

Seager, A. "The Synagogue at Sardis." In *Ancient Synagogues Revealed*, edited by Lee I. Levine, 178–84. Jerusalem: Israel Exploration Society, 1981.

Sekunda, N. "Achaemenid Settlement in Caria, Lycia and Greater Phrygia." In *Achaemenid History VI*, edited by Heleen Sancisi-Weerdenburg and Amélie Kuhrt, 83–143.

Proceedings of the Groningen 1988 Achaemenid History Workshop. Leiden: Nederlands Institute voor het Nabije Oosten, 1991.

Shahbazi, Alireza. *The Irano-Lycian Monuments: The Principal Antiquities of Xanthos and its Region as Evidence for Iranian Aspects of Achaemenid Lycia*. 1973. Tehran: International Communicators, 1975.

Smith, Morton. "II Isaiah and the Persians." *JAOS* 83 (1963) 415–21.

Stern, Ephraim. "Achaemenian Tombs from Shechem." *Levant* 12 (1980) 90–111.

———. *Material Culture of the Land of the Bible in the Persian Period 538–332 B.C.* Translated by Essa Cindorf. Warminster: Aris & Philips, 1982.

———. "New Evidence on the Administrative Division of Palestine in the Persian Period." In *Achaemenid History IV: Centre and Periphery*, edited by Heleen Sancisi-Weerdenburg and Amélie Kuhrt, 221–26. Leiden: Nederlands Institute voor het Nabije Oosten, 1990.

Strabo. *The Geography of Strabo, V*. Translated by Horace Leonard Jones. LCL London: Heinemann, 1928.

———. *The Geography of Strabo VI*. Translated by Horace Leonard Jones. LCL. London: Heinemann, 1929.

———. *The Geography of Strabo VII*. Translated by Horace Leonard Jones. LCL. London: Heinemann, 1930.

Summers, Geoffrey D. "Aspects of Material Culture at the Iron Age Capital on the Kerkenes Dağ in Central Anatolia." *ANES* 43 (2006) 164–202.

———. "The Median Empire Reconsidered: A View from Kerkenes Dağ." *AnSt* 50 (2000) 55–73.

Tadmor, Miryam. "Fragments from an Achaemenid Throne from Samaria." *IEJ* 24 (1974) 37–43.

Trebilco, Paul R. *Jewish Communities in Asia Minor*. SNTSMS 69. Cambridge: Cambridge University Press, 1991.

Uehlinger, C. "'Powerful Persianisms' in Glyptic Iconography of Persian Period Palestine." In *The Crisis of Israelite Religion: Transformation of Religious Tradition in Exilic and Post-Exilic Times*, edited by Bob Becking and Marjo C. A. Korpel, 134–82. OtSt 42. Leiden: Brill, 1999.

Vanderhooft, David. "Cyrus II, Liberator or Conqueror? Ancient Historiography concerning Cyrus in Babylon." In *Judah and the Judeans in the Persian Period*, edited by Oded Lipschits and Manfred Oeming, 351–72. Winona Lake, IN: Eisenbrauns, 2006.

Wapnish, Paula, and Brian Hesse. "Pampered Pooches or Plain Pariahs? The Ashkelon Dog Burials." *BA* 56 (1993) 55–80.

Watts, James W., editor. *Persia and Torah: The Theory of Imperial Authorization of the Pentateuch*. SBLSymS 17. Atlanta: SBL, 2001.

Watts, John D. W. *The Books of Joel, Obadiah, Jonah, Nahum, Habakkuk, and Zephaniah*. The CBC. Cambridge: Cambridge University Press, 1975.

Widengren, Geo. *Iranisch-semitische Kulturbegegnung in parthischer Zeit*. Arbeitsgemeinschaft für Forschung des Landes Nordrhein-Westfalen 70. Cologne: Westdeutscher, 1960.

Winn Leith, Mary Joan. *Wadi Daliyeh I: The Wadi Daliyeh Seal Impressions*. DJD 24. Oxford: Clarendon, 1997.

Xenophon. *Anabasis*. Translated by Carleton L. Brownson and John Dillery. LCL 90. Cambridge, MA: Harvard University Press, 2006.

———. *Cyropaedia: Books 5–8*. Translated by Walter Miller. LCL. Cambridge: Harvard University Press, 2000.

Yarshater, Ehsan. "Iranian Common Beliefs and World-View." In *The Cambridge History of Iran*, edited by Ehsan Yarshater, 3.1:343—58. 7 vols. in 8 bks. Cambridge: Cambridge University Press, 1983.

Younger, K. Lawson, Jr. "The Deportations of the Israelites." *JBL* 117 (1998) 201–27.

Zadok, Ran. "Iranians and Individuals Bearing Iranian Names in Achaemenid Babylonia." *Israel Oriental Studies* 7 (1977) 89–138.

———. *The Jews in Babylonia during the Chaldean and Achaemenian Periods*. Studies in the History of the Jewish People and the Land of Israel, Monograh Series 3. Haifa: University of Haifa, 1979.

———. "On the Connections between Iran and Babylonia in the Sixth Century B.C." *Iran* 14 (1976) 61–78.

———. *On West Semites in Babylonia during the Chaldean and Achaemenian Periods: An Onomastic Study*. Rev. ed. Jerusalem: Wanaarta, 1978.

Zaehner, R. C. *The Dawn and Twilight of Zoroastrianism*. 1961. History of Religion. London: Phoenix, 2003.

Zahle, Jan. "Achaemenid Influences in Lycia (Coinage, Sculpture, Architecture). Evidence for Political Changes during the 5th Cent. B.C." In *Achaemenid History VI: Asia Minor and Egypt; Two Old Cultures in a New Empitre*, edited by Heleen Sancisi-Weerdenburg and Amélie Kuhrt, 145–60. Proceedings of the Groningen 1988 Achaemenid History Workshop. Leiden: Nederlands Institute voor het Nabije Oosten, 1991.

# 8

## How *Not* to Raise Children

*From Adam to David—A Contemporary Theological Perspective*

Peter Admirand

Trinity College Dublin

### INTRODUCTION

THIS STUDY IS A search for a positive fatherly role model depicted within the biblical narrative. I am not looking for *mitzvah*s or commandments but actual flesh-and-blood father-child interactions that can serve as fatherly examples to emulate. Thus, I will not look at a God/human relationship in a parent-child context, though this, too, may not be without problems.[1] Note that I whole-heartedly concede that I am reading the Bible through the lens of a twenty-first-century, supposedly enlightened father of three young children. Looking to an Abraham or David as a parental guide may thus be unfair and anachronistic, but if the Bible is the Living Word of God, surely it should have something substantial to say to me today as a father.

Moreover, the basic absence of such a fundamental relationship in the Bible could shed important light, not only on the role fathers played during the periods these biblical stories were composed, but on how the role of fatherhood has been envisioned and practiced in societies, like our

---

1. For an engaging but radical accusation of God as a parental abuser, see Blumenthal, *Facing the Abusing God*.

own, that have been shaped by the Bible. Thus the Bible's potentially nonexistent or antiquated depiction of fatherhood is of far greater relevance than its silence on some other banal or uniquely contemporary issue.[2] Moreover, if the Bible is deemed an inadequate source for guidance in fatherhood, then one needs to find appropriate theological sources for this topic of paramount importance, which is often neglected in theological and church-related circles.

I concede that we do not need to find a perfect father, for what makes the Bible special is the gallery of saints-sometimes-rogues who fill its portraits and scenes. Nevertheless, I will argue that becoming a father in the Bible predominantly seems a sexual or genealogical feat (though also a covenantal act). There is little textual evidence that one embodies a father in the modern sense of the term by getting one's hands dirty and dealing with dirty diapers, toddler temper tantrums, and the drama of teenage dilemmas. Such a gap needs to be addressed to galvanize the spiritual and religious calling for fathers to care and nurture those within and outside one's home. It is a calling to tackle the rampant reality of uninvolved (or rarely-involved), absentee, alcoholic, or abusive fathers who sully and batter their loved ones with rage, absence, or outdated claims of masculinity and specious notions of what should and should not be a "man's job."

For the sake of brevity, I will predominantly focus on scenes of fatherhood in Genesis, though I will touch upon instances of father-child interactions in other biblical books as well.

## ABSENCE AS PRESENCE: DETACHMENT PARENTING[3]

In my biblical reading, I recognize absence as much as presence within a text and scour for the subtly of the unsaid or unrecognized. Keeping this practice in mind, let us begin with those dwellers in Eden. Alas, there is no interaction between Adam and his children even after one of his sons commits fratricide. It is the Lord and not Adam who castigates Cain. The only "response" of Adam is that he helps to produce more babies, though no information is given on his raising them. Eve at least remarks that

---

2. The Bible does not address root canal, for example, or (at least explicitly) human cloning.

3. For an informative, practical overview and parent guide for "attachment parenting," see Sears and Sears, *The Baby Book*.

Seth was granted in place of Abel.[4] With its roots in our primordial father, fatherly detachment will be a predominant theme in these stories.

Interestingly, the first father to comment on his child is Lamech, Noah's dad, who boasts of his own violent exploits and seems to challenge God the way Browning's "Porphyria's Lover" does after he strangles her with "one long yellow string" and remarks that "all night long we have not stirred / And yet God has not said a word!" At the age of 182, Lamech is glad that his child will "bring us relief from our work and the toil of our hands."[5] This is the same reason the presumably overworked Mesopotamian gods produced humanity. The Hebrew God, of course, was said to create us out of love and for our own sake—to "be fruitful and multiply and fill the earth."[6] If Lamech also exudes any parental affection, the text is silent. Either way, there is soon the great deluge. All but Noah and his immediate family are deemed wicked and drown from their own selfishness and disordered desires.

The first post-deluge father-child interaction is the drunken Noah episode. Ham does not immediately cover his father's nakedness, but the other two brothers do, so they get blessed and Ham's child is cursed as a slave of his brothers.[7] The scene is about an affront of honor to Noah and so speaks of how children should respect their parents. While the curse may be somewhat harsh, at least Noah, unlike Adam, takes responsibility to correct his child. One problem is he curses his grandson and not the perpetrator of the deed. In *The City of God*, though, Augustine writes that Noah did so because "he knew, by prophetic insight, what was to happen in the far-distant future."[8] Prophetic powers aside, we need to skip a number of generations to Abram (Abraham) to assess a father-child relationship in more detail.

## THE PAWN

Abraham, the father of faith, is an interesting model as a parent, though with Kierkegaard, one can say, "I cannot understand him, I can only admire

---

4. Gen 4:25.
5. Gen 5:29.
6. Gen 1:28.
7. Gen 9:20–28.
8. Augustine, *City of God*, 649.

him."[9] While I will maintain the first assertion, I will suspend judgment on the second part for now. Abraham can certainly be kind and generous. Recall how he sent his servant to find a wife for Isaac. While part of the motive was to prevent intermarriage with a Canaanite, at least Rebekah, who brings his son so much initial peace, is the result. In another instance we are told how "Abraham gave all he had to Isaac."[10] It is a telling passage because surrounding the verse is the statement that Abraham took another wife after Sarah's death, the first time she is mentioned after the sacrifice.

Abraham's treatment of Hagar and their love child offers mixed results. "To keep the household peace" as the rabbis might say, Abraham yields to his wife's envy of Hagar and turns a blind eye to her abuse of her maidservant or slave[11] and allows the pregnant Hagar to be banished. After she returns to the household and gives birth to Ishmael, Abraham's only fatherly action is to circumcise him (though to be fair to him, Abraham was also circumcised on the same day). No father-child interaction is depicted before Ishmael and Hagar are banished permanently.

### A Digression: Lot's Fatherless Act

The biblical books often contain tales which weave multiple stories sometimes within one overriding narrative. Amidst the Ishmael and Isaac episodes is the destruction of Sodom. Here, perhaps not surprisingly, fatherly affection is wanting, though it is displayed in the one father who is saved from that cursed city. Lot, pressured by an angry mob who wants to "know" his guests (who happen to be angels), offers up his virginal daughters and tells the mob to "do to them as you please."[12] He wins points in the hospitality column, less so in the parental one.

Retribution comes, though, as the still virginal daughters, in fear that the end of the world is nigh, later seduce and lay with their now-widowed father and subsequently give birth to the children who would become the Moabites and Ammonites. Of course, Lot was not aware of their lying down nor of their getting up,[13] and the Bible never tells us how this

---

9. Kierkegaard, *Fear and Trembling*, 136.
10. Gen 25:5.
11. Gen 16:6.
12. Gen 19:8.
13. Gen 19:33.

incestuous relationship works out. In *Genesis Rabbah*, while the rabbis are not unanimous on Lot's desire in the propagating, we read, "On the basis of the following verse: 'He who separates himself seeks desire' (Prov 18:1) it is clear that Lot lusted after his daughters."[14]

Another Midrash uses the story to explain why the Israelites were eventually offered Torah—in part, because they were the only ones to accept it: "He revealed himself to the Ammonites and the Moabites and said to them: 'Will you accept the Torah?' They said to him: 'What is written on it?' He said to them: 'You shall not commit adultery' (Exod 20:13). They said to Him that they were all the offspring of adultery."[15] Regardless, if a fatherly ideal exists, it also seems to have been lost in the smouldering ruins of Sodom.

### Circumcision and Banishment

After the birth of Isaac, Abraham circumcises his child, which is his only direct action towards him before the Akedah. Soon, Sarah's jealousy stirs again and she demands of Abraham, "Cast out this slave woman with her son; for the son of this slave woman should not inherit along with my son Isaac."[16] While he again yields to her, the text notes, "The matter was very distressing to Abraham on account of his son."[17] While his acquiescence in the banishing remains blameworthy, his fears are assuaged by God's promises that Ishmael will also found a great nation. What follows is certainly a tender moment as Abraham gives Hagar some bread and water and places the child on her back before sending them away. Still, this is not evidence of a fatherly exemplum.

### The Test God and Man Failed

Because fear of God today is often a surreptitious or less heralded position, one has to be careful to dismiss too easily Abraham's fatherly status on account of his agreeing to sacrifice Isaac, for to say "no" to such a God in a world full of temperamental ones is no light matter. As many of us learned as children, the purpose of the *Akedah* was to emphasize how the God of Abraham was different because such a God values human life and

14. Neusner, *Genesis Rabbah*, 2:228.
15. Hammer, *The Classic Midrash*, 146.
16. Gen 21:10.
17. Gen 21:11.

has no need for the blood and entrails of little first-born children, or adult males (if one Midrash is right about Isaac's age). Recall how absence pervades the story: Sarah seems to disappear from the narrative, for example. One can also speculate about the trauma and baggage Isaac had to endure from the sacrifice, as Anita Diamant brilliantly sketches in her novel *The Red Tent*. But the Bible is too supple for that and so one must search for—and sometimes, invent—clues.

To be fair, Abraham clearly loves Isaac, whom the text refers to as his "beloved."[18] Augustine adds, with interpretive creativity, "Abraham, we can be sure, could never have believed that God delights in human victims; and yet the thunder of a divine command must be obeyed without argument. However, Abraham is to be praised in that he believed, without hesitation, that his son would rise again when he had been sacrificed."[19] Further minimizing Abraham's moral involvement, the Qur'an reveals Abraham has a dream about the sacrifice and tells Isaac, who is a willing participant.[20] More starkly, Maimonides, in *The Guide for the Perplexed*, writes, "How great must have been his delight in the child! How intensely must he have loved him! And yet, because he feared God, and loved to do what God commanded, he thought little of that beloved child, and set aside all his hopes concerning him, and consented to kill him after a journey of three days." After noting how such a time frame necessitated proper reflection and consideration on the act, Maimonides adds, "For Abraham did not hasten to kill Isaac out of fear that God might slay him or make him poor, but solely because it is man's duty to love and fear God, even without hope or reward or fear of punishment."[21] *Genesis Rabbah* echoes similar praise of Abraham and argues why it was just for Abraham to be tested by God.[22]

The fact that Abraham woke up early the next day to fulfill God's test and did not linger can be read in different ways. Kierkegaard writes, "He hurried as though to some celebration, and he was at the appointed place, the mountain in Moriah, early in the morning. He said nothing to Sarah,

---

18. Gen 22:13.
19. Augustine, *City of God*, 694.
20. Dawood, *The Koran*, "The Ranks," 315.
21. Maimonides, *The Guide for the Perplexed*, 306.
22. Neusner, *Genesis Rabbah*, 55:2 1.A, 268.

nothing to Eleazar. After all, who could have understood him?"[23] Given this inability to understand him, one needs to tread cautiously in judging him. If the story contains a relevant moral for contemporary times, it was sacrificed for a less important one. So, at best, Abraham becomes a pawn for the sake of a once crucial moral that needed to be conveyed by whatever means necessary. He may still deserve the title "father of faith," though he is linked with a faith-practice that remains severed from one that requires parents to sacrifice for their children but not their actual children.

After the *Akedah*, there is no more father-son interaction except off scene. The narrator notes that Isaac and Ishmael bury their father next to his wife Sarah, another scene pregnant with meaning, though tangential to my purposes.

## PLAYING FAVORITES

"Isaac preferred Esau," and so begins a family trait passed from one generation to another, often with violent results. In addition to the tendency for detachment parenting, the other predominant fatherly parenting style is blatant favoritism of one son at the cost of the development of the other children, particularly the daughters. For example, from Joseph and Amnon's standpoint, their fathers are no doubt the great patriarchs they are said to be, but the portrait fades and tarnishes from the perspective of their siblings, Dinah and Tamar, respectively.

While Abraham ultimately favors Isaac, Isaac also has a clear favorite, preferring Esau. Such child favoritism also slips into marital unity and happiness as Rebekah prefers Jacob. The subsequent story of the "deception and switch" at the expense of the blind Isaac is well known, but here is a key point to highlight: there is an understated connection between father and son in Isaac's request to Esau. Isaac tells him to get his quiver and bow—he loves Esau for being a man of the land—and tells him to prepare "savory food, such as I like."[24] Since Esau later prepares such a dish, he knows what his father enjoys to eat. Rebekah's wiles work, though. Isaac is deceived. Fraternal enmity results.

Further favoritism or a questionable parental reaction occurs when Jacob's daughter Dinah is raped, or at the least, is later held captive by

23. Kierkegaard, *Fear and Trembling*, 55.
24. Gen 27:4.

Shechem (as Meir Sternberg argues.)[25] Jacob responds politically (or indifferently) and is later eclipsed in the story by his sons, especially the full-blooded brothers of Dinah, Simeon and Levi. Jacob only re-enters the story when he rebukes Simeon and Levi for bringing trouble upon him.[26] He says nothing of the other brothers who did the looting and pillaging. Simeon and Levi, however, retort, "Should our sister be treated like a whore?"[27] Jacob as a father comes across as weak and self-centered. It is also fitting that the narrator cedes the last word to the brothers. Soon, however, Joseph is Jacob's favorite, which sets in motion another dastardly plot and causes bitterness among the children. At least, perhaps, the brothers only sell Joseph into slavery and do not kill him, as originally devised.

With Joseph seemingly dead, Benjamin becomes especially loved by Jacob, as he, too, is a son of Rachel. Rachel, however, dies delivering him.[28] It is also pertinent to note that Jacob overruled the name the dying Rachel wanted to give her son, though perhaps justly with its mournful meaning ("son of my sorrow", instead of "son of my right hand").

## LIKE FATHER, LIKE SON

While there has been little to no father-child interactions so far, the recurring themes and narrative patterns or tropes do suggest that sons followed their fathers' examples or blindly stumbled down similar paths. As a negative example, we see that, like his father, Isaac enters a foreign land and puts his wife's honor and safety at risk by pretending she is his cousin. So lessons were presumably taught. But aside from some other uninspiring or egregious examples, there is no evidence that anyone has a fatherly epiphany in the Genesis narrative.

Yet, word should be saved for Joseph, who, unlike Judah, is able to control his sexual appetite and refuse the advances of Potiphar's wife. While Joseph's initial treatment of his brothers can be interpreted as revenge or calculated and prudent testing, ultimately Genesis is about forgiveness, and so he could be our best model of a father. Unfortunately little narrative is available to extrapolate, save that he took his sons to receive

---

25. See Sternberg, *Poetics of Biblical Narrative*.
26. Gen 34:30.
27. Gen 34:31.
28. Gen 35:18.

a blessing from their grandfather.[29] Genesis also notes that Joseph lived to see his great, great grandchildren born on "Joseph's knees."[30] While the text is sparing, there is a potential father to emulate, but one would have to turn to stories outside the Bible for anything of substance regarding Joseph.[31]

## OTHER BIBLICAL BOOKS, BRIEFLY

Looking at other biblical books, one cannot nominate David in lieu of Tamar. Jepthah is clearly upset that his foolish vow entailed the sacrifice of his daughter and only child, but instead of showing proper remorse and tenderness, he unjustly blames her. He does at least give her some time to frolic with her friends on the mountain.[32]

Samson's father seems like an honorable man, though no information is given after the birth of his hot-headed and thick son.[33] The same praise can be said of Boaz, perhaps, though the text is more concerned to trace the future descendents of the child he had with Ruth the Moabite. Overzealous Job was said to offer sacrifices for his children,[34] though the text never acknowledges that the "new" children he received could never "make up" for the ones he lost. I, at least, hold that against Job, though some rabbis have claimed the children were wicked, which was why he offered sacrifices on their behalf. Sirach deserves mention for his advice to his son, as does Mattathias's speech to his sons before his martyrdom.[35] But there is little sustained narrative interaction between a father and his child.

## A POTENTIAL ANSWER: TOBIT AND TOBIAH

While the book of Tobit is not canonical for Protestants or Jews, the relationship between Tobit and his son Tobiah is the most promising model

---

29. Gen. 48:10.
30. Gen. 50:23.
31. See, for example, the surah "Joseph" in the Qur'an, which further highlights his exemplary character, though not with any specific details of Joseph as a father.
32. Judg 11:35.
33. Judg 13:1–25.
34. Job 1:5.
35. 1 Macc 2:49–64.

for my inquiry. As a model of virtue and kindness,[36] Tobit passes on his moral example to his son through both word and deed. While the narrative does not include stories of Tobit raising his son, in their first interaction in the narrative, he tells Tobiah (who is of marrying age) to find a poor, pious kinsman from the streets and bring him home to share in the Pentecost feast. Tobiah dutifully obeys, though bringing news back of a murder, which leads to Tobit retrieving the body and placing the cadaver in a room for burial after sunset. Calamitous events follow: Tobit is mocked for his actions towards the body and later becomes blind by a freak accident from bird droppings. After an argument with his wife, he soon asks God for death. Expecting the end, he tells Tobiah to retrieve money that he had left in Media.

Tobit then offers fatherly advice and instruction, similar to material in the Book of Sirach, advocating Tobiah to follow God's commandments, aid the poor, honor his parents, and marry one of his kinswomen. Tobiah, a dutiful son, replies: "I will do everything that you have commanded me, father."[37] After working together to find a suitable companion (who is actually the angel Raphael) for Tobiah's journey, Tobiah kisses his parents goodbye and leaves.

Skipping to the end of the tale, we hear of Tobit's worry about hearing no news of his son[38] followed by his joy when they are reunited. After Tobiah cures him of his blindness, Tobit refers to him as "the light of my eyes!"[39] When Tobit meets his daughter-in-law, he showers her with praise. Finally, before Tobit dies at a ripe old age, he blesses his son and grandsons and warns them to flee Nineveh. Tobiah gives his father and his mother honorable burials and later flees from Nineveh before it is destroyed.

## THE CHRISTIAN SCRIPTURES

The Christian Scriptures offer surprisingly few father role models and exhibit little father-child interactions. While Joseph, the son of Heli, is the patron saint of fathers for Catholics, it must be conceded that there is little to no narrative interaction between Jesus and Joseph. In Matthew's gospel,

36. Tob 1:3.
37. Tob 5:1.
38. Tob 10:3.
39. Tob 11:14.

Joseph moves the family to Egypt to protect them[40] and later settles them in Nazareth where it is safer,[41] but he is not heard from after. In Luke's gospel, there is the additional scene of Jesus not returning with his parents to Nazareth and instead remaining in the Temple. When he is found after three days, Mary says, "Child, why have you treated us like this? Look, your father and I have been searching for you in great anxiety."[42]

In fact, fathers in general are conspicuously absent or voiceless (think of Zechariah) in the Christian Scriptures. The two principal figures in the early parts of the Gospels, John the Baptist and Jesus of Nazareth, are not married and have no children. While we know Peter was married, neither he nor any of the Twelve are said to have children. Paul chooses chastity over marriage and children. Of those Jesus heals, Jairus poignantly gives obeisance to Jesus and repeatedly begs him to heal his daughter.[43] The only father-child interaction in the narrative, however, is between Herod and his daughter, a macabre scene that begins with Herodias's mesmerizing dance. Herod foolishly promises to give her whatever she asks, up to half his kingdom, and then reluctantly accedes to her (mother's) request for John the Baptist's head on a platter.[44]

There is more promise in the story of the prodigal son, though strictly speaking, the father is a fictional (or allegorical) character in one of Jesus' parables, and it must be noted (even if such a practice was the norm for that time), he is said to have "slaves."[45] Nevertheless, the father's unceasing love for both of his sons, embodying the virtues of forgiveness, compassion, and disinterested love, provide a brief but potentially rich model further to flesh out and build upon.

## ONE FINAL NOTE

While the relationship of Tobit and Tobiah is an exception to the general rule (and still does not address the issue of raising a child) and the father in the story of the prodigal son offers tantalizing evidence as a potential model, on the whole, I have found scant narrative material that shows

---

40. Matt 2:14.
41. Matt 2:22–23.
42. Luke 2:49.
43. Mark 5:22.
44. Mark 6:22–29.
45. Luke 15:25.

a father caring, nurturing, instructing, feeding, clothing, or positively interacting with his children in the Bible. Perhaps such scenes were too frequent offstage and had to be sacrificed to maintain the pace, purpose, and themes of these biblical stories. Perhaps, as always, the titillating and scandalous bits were more interesting. Perhaps those stories were retold and snickered about over campfires, while quiet moments of Abraham tickling Isaac or Joseph impersonating a snake before his sons were simply neglected and forgotten. While examples of salvation may occur in dramatic scenes like the parting of the Red Sea or the various battles to conquer the Holy Land, sometimes the most authentic and challenging expression of religious belief resides in the daily and the banal, and it is within those moments, especially between a parent and child, where the Sprit of God may be clearly discerned.

The absence of positive examples of fatherly parenting in the biblical narratives is a noteworthy and unfortunate silence that very likely has had effects in how fathers raised—or more likely, failed to nurture and raise properly—their children. Such neglect has very likely had pastoral, liturgical, catechetical, and sacramental consequences, a possibility worthy of further in-depth analysis and investigation. At the least, such an absence has not helped to solve these societal problems.

Finally, recognizing such an absence and need may also help to identify other resources that are more useful and spiritually enriching, both within and outside the Bible. As a start, one may begin with the *Shema*, which so beautifully describes the holistic love of God, with the instructions to "recite them to your children."[46] Perhaps, typically, though, even this phrase may not be so clear. There is a Midrash that refers to children as disciples: "Were they really children of the prophets? Were they not disciples of the prophets? This teaches us that disciples are always called 'children.'"[47] The search thus continues.

---

46. Deut 6:7. See also Deut 6:20–25.
47. See Hammer, *The Classic Midrash*, 317–18.

## BIBLIOGRAPHY

Alter, Robert. *The Art of Biblical Narrative*. London: Allen & Unwin, 1981.
Augustine. *City of God*. Translated by Henry Bettenson. Edited by David Knowles. 1972. Middlesex, UK: Penguin, 1980.
Benedict XVI, Pope. *Jesus of Nazareth: From the Baptism in the Jordan to the Transfiguration*. Translated by Adrian J. Walker. New York: Doubleday, 2007.
Blumenthal, David R. *Facing the Abusing God: A Theology of Protest*. Louisville: Westminster John Knox, 1993.
Dawood, N. J., translator. *The Koran*. Penguin Classics. London: Ivy Books, 1993.
Diamant, Anita. *The Red Tent*. New York: Picador, 2007.
Hammer, Reuven, translator and editor. *The Classic Midrash: Tannaitic Commentaries on the Bible*. Classics of Western Spirituality. New York: Paulist, 1995.
Kierkegaard, Søren. *Fear and Trembling*. Translated by Alastair Hannay. Harmondsworth, UK: Penguin, 1985.
Maimonides, Moses. *The Guide for the Perplexed*. Translated by M. Friedländer. New York: Dover, 1956.
Myers, Ched. *Say to This Mountain: Mark's Story of Discipleship*. Maryknoll, NY: Orbis, 1997.
Neusner, Jacob, translator and editor. *Genesis Rabbah: The Judaic Commentary to the Book of Genesis: A New American Translation*. 3 vols. BJS 104–106. Atlanta: Scholars, 1985.
Sears, William, and Martha Sears. *The Baby Book: Everything You Need to Know about Your Baby from Birth to Age Two*. Rev. ed. Boston: Little, Brown, 2003.
Sternberg, Meir. *The Poetics of Biblical Narrative: Ideological Literature and the Drama of Reading*. Indiana Studies in Biblical Literature. Bloomington: Indiana University Press, 1987.

# 9

## Ethics as Cross-Cultural Reaction

*Deuteronomic Ethics as a Reaction to Manassean Multiculturalism*

CARLY L. CROUCH

University of Oxford

### INTRODUCTION

THIS CHAPTER ARGUES THAT the core of the book of Deuteronomy was developed as an ideologically-charged, nationalistic response to the rapid increase in cross-cultural interaction which occurred during the reign of the Judahite king Manasseh and to a corresponding surge in (multi-)cultural imitation and assimilation. This nationalistic legal theology was developed as reaction to a perceived threat to Judahite culture from encroaching "foreign" practices, and as a result the core of Deuteronomy exhibits an intense concern to establish clear and distinctive boundaries between Judahite culture—archaized as "Israelite"—and the cultures of Judah's near eastern neighbors.

A version of this thesis was put forth by Norbert Lohfink in his 1977 article "Culture Shock and Theology," in which he wrote, "Would not the crisis which Deuteronomy encounters be really that culture shock in which Judah of necessity must have fallen when it came under an Assyrian sovereignty?"[1] While suggestive, Lohfink's conclusions did not go nearly far enough in extrapolating the effect which the historical situ-

---

1. Lohfink, "Culture Shock and Theology," 18.

ation has had on Deuteronomy, nor in calculating the extent to which the book also reacts against non-Assyrian cultural elements. Lohfink went no further than to characterize Deuteronomy as a systematization of old traditions, for the purpose of presenting a monolithic alternative to Assyrian religion and culture. Furthermore, he limited the interaction between Deuteronomy's commandments and neighboring cultures to the work's presentation in a treaty form; he contended that as "to conclude a treaty was the greatest fashion," this form allowed "an integration of the competition which in this way is rendered harmless."[2]

As will become clear in this study, the extent of interaction between Deuteronomy and "foreign" cultural elements was much greater than Lohfink allowed. Specifically, this paper argues that a significant strand of deuteronomic ethics is based on a fundamentally ideological alignment of the activities of "the nations" with evil, and bases the moral superiority of the "Israelites"/Judahites on their rejection of these "foreign" practices. The focus of Deuteronomy's boundary delineation was on religious practice, and the close ancient connection between cult and morality meant that Deuteronomy's ethical considerations were considerably influenced by the work's ideological slant.

## HISTORIOGRAPHICAL CONCERNS

Discerning the historical facts of the seventh century Judahite monarchy and of the origins of Deuteronomy is among the most problematic issues of biblical studies. Hypotheses regarding the date of Deuteronomy's composition tend to revolve around the Josianic reforms, following Wilhelm M. L. de Wette's association of some form of Deuteronomy with the law book found in the temple. According to de Wette's classical hypothesis, the book of the law found in the temple was some earlier form of the present book of Deuteronomy, which by its discovery provoked fervor for religious reform.[3] Given the lack of clarity regarding the Josian reforms and the role of the law book in them, however, some scholars have questioned the originality of the association between the two. Thus Andrew D. H. Mayes argues that Martin Noth's Deuteronomistic Historian (DtrH), responsible for the historical narrative of the former prophets, is similarly responsible for the Kings account of Josiah's reform, and argues that

2. Lohfink, "Culture Shock and Theology," 20.
3. See Nicholson, *Deuteronomy and Tradition*, 3.

the removal of secondary deuteronomic layers of editing in the account leaves no reference to the book of the law.[4]

While the debate continues, most scholars believe that Deuteronomy is pre-exilic. Though a few, such as Johannes Pedersen, argue for an exilic or post-exilic origin for the book (generally on the grounds that its commands tend towards the ideal or utopian and thus could not have originated during the actual existence of the nation), DtrH concludes with the release of Jehoiachin from prison in Babylon in 562 BCE. This suggests that a more or less final version of DtrH was completed around this time, and the lack of mention of a return from exile makes almost certain that DtrH had been concluded before the exiles began to return in 538. DtrH is called deuteronomistic because of its close connection to the laws and style of Deuteronomy, so if the end-date for DtrH is the middle of the sixth century BCE, this provides a second *terminus ad quem* for Deuteronomy, if Josiah's reforms are considered too unreliable. And though an earlier date is impossible to pin down, the reliance of DtrH on Deuteronomy makes likely that the origins of Deuteronomy pre-date it. With the exile beginning in 597, it is therefore highly probable that Deuteronomy had come into written existence prior to the exile.

This concludes a general date for Deuteronomy in the seventh century with reasonable confidence, and this paper will further secure this date by providing a suitable context for Deuteronomy's ideology in this century.

The driving character behind the plot of Deuteronomy's seventh-century development is Manasseh, king of Judah for over half of that century. According to the Kings writer, Manasseh was the most evil king who ever reigned over Judah. Key to this condemnation is Manasseh's allegedly syncretistic religious practice, which I argue provided the impetus for Deuteronomy's reactionary imprecations.

In the most recent major study of Manasseh, however, Francesca Stavrakopoulou argues that the historicity of the Kings narrative with respect to Manasseh's reign is effectively nil and that the ideological concerns of the writer overshadow any interest in an accurate portrayal of the king and his activities. Similarly, Stuart Lasine complains that the Kings portrait of Manasseh "is not the portrait of an individual at all," but rather

---

4. Mayes, *Deuteronomy*, 90–98, but, compare the objections of Nicholson.

"the inverted image of a glorified Josiah."[5] The Kings description of Josiah does indeed deliberately recall the description of Manasseh, making it difficult to tell the extent to which the detailed similarities are literary creations to serve a point and the extent to which they are based in historical fact.[6]

If there is no truth in it at all, then the text is useless for discerning the historical circumstances leading up to the time of Deuteronomy's composition. The evidence overall, however, suggests that the accusations of syncretism in Kings are plausible in the broader historical context, and the broad accuracy of the accusations may provide the best explanation of certain elements of Deuteronomy, namely its cultural and cultic reactionism.

## THE COMMERCIAL CONTEXT

Most notably, Stavrakopoulou argues that Manasseh followed a policy of economic expansion to take advantage of the land left to Judah after Sennacherib's campaign of 701 BCE. "King Manasseh of history," she writes, "may well have masterminded the transformation of his floundering city-state into a strengthened and prospering kingdom."[7]

The *pax assyriaca* which characterized the first half of the seventh century produced a political stability across the Near East which meant that international commerce could proceed relatively securely.[8] Prior to this period, archaeological evidence suggests that Judah's borders were closed to outsiders, leading to a high level of ideological and religious insularity. In the seventh century, Judah's borders eased dramatically.[9] There is considerable evidence to suggest that the country was engaged in a number of international commercial and trading activities with both nearby neighbors, such as the Philistines, and more far-flung ones like the Assyrians. Judah was well integrated into the international trading system, and the country was undoubtedly exposed through trade to an extensive range of foreign cultures. One Judahite reaction to this increase

---

5. Lasine, "Manasseh as Villain and Scapegoat," 163, 177.
6. Stavrakopoulou, *King Manasseh and Child Sacrifice*, 38.
7. Ibid., 72.
8. Faust and Weiss, "Judah, Philistia, and the Mediterranean World," 72.
9. Na'aman, *Ancient Israel and Its Neighbors*, 213, 231.

in internationalism was a heightened nationalism and an increased concern to preserve a distinctive Judahite identity.

Inland Philistine population centers flourished as never before during the *pax assyriaca*, and the variety of cultural remains found at Philistine sites indicate the extent to which an extensive international trade was also part of their success.[10] In particular, finds provide clear evidence of commercial contacts with Judah. Discoveries at Ekron include inland Judahite ceramic forms and the Judahite shekel-weight, both of which indicate the presence of Judahite traders in the city, and the latter of which suggests trade extensive enough for the shekel-weight to achieve the status of legitimate trade currency.[11] Avi Faust and Ehud Weiss also argue that Judah was a major source of wheat in the Ancient Near East, noting that the method of transport used in that particular commerce was almost certainly bags, which have of course disappeared from the archaeological record.[12]

Whilst in Ekron Judahite merchants would have been in contact with visitors from many other nations; archaeologists have also found material support for influences on Ekronite culture from numerous other sources, including Egypt and Assyria.[13] Cross-cultural interaction among the scribal classes specifically is assured by palaeographers' conclusions that the seventh-century Philistines wrote in a script adopted from Judah.[14]

Less definitive but also suggestive of Philistine influence over Judah during the seventh century is that, while Judah experienced a major decline in population between the eighth and seventh centuries due to the deportations in 701 BCE and was still small into the time of Josiah, Ekron experienced a significant increase in size and power during this period.[15] The weakening of Judah concurrent with Ekron gaining in strength may well have resulted in a larger "sphere of influence" for Ekron and a greater

---

10. Erlich, *The Philistines in Transition*, 1.

11. Gitin, "Tel Miqne-Ekron in the 7th Century BCE," 70. It is of course also possible that some of these Judahite goods were transported to Ekron by Philistine traders returning from Judah, probably Jerusalem.

12. Faust and Weiss, "Judah, Philistia, and the Mediterranean World," 76ff.

13. Schäfer-Lichtenberger, "The Goddess of Ekron," 86; Dothan et al., "A Royal Dedicatory Inscription from Ekron," 7–8; Gitin, "Tel Miqne-Ekron in the 7th Century BCE," 70.

14. Dothan, et al., "A Royal Dedicatory Inscription from Ekron," 13.

15. Na'aman, *Ancient Israel and Its Neighbors*, 210.

level of exposure to Philistine culture on the part of a weakened Judah. The prophet Zephaniah, whose career is dated to the reign of Josiah, even describes the imitation of Philistine dress and mannerisms in Jerusalem (1:8–9).

Interaction with other western neighbors is indicated by the large selection of fish bones found in Jerusalem, which suggest a fairly intensive trade with the Mediterranean and southern coastal plain.[16] Judah was also in commercial contact with Edom during this period, and luxury goods from regions as far flung as northern Syria, Mesopotamia, the Red Sea, the Aegean, Assyria, and Egypt all point toward trade and cultural interaction between Judah and most of the nations and peoples of the ancient world.[17] Judah was certainly well-integrated into the seventh century's larger economic system.[18]

Assyrian hegemony during the second half of the eighth and first half of the seventh centuries also led to an increase in intercultural interaction to the east, via trade and diplomacy.[19] In Nineveh, the sale of wheat is described in terms of the "Judahite se'ah," again suggesting trade sufficiently frequent as to make feasible the use of the measure in a commercial document.[20] There was also, as is well known, extensive political involvement by the Assyrians in the politics of its provinces and vassal states in the west.

The rapid decrease of Judah's political and economic isolation could only have been a significant shock to its cultural identity, which was suddenly faced with beliefs and practices threatening to ingratiate themselves into Judahite practice. This essay suggests that the reaction of the elites to the Manassean increase in international commerce was not a unified insularity (as Stavrakopoulou contends), but rather that the Jerusalem elites were divided amongst themselves with regard to the results of these economic developments.[21] Many of those for whom the increase in internationalism proved personally profitable were undoubtedly tempted to assimilate the cultural and religious practices of their new friends and

16. Faust and Weiss, "Judah, Philistia, and the Mediterranean World," 75.
17. Berlin, *Zephaniah*, 121; Faust and Weiss, "Judah, Philistia, and the Mediterranean World," 71.
18. Faust and Weiss, "Judah, Philistia, and the Mediterranean World," 75.
19. Cogan, *Imperialism and Religion*, 92–93.
20. Faust and Weiss, "Judah, Philistia, and the Mediterranean World," 82.
21. Stavrakopoulou, *King Manasseh and Child Sacrifice*, 109–10.

associates. Still others may have been attracted to these influences for political reasons, or because they were exotic and exciting. This cultural malleability produced a vehement counter-reaction among those who feared the erosion of a distinctive Judahite cultural and religious identity, and the eventual literary result of this fear was the core of Deuteronomy.

## THE INTERNATIONAL POLITICAL SCENE

The international political situation of the seventh century also contributed to the rapid increase in international influence on Judahite culture and religion. Politically, Sennacherib's campaign in 701 increased Judah's subjugation, Assyrian involvement in Judahite affairs, and "foreign" influences on Judah's cult and culture.[22] Upon Manasseh's accession the disaster of 701 would have been fresh in many people's minds; hopes of independence waned in proportion to Assyria's rising fortunes. John McKay argues that this may have led to a decrease in religious fervor and an atmosphere ripe for polytheism.[23] The later chastisements of Zephaniah and Jeremiah certainly indicate that by the end of the century multiculturalism and religious syncretism were in full force in Jerusalem. Earlier nationalistic sentiments, grown out of Judah's centuries of isolation, may have suddenly seemed implausible in the face of Assyrian power and the survival of only a stripped-down city-state centered on Jerusalem. The waning of this traditional nationalism among most Judahites could have readily prompted a reactionary attempt to encourage and re-institute it, even without the additional threat of direct international influence on Judah's culture and religion.

The influence of the neo-Assyrian empire on its vassal kingdoms was significant, due primarily to the extensive acculturation which normally followed in its political and military wake.[24] Mordecai Cogan writes, "The diminutive Judahite state was buffeted on all sides by the cultural patterns dominant in the Assyrian empire. Although Assyria made no formal demands for cultural uniformity among its subjects, one of the by-products of political and economic subjugation was a tendency toward cultural homogeneity. Involved as it was in imperial affairs, Judah was faced with

---

22. Na'aman, *Ancient Israel and Its Neighbors*, 330.
23. McKay, *Religion in Judah under the Assyrians*, 26–27.
24. Na'aman, "Ekron under the Assyrian and Egyptian Empires," 87.

the problem of assimilation of foreign norms, on a national scale, for the first time in its history."[25]

Describing the effect of Assyrian imperial ideology on the cultural content of the empire, Mario Liverani speaks of a process of "de-culturation" in conquered countries, which ultimately leads to "an impoverishment and a levelling out of culture throughout the empire."[26]

Judah's cross-cultural exposure was heightened by the nearness of the defeated northern state of Israel, by the seventh century transformed into an Assyrian province. As a province, the Assyrian cult would almost certainly have been incorporated in its temples.[27] In addition, a large number of cultures came into contact with Judah via the Assyrians' deportation of conquered peoples to Samaria. With such a variety of cults and cultures on its doorstep, Judah could hardly have been immune to the political and religious temptations to syncretism; Adele Berlin observes that "many in Judah, especially in the ruling elite, would have found the practices of a wealthy and successful empire very attractive and would have promoted a degree of cultural and religious imitation if not assimilation."[28] Hermann Spieckermann contends that Judah would have been under just as much pressure to incorporate Assyrian practices as territories incorporated directly into the provincial system.[29]

After Samaria fell in 721 at least some refugees probably made their way south, and it is hardly implausible to suggest that among the latecomers there may have been those who had seen the demise of a distinctively Israelite identity in the wake of cultural assimilation to the Assyrians. Deuteronomy is widely acknowledged to exhibit northern influences, and the urgency of resistance to a similar threat in Judah must have been heightened by reports of the failure of the Israelites to do likewise, and the inevitable results of that failure.[30]

---

25. Cogan, *Imperialism and Religion*, 95.

26. Liverani, "The Ideology of the Assyrian Empire," 300.

27. Cogan, *Imperialism and Religion*, 42–60; see also Spieckermann, *Juda unter Assur in der Sargonidenzeit*.

28. Berlin, *Zephaniah*, 45.

29. Speickermann, *Juda unter Assur in der Sargonidenzeit*, 369–70.

30. Note especially the similarities to the prophetic book of Hosea. See von Rad, *Deuteronomy*, 26; and von Rad, *Studies in Deuteronomy*, 68; Nicholson, *Deuteronomy and Tradition*, 94–101; Clements, "Deuteronomy and the Jerusalem Cult Tradition," 300–301.

When the immigrants came even closer to Jerusalem through the annexation of most of Judah's territory to Assyria after 701, the proximity of strange cultures and religions to the religious, political, and intellectual core of Judah would have reached a point unparalleled in its history. Cogan notes that the nearness of these foreign populations to the remaining countryside Judahites would have meant that intermingling would have occurred at an even higher level there, while Nadav Na'aman observes rather nonchalantly that "[t]he considerable changes in the ethnic composition of the population may well have brought similar changes in society, economy, cult, etc."[31]

Exacerbating rising nationalistic concerns about the effect of this intermingling on Judahite culture may well have been the king's own uncertainty about opposing it. More than one scholar observes the apparently northern origins of Manasseh's wife, and suggests that the international atmosphere of her conquered country may well have found its way into her husband's court.[32] Having seen the events of 701 as a child, Manasseh would have been unlikely to have risked rebellion, and while Chronicles attempts to portray a Manasseh whose activities led to his arrest by Assyrian forces, the Assyrian annals mention Manasseh only as a loyal vassal.[33] Manasseh's lack of active rejection of foreign encroachments on Judahite culture—indeed his encouragement of them through his encouragement of international commercial and political contacts—almost certainly played a significant role in his vilification by the historians of the next generation, who viewed his tolerance as tantamount to a death warrant for the distinctiveness of Judahite culture and a betrayal of the national identity.

In the midst of the cultural and political dependence of Judah, a strong anti-Manasseh sentiment may well have arisen among those who sought more independence—those who rejected the increasing internationalism and its assimilationist implications—perhaps because they recognized the potential for the disintegration of Judahite identity into Assyrian and other Near Eastern cultures. Manasseh was not "pro-Assyria and anti-nationalistic" in that he would have prioritized

---

31. Cogan, *Imperialism and Religion*, 93; Na'aman, *Ancient Israel*, 215.

32. Cogan, *Imperialism and Religion*, 91; Stavrakopoulou, *King Manasseh and Child Sacrifice*, 51–52; McKay, *Religion in Judah under the Assyrians*, 23–25.

33. Stavrakopoulou, *King Manasseh and Child Sacrifice*, 114; Cogan, *Imperialism and Religion*, 67–68.

Assyrian interests over Judahite interests, but it is quite possible that this diplomatically middle ground was not nearly as nationalistic as some would have liked.[34]

## ASSIMILATIONISM AND IDEOLOGY

The part that religious ideology plays in this historical picture is impossible to overestimate. Religion plays a key role in delineating the identifying characteristics of a given group; expressed negatively, this means that religious ideology is centered on the rejection of characteristics which are not essentially part of the identity of the group. To this effect, Norman Gottwald described the purpose of "Israelite" religion as "*to define and energize the Israelite social system oppositionally or polemically over against other social systems.*"[35] Religious ideology in particular acts as a safeguard against the encroachment of cultural characteristics whose adoption by the group could lead to the eventual disintegration of its distinctiveness.

In the context of seventh century Judah, the political and economic revival under Manasseh led to a sharp increase in the Judahites' exposure to foreign cultural characteristics. It was the shock of this new internationalism that led to the nationalistic, ideologically inspired counter-reaction of Deuteronomy. Louis Stuhlman explains, "The deuteronomic law code aims to restore a people whose social and political (and religious) boundaries have been broken down, in which Israelites faithful to the past are confused with Israelites assimilated to the peoples of the environment. It tries to persuade faithful Israelites to separate themselves from those who threaten her with internal disintegration."[36] While Stuhlman makes these remarks in the context of a theory of exilic redaction of Deuteronomy, his description of the purpose of the law code fits perfectly with the theory that the origins of Deuteronomy lie in a mid-seventh-century reaction to the multiculturalism which characterized the reign of Manasseh.

Cultures with which a group shares much in common pose a particular threat to the attempt to delineate identity boundaries, as cultural familiarity readily leads to the sharing of previously distinctive practices, and ultimately to the disintegration of group boundaries. It is thus hardly surprising that Deuteronomy's greatest vitriol is directed at the nations in

---

34. Stavrakopoulou, *King Manasseh and Child Sacrifice*, 119.
35. Quoted in Mayes, "Deuteronomistic Ideology," 64 (italics original).
36. Paraphrased in Mayes, "Deuteronomistic Ideology," 79.

the immediate vicinity of "Israel," whose religious and cultural characteristics have been increasingly recognized to be quite similar to those of the "Israelites."[37]

How, though, does the desire to preserve religious and cultural identity take on an ethical dimension? While an inherent connection between correct cultic practice and moral virtue may not now seem inevitable, both biblical and extra-biblical texts demonstrate that correct religious practice was one of the most essential factors in ancient morality. An obvious example is the direct correlation between the moral assessments of Judahite and Israelite rulers made by the Kings writer(s) and those rulers' cultic activities.

While post-exilic texts begin to play down the indispensability of the cult in leading a moral life, pre-exilic Judah held the two in close connection. Even clearer evidence that the preservation of religious and cultural identity could be construed as a moral issue is found among Ugaritic texts. There, cultic texts record offerings made for the forgiveness of sins which had been incurred through actions "according to the custom" of other nations.[38] These sins, according to Gregorio del Olmo Lete, were most probably habits "in which the 'sons of Ugarit' have fallen no doubt through adopting their customs (social? cultic?) and abandoning their own."[39] He particularly notes the similarity between the Ugaritic injunctions in this context regarding pursuit of foreign gods and the biblical prophets' admonitions on the topic, but this striking conjunction of religion and moral standing also provides a highly enlightening parallel to the ideological framework of Deuteronomy.

## SOURCES OF CROSS-CULTURAL INFLUENCE

The precise details of the cults and cultures whose influence on Judah were tolerated by Manasseh and so opposed by the nationalists are difficult to come by. The details of which cults appeared in and around Judah at this time are unclear, as is whether they were adopted by the king as part of a wider assimilationist trend or were actively promoted by him. Further exacerbating these difficulties is that, on the whole, very little is known

---

37. See Cogan, *Imperialism and Religion*, 85–86; Stavrakopoulou, *King Manasseh and Child Sacrifice*.

38. Olmo Lete, *Canaanite Religion*, 146–47.

39. Ibid., 157.

about religious beliefs and practices in Judah and neighboring countries outside of what is described in the Bible.

The problem, of course, returns to the reliability of the Kings narrative with regards to the practices which were supposedly introduced by Manasseh.

The excess attributed to Manasseh exacerbates historians' suspicions—the list of cult syncretisms attributed to him is the longest of any in Kings, and it intensifies all the crimes attributed to other kings.[40] While Manasseh may have introduced all these practices into the cult, one must wonder whether Kings is making a theological point or searching for a scapegoat for Judah's ultimate demise.[41] Even more suspicious is that every transgression of which Manasseh is accused is specifically prohibited in Deuteronomy, and the direction of causation is usually thought to run from Deuteronomy to Kings.[42]

I will not dispute the consensus proposal that the specificities of Manasseh's cultic crimes as they are presented by Kings are sketched from the legalities laid down in Deuteronomy. I would, however, propose that an underlying causality exists in the opposite direction: from the historical Manasseh, as the figurehead of a country increasingly immersed in international politics and exposed to foreign cultural practices, to the prohibitions of Deuteronomy, which sought to limit the assimilation of those practices—prohibitions used by a later generation to give specific articulation to the king's characterization. This essay, therefore, cautiously operates on the premise that there is some historical basis to cults and influences which are attributed to Manasseh in 2 Kings, with special credibility awarded to those which have some form of corroborating historical information.

## DEUTERONOMY

Having established an historical framework for my hypothesis, direct analysis of Deuteronomy's core and of the impact of this agenda on its ethical concerns may be undertaken. As to the identification of the "core" of Deuteronomy, suffice it to say that the central section of the book is largely agreed to be a fairly unified composition, albeit composed in part

---

40. Stavrakopoulou, *King Manasseh and Child Sacrifice*, 27–28.
41. See Lasine, "Manasseh as Villain and Scapegoat."
42. Stavrakopoulou, *King Manasseh and Child Sacrifice*, 29.

of multiple pre-existing blocks of legal material.[43] For the purposes of the relationship between Deuteronomy's nationalism and its ethics, there seems to be little significant difference derived from the inclusion or exclusion of individual verses in the core of the book, and therefore this discussion will use the majority of chapters 6–26 as its evidence.

Of final importance is a brief return to that aforementioned debate over the relationship of the law book in the temple to the core of Deuteronomy. Mayes considers the tradition "unlikely" and argues specifically on the basis that the book is a "covenant" book in Kings and the covenant aspect of Deuteronomy is a deuteronomistic redaction.[44] Mayes, however, is a proponent of the minute dissection of the text into redactional layers, and one must note that in this way the covenant aspect of Kings may itself be readily eliminated, by excising nothing more than 2 Kgs 23:1–3 and "as it is written in the book of the covenant" from 2 Kgs 23:21b, which does no damage to the sense—perhaps indicating that the covenant aspect of Kings was merely the beginning of the emphasis on covenant found to such greater effect in Chronicles. What is then left is heavily focused on the elimination of foreign cultic elements as commanded in the book which was found in the temple—correlating well to Deuteronomy's nationalism and its focus on the rejection of foreign gods and practices.

One point on which I agree most wholeheartedly with Mayes, however, is his statement that "Deuteronomy lends itself to being described as the expression of an intensely nationalistic faith."[45] The effect of this nationalism on the moral character of the book, however, has not been fully appreciated.

## Deuteronomy's Ethics

While many commandments are advocated without apparent care for the actions of the nations, a striking number of practices and beliefs are banned by making explicit reference to the fact that they are characteristic

---

43. Mayes breaks up a good deal of chapters 6–14, but attributes nearly all of 14:22—26:16 to the "original" Deuteronomy; Nelson sees little in the way of obvious redactional layers in the entirety of chapters 6–26, and 28, with a few exceptions (Mayes, *Deuteronomy*, 48; Nelson, *Deuteronomy*, 5). Miller is even broader in his attribution, considering 4:44—28:68 to be largely uniform (Miller, *Deuteronomy*, 3).

44. Mayes, *Deuteronomy*, 101–2.

45. Mayes, *Deuteronomy*, 55.

of foreigners. In Deuteronomy there may be found with regular frequency commandments which exhibit a reliance on an underlying premise, more or less explicit, that what the nations do is evil *because the nations do it* (and not for any more substantial reason). The Israelites' moral superiority lies in their rejection of the practices of the nations. The seventh-century encroachment of other nations and cultures into the political, economic, and religious affairs of Judah provides a perfectly suited historical context for this ideology.

Anyone familiar with Deuteronomy will be familiar with its highly nationalistic language. In the first several chapters of the core, the primary focus of this concern is the worship of the one God Yahweh. This concern is persistently and clearly articulated with reference to rejecting the practices of the nations. Thus, "You shall not go after other gods, of the gods of the peoples who are round about you" (6:14), and "you shall destroy all the peoples that Yahweh your God will give over to you, your eye shall not pity them; neither shall you serve their gods, for that would be a snare to you" (7:16; cf. 7:22–26). Note particularly the justification of genocide here on the grounds of keeping the Israelites uncontaminated, and the great sense of fear of these peoples' practices which emanates from the description of them as "a snare."

Deuteronomy 13:17 similarly instructs the Israelites to put to death any prophets and other persons who advocate serving "the gods of the peoples that are round about you, whether near you or far off from you, from the one end of the earth to the other." Earlier, there is this warning: "When Yahweh your God cuts off before you the nations whom you go in to dispossess, and you dispossess them and dwell in their land, take heed that you be not ensnared to follow them, after they have been destroyed before you, and that you do not inquire about their gods, saying, 'How did these nations serve their gods?—that I also may do likewise.' You shall not do so to Yahweh your God; for every abominable thing which Yahweh hates they have done for their gods; for they even burn their sons and their daughters in the fire to their gods" (12:29–31).

This last excerpt occurs immediately on the heels of that chapter's centralization imperatives—a program eminently sensible for a group attempting to minimize the influence of outsiders on the religious culture of Judah, since centralization would bring that culture under the close eye of a watchful, anti-syncretistic elite (however extensive this program is thought to have been in the original text of the book). The explicit reference to the threat posed by cultural assimilation is highly suggestive of a culturally reactionary motivation behind the centralization of the cult.

The sacrifice of children is mentioned as an especially characteristic and abhorrent feature of non-Israelite practice. It is, as Stavrakopoulou's study made clear, a highly polemicized issue in the Hebrew Bible. The practice is prohibited a second time in 18:10, where it is called "abominable"—a word which Erhard Gerstenberger defines as expressing emotional revulsion against that which is strange.[46] While Cogan argues that "[a]t best, the evidence tells of vestigial human sacrifice amidst eighth century BCE Assyro-Aramaean cultural traditions," Stavrakopoulou convincingly argues that, while the extant biblical texts claim that the Israelites did not practice such sacrifice, this does not indicate a long-held rejection of the practice but rather wishful thinking by a late generation of Israelites.[47] It is intriguing to consider the possibility that the rejection of child sacrifice occurred during this seventh-century period as part of a wide-ranging rejection of practices which might confuse the religio-cultural identity of the "Israelites" with those of their neighbors. That is, the rejection of the sacrifice of children occurred as part of an attempt to create a clearly identifiable distinction between the religious practices of Judahites and non-Judahites, rather than having been derived from a theologically-based, moral objection to the practice.

The ideal of complete separation from other cultures is also exemplified in 7:1–3, which again propounds genocide, and then bans intermarriage (suggesting that the implementation of genocide, at least, was more theoretical than actual): "When Yahweh your God brings you into the land which you are entering to take possession of it, and clears away many nations before you ... then you must utterly destroy them; you shall make no covenant with them, and show no mercy to them. You shall not make marriages with them, giving your daughters to their sons or taking their daughters for your sons."

The war rules in Deut 20 similarly justify the complete destruction of the nations, and the isolationist, anti-assimilationist rationale is eminently clear: "... that they may not teach you to do according to all their abominable practices which they have done in the service of their gods, and so to sin against Yahweh your God" (20:18). Again and again, the

---

46. Gerstenberger, "תעב (tʿb pi). *to abhor*," 1431.

47. Cogan, *Imperialism and Religion*, 83; see Stavrakopoulou, *King Manasseh and Child Sacrifice*.

moralized commandments to demolish the nations are grounded in the need for cultural and religious isolation for the Israelites.

More than a third of the core is devoted to admonishments relating to monolatry, and it is not until Deut 14 that an independent topic arises. The issue is rites of mourning, and the command is striking evidence for this paper's case: "You are the sons of Yahweh your God; you shall not cut yourselves or make any baldness on your foreheads for the dead. For you are a people holy to Yahweh your God, and Yahweh has chosen you to be a people for his own possession, out of all the peoples that are on the face of the earth" (14:1–2).

The practices of laceration and shaving of the head in mourning are well-known from the Ancient Near East. The most detailed description comes in an epic mythical text from Ugarit:

> [H]e [Iln] sprinkled ash of affliction on his head,
> dust of humiliation on his skull,
> for clothing he covered himself with a ritual tunic;
> (his) skin with a stone (knife) he gashed,
> the two tresses with a razor,
> he lacerated (his) cheeks and chin;
> harrowed the bone of his arm,
> ploughed like a garden his chest,
> like a valley harrowed his back.[48]

The mourning rites rejected in Deut 14 are clearly and directly linked to the notion of a unique and differentiated role which is the special provenance of the Israelites; it is the threat which these rites pose to this role which set them out as morally objectionable. The nationalistic motivation clause in 14:2 makes clear that the rationale behind this commandment is grounded in the distinction between Israel and the nations, and the extra-biblical evidence grounds the rejection firmly on known Ancient Near Eastern practice.

The deuteronomic dietary laws also appear in Deut 14. While the passage lacks the nationalistic motivation of its predecessor, some scholars, including Noth and Roland de Vaux, have argued that the logic of clean and unclean animals is based in the use or disuse of certain types of animals in Canaanite sacrifices (though probably other concerns were

---

48. del Olmo Lete, *Canaanite Religion*, 161–62.

also involved in the division of animals into clean and unclean).[49] The anthropologist Mary Douglas, whose work on purity and taboo is well-known, rejected the connection between the Levitical division of animals into clean and unclean and the practices of the Judahites' neighbors as a comprehensive explanation for their prohibition on the grounds that not all foreign practices were rejected.[50] It seems at least plausible, however, that those practices which were considered particularly characteristic of foreign encroachment were singled out for particular attention. As Mayes writes, the dietary laws "are the means by which the people of Yahweh are to demonstrate their separateness from the peoples and cultures of their environment."[51]

Douglas also complains that the foreign-practices proposal fails to explain why Judahite culture soaked up foreign influence one minute and rejected it the next.[52] Hardly least among the reasons for this can be the conflicts internal to Judahite culture at the time, with the incongruity between ideology and social reality observed by Stuhlman resulting in inconsistency in the text.[53] More broadly, Douglas provides an answer to her own question in the context of a discussion of the Indian caste system, where she observes that "food is not likely to be polluting at all unless the external boundaries of the social system are under pressure."[54] The priestly purity laws in Leviticus may be aptly described as a response to such pressures during the exile, and the Deuteronomic laws provide an excellent parallel in late pre-exilic Judah.

Further examples of the rejection of practices on the grounds of foreignness are the bans against the erection of trees and asherahs, which are of course well-attested as part of Canaanite religious practice. Indeed the involvement of asherah—whatever or whoever it is—in Judahite and Israelite worship is now commonly acknowledged. Speaking generally

---

49. See Wenham, "The Theology of Unclean Food," 8, for a review of the history of interpretation. Note also Mayes's argument, on sociological grounds, that the dietary laws are a post-exilic insertion (Mayes, "Deuteronomy," 181).

50. Douglas, *Purity and Danger*, 60–62.

51. Mayes, "Deuteronomy," 165. Note, however, that Mayes ultimately argues for the dietary laws as a late, post-exilic addition to Deuteronomy on the basis of it presupposing a world view distinct from that of the rest of Deuteronomy (180–81).

52. Douglas, *Purity and Danger*, 61.

53. See Mayes, "Deuteronomy," 79.

54. Douglas, *Purity and Danger*, 157.

regarding the myriad "foreign" cults which Kings accuses Manasseh of introducing, Stavrakopoulou observes that many of these practices were probably part of the "normative and native polytheism of Judah."[55] The enduring persistence of the worship of goddesses in Judah—the Queen of Heaven mentioned in Jeremiah, among probable others—attests to the deeply rooted history of the cult in Judah.[56] The portrayal of these practices as foreign by both Kings and Deuteronomy, however, seems to have been part of a process of deliberate alienation, aiming to eliminate practices which blurred the lines between Judah and its neighbors. The same process seems to have been at work on the rejection of asherah as in the rejection of child sacrifice.

The problem of Israelite monolatry resurfaces in Deut 17 with the worship of yet other foreign gods, specifically the sun, moon, and host of heaven. The first instance of the death penalty—the ultimate punishment—is invoked against those who worship such gods.[57] Pinpointing which foreign nation's practice is in mind at this point in Deuteronomy, however, is nearly impossible, as astral worship was very common in the Ancient Near East; worship of the sun is attested in nearly every country in the ancient world.[58] The moon god, Sin, was particularly popular among the Aramaeans of northern Syria, and Cogan argues that the Mesopotamian astral elements discernable in Judah (textually and archaeologically) were most likely assimilated via Aramaean mediation.[59]

McKay also argues that the astral deities mentioned here and in Kings could be indigenous Canaanite gods.[60] The worship of astral deities in Judah during this period may also be attributed to Assyrian influence; McKay notes that all references to astral deities and worship in the Hebrew Bible occur during the period of Assyrian domination.[61] Even if the Assyrians did not impose their religion on vassal states—though Spieckermann is probably correct that they did—it is hardly far-fetched to suggest that the Assyrian gods, whose power and patronage would

---

55. Stavrakopoulou, *King Manasseh and Child Sacrifice*, 111.
56. See Cogan, *Imperialism and Religion*, 85.
57. Zephaniah, whose book is dated to early in Josiah's reign, also mentions worship of the heavenly host during that period (1:5).
58. McKay, *Religion in Judah under the Assyrians*, 32.
59. Cogan, *Imperialism and Religion*, 86–88.
60. McKay, *Religion in Judah under the Assyrians*, 20–21.
61. Ibid., 45.

have been understood to undergird the Assyrian empire, were readily adopted by eager subjects.[62] The religious and cultural threat which this adoption posed to Judahite identity led the purists to condemn these gods as "abominable" and "an evil thing"—a crime so great as to demand the penalty of death.

Equally "abominable"—recall the cultural connotations described by Gerstenberger—are divination, soothsaying and other similar "magical" practices. These are listed at 18:9–14, and described twice as practices which the nations follow. Divinatory activities are well-attested across the Ancient Near East, by the extensive library of divinatory texts found in Assyria and by texts at Ugarit describing offerings to the underworld gods for purposes of divination.[63] Even the Hebrew Bible, which opposes these practices, reports Saul resorting to a consultation of the necromancer of Endor (1 Sam 28). At Ugarit, the king acted as mediator between the living and the dead; perhaps Manasseh himself followed suit.[64] Once again, practices probably widely known in Judah itself seem to have undergone in this period an ideological realignment to define them as objectionable activities of the nations. To demarcate Judahites from the indiscriminate sea of Ancient Near Eastern culture, Deuteronomy established a moral binary between the abominations of the nations and Judah's path of moral right.

## CONCLUSIONS

While many commandments in Deuteronomy's core are typical to the Ancient Near Eastern legal tradition and the core no doubt incorporates pre-existing blocks of legal material, there is nonetheless a striking persistence of injunctions among these commands whose rationale is explicitly or implicitly based in the rejection of the practices of Judah's neighbors. Besides the underlying Ancient Near Eastern assumption of an inherent link between religion and ethics, a number of these also use explicit language of evil and abomination to equate the practices of the nations with

---

62. Lohfink observes, "The highest degree of danger is reached, if the competitive worldview establishes its superiority through the most convincing of all proofs: power and success" (Lohfink, "Culture Shock and Theology," 13).

63. del Olmo Lete, *Canaanite Religion*, 143.

64. Ibid., 346.

moral wrong, and to identify the course of moral rightness for Judah as one in which the foreigner and his practices are rejected.

This effort to delineate the boundaries of Judahite identity is firmly rooted in the political and economic culture of the seventh century, in which Manasseh presided over an economic expansion and Assyrian power came directly to Judah's doorstep. The temptations of assimilation provoked a fear that the cultural and religious identity of the Judahites, who had until that time been largely politically and economically isolated, would be lost in an ever-increasing wave of cultural assimilationism. Deuteronomy arose as a response to this threat, and the core of the book strongly reflects the nationalistic and isolationist concerns of its creators. It is hardly surprising that the book repeatedly merges the language of religion and ethics in its attempts to encourage seventh-century Judahites to safeguard their culture and reject foreign practices.[65]

---

65. [For a significantly expanded and revised analysis of Deuteronomy's sociological context, see my forthcoming *Ethics and Identity: a Study of Deuteronomy's Origins* —CC.]

# BIBLIOGRAPHY

Berlin, Adele. *Zephaniah: A New Translation with Introduction and Commentary.* AB 25A New York: Doubleday, 1994.

Clements, Ronald E. "Deuteronomy and the Jerusalem Cult Tradition." *VT* 15 (1965) 300–312.

Cogan, Mordechai. *Imperialism and Religion: Assyria, Judah and Israel in the Eighth and Seventh Centuries B.C.E.* SBLMS 19. Missoula: SBL, 1974.

Cogan, Mordechai, and Hayim Tadmor. *II Kings: A New Translation with Introduction and Commentary.* AB 11. Garden City, NY: Doubleday, 1998.

Craigie, Peter C. *The Book of Deuteronomy.* NICOT. Grand Rapids: Eerdmans, 1976.

Demsky, Aaron. "The Name of the Goddess of Ekron: A New Reading." *JANES* 25 (1997) 1–5.

Dothan, Trude. "Tel Miqne-Ekron: The Aegean Affinities of the Sea Peoples' (Philistines') Settlement in Canaan in Iron Age I." In *Recent Excavations in Israel: A View to the West; Reports on Kabr, Nami, Miqne-Ekron, Dor and Ashkelon*, edited by Seymour Gitin, 41–59. Colloquia and Conference Papers 1. Dubuque: Kendall/Hunt, 1995.

———. *The Philistines and Their Material Culture.* Jerusalem: Israel Exploration Society, 1982.

Dothan, Trude et al. "A Royal Dedicatory Inscription from Ekron." *IEJ* 47 (1997) 1–16.

Douglas, Mary. *Implicit Meanings: Essays in Anthropology.* London: Routledge & Kegan Paul, 1975.

———. *Purity and Danger: An Analysis of Concept of Pollution and Taboo.* London: Routledge, 2004.

Edelman, Diana. Review of *Biblical Peoples and Ethnicity: An Archaeological Study of Egyptians, Canaanites, Philistines, and Early Israel 1300–1100 B.C.E.*, by Ann E. Killebrew. *RBL* (2006). Online: http://www.bookreviews.org/.

Erlich, Carl S. *The Philistines in Transition: A History from ca. 1000–730 B.C.E.* Studies in the History and Culture of the Ancient Near East 10. Leiden: Brill, 1996.

Faust, Avi, and Ehud Weiss. "Judah, Philistia, and the Mediterranean World: Reconstructing the Economic System of the Seventh Century B.C.E." *BASOR* 338 (2005) 71–92.

Gerstenberger, Erhard. "תעב (tᵉb pi). *to abhor*." In *Theological Lexicon of the Old Testament*, edited by Ernst Jenni and Claus Westermann, 3:1428–31. 3 vols. Peabody, MA: Hendrickson, 1997.

Gitin, Seymour. "Tel Miqne-Ekron in the 7th Century B.C.E.: The Impact of Economic Innovation and Foreign Cultural Influences on a Neo-Assyrian Vassal City-State." In *Recent Excavations in Israel: A View to the West; Reports on Kabr, Nami, Miqne-Ekron, Dor and Ashkelon*, edited by Seymour Gitin, 61–79. Colloquia and Conference Papers 1. Dubuque: Kendall/Hunt, 1995.

Killebrew, Ann E. *Biblical Peoples and Ethnicity: An Archaeological Study of Egyptians, Canaanites, Philistines, and Early Israel 1300–1100 B.C.E.* SBLABS 9. Leiden: Brill, 2005.

Lasine, Stuart. "Manasseh as Villain and Scapegoat." In *The New Literary Criticism and the Hebrew Bible*, edited by Cheryl Exum and David J. A. Clines, 163–83. JSOTSup 143. Sheffield, UK: JSOT Press, 1993.

Liverani, Mario. "The Ideology of the Assyrian Empire." In *Power and Propaganda: A Symposium on Ancient Empires*, edited by Mogens Trolle Larsen, 297–317. Mesopotamia 1. Copenhagen: Akademisk, 1979.

Lohfink, Norbert. "Culture Shock and Theology." *BTB* 7 (1977) 12–22.
Maeir, Aren M. "The Relations between Egypt and the Southern Levant during the Late Iron Age: The Material Evidence from Egypt." *Ägypten und Levante* 12 (2002) 235–46.
Mayes, A. D. H. "Deuteronomistic Ideology and the Theology of the Old Testament." *JSOT* 82 (1999) 57–82.
———. *Deuteronomy*. NCB. London: Marshall, Morgan & Scott, 1981.
———. "Deuteronomy 14 and the Deuteronomic World View." In *Studies in Deuteronomy: In Honour of C. J. Labuschange on the Occasion of His 65th Birthday*, edited by F. García Martínez, et al., 165–81. VTSup 53. Leiden: Brill, 1994.
McKay, J. W. *Religion in Judah under the Assyrians, 732–609*. SBT (2nd ser.), 26. London: SCM, 1973.
Miller, Patrick D. *Deuteronomy*. IBC. Louisville: Westminster John Knox, 1990.
Na'aman, Nadav. *Ancient Israel and Its Neighbors: Interaction and Counteraction*. Colllected Essays 1. Winona Lake: Eisenbrauns, 2005.
———. "Ekron under the Assyrian and Egyptian Empires." *BASOR* 332 (2003) 81–91.
Nelson, Richard D. *Deuteronomy: A Commentary*. OTL. Louisville: Westminster John Knox, 2002.
Nicholson, E. W. *Deuteronomy and Tradition*. Oxford: Blackwell, 1967.
Olmo Lete, Gregorio del. *Canaanite Religion: According to the Liturgical Texts of Ugarit*. Translated by Wilfred G. E. Watson. Bethesda: CDL, 1999.
Pongratz-Leisten, Beate. "The Other and the Enemy in the Mesopotamian Conception of the World." In *Mythology and Mythologies*, edited by Robert M. Whiting, 195–231. Helsinki: The Neo-Assyrian Text Corpus Project, 2001.
Rad, Gerhard von. *Deuteronomy: A Commentary*. Translated by Dorothea Barton. OTL. London: SCM, 1966.
———. *Studies in Deuteronomy*. London: SCM, 1963.
Schäfer-Lichtenberger, Christa. "The Goddess of Ekron and the Religious-Cultural Background of the Philistines." *IEJ* 50 (2000) 82–91.
Seitz, Christopher R. *Isaiah 1–39*. IBC. Louisville: John Knox, 1993.
Spieckermann, Hermann. *Juda unter Assur in der Sargonidenzeit*. FRLANT 129. Göttingen: Vandenhoeck & Ruprecht, 1982.
Sprinkle, Joe M. "The Rationale of the Laws of Clean and Unclean in the Old Testament." *JETS* 43 (2000) 637–57.
Stavrakopoulou, Francesca. *King Manasseh and Child Sacrifice: Biblical Distortions of Historical Realities*. BZAW 338. Berlin: de Gruyter, 2004.
Stern, Ephraim. "Tel-Dor: A Phoenician-Israelite Trading Center." In *Recent Excavations in Israel: A View to the West; Reports on Kabr, Nami, Miqne-Ekron, Dor and Ashkelon*, edited by Seymour Gitin, 81–94. Colloquia and Conference Papers 1. Dubuque: Kendall/Hunt, 1995.
Wenham, Gordon J. "The Theology of Unclean Food." *EQ* 53 (1981) 6–15.

# 10

## Illuminating Darkness

### Mystical Strategies for Biblical Interpretation in Judaism and Christianity

JOHN ROBINSON

Irish School of Ecumenics, Trinity College Dublin

## INTRODUCTION

IT IS PERHAPS A truism to aver that every age has its own specific character which in turn marks its search for truth, but it is surely a point worth recalling. Any such character will, of course, be multidimensional and possibly can only be adequately understood by later commentators. Yet, certain aspects will stand out as egregious even at the time, and for those of us working in the field of theology, the growing alienation of theology from historical-critical Biblical Studies deserves particular attention and analysis as a matter of gravity, and one which poses particular questions to theology. It must also be said that a large part of this problem is the consistent failure of theology to adequately integrate the findings of historical-critical biblical research into its thought. This is often motivated, I think, by a fear occasioned by the knowledge that such studies, in their rigorous criticism of the biblical texts, have shown that things did not happen historically in accordance with the picture presented to us by the biblical authors.

The shock administered by this refutation of what is understood to be the literal sense of the text is not to be underestimated, even though it is seldom given any direct examination in theology. The question is raised, however, of how we theologically interpret the biblical texts in the knowledge that we cannot regard them as accurately reflecting things as they actually took place in terms of what we would normally understand as history. Even more than that—do the findings of modern biblical criticism mean that the view of history as revelatory is in many respects debunked, thus rendering the understanding present in theological tradition effectively obsolete?

Obviously, it is impossible to give a comprehensive answer in an essay such as this, but I hope at least to suggest that this is not the case, and that, far from historical-critical exegesis being something theologians ought to fear, the grammar of Judaism and Christianity, as present in their respective mystical traditions, can provide a means of integrating this new knowledge coming to light that is at once rooted in the traditions of both faiths and yet can fully respect the autonomy and methodology of this approach to biblical studies. To do this, I will start by examining mystical views of revelation in Judaism and Christianity—and the interpretive strategies that emerge from them—by looking at the work of Gershom Scholem and Mark McIntosh. I will then look at what sort of application of these is possible in the task of interpreting the biblical texts in the contemporary context.

## GERSHOM SCHOLEM AND MYSTICAL VIEWS OF REVELATION IN JUDAISM

It is fair to say that in the modern study of the Jewish mystical tradition, Gershom Scholem occupies a unique and preeminent place. Indeed, it was Scholem who pioneered the historical-critical study of Kabbalistic texts and based a critical philosophy on them in a way which had not previously been done. Consequently, he is a particularly apt thinker with whom to engage in the search for a critical hermeneutic of biblical interpretation based on the sources of the Jewish mystical tradition.

Scholem himself occupied a position which in some way mirrored the liminality of the texts he expounded. Unorthodox in religious terms, he saw revelation as an integral phenomenon in human existence, was deeply troubled by the lack of belief within modernity, and sought to find some way in which a bridge could be thrown up between modern consciousness and the fundaments of Jewish religious consciousness. His analysis of revelation led him to posit a threefold structure expressed most clearly in his essay, "Revelation and Tradition as Religious Categories in Judaism." In it he listed the development of the categories of revelation as the stabilization of the initial event of revelation in the written text, the commentary and reflection of the sages which came to be designated as oral Torah, and finally, the culmination in the speculative thought of the Kabbalists. It was, of course, the third of these upon which Scholem focused and upon which he based his thought.

The underlying supposition of the Kabbalists' view of Torah was that God could only reveal his own essence and that the Torah was in fact the revelation of the name of God which was, by its nature, something which humanity could not begin to comprehend in any unmediated sense. The written Torah, then, was a texture fashioned from the name of God, and the plain sense of the text, such as we read it, is itself mediation. Scholem puts it thus:

> Thus, the very words that we read in the Written Torah and that constitute the audible "word of God" and communicate a comprehensible message, are in reality mediations through which the absolute word, incomprehensible to us, is offered. This absolute word is originally communicated in its limitless fullness, but—and this is the key point—this communication is incomprehensible! It is not a communication which provides comprehension; being basically nothing but the expression of essence, it becomes a comprehensible communication only when it is mediated.[1]

This, for Scholem, culminated in the articulation of the polysemy of the words of Torah which, in an organic growth of continuity with tradition, assumes meaning in a dialectical relationship with history. Equally, language itself is seen as possessing an ontological status to the point where it can function as a symbol of the divine and is capable of rendering the communicative word of God in a form which can both signify and make concrete the ineffable which it sets out to express.

In the view put forward here, revelation is seen as an ongoing development and expansion of meaning latent in the text, with the words of the text possessing a polysemy which makes such expansion possible. Revelation is the revelation of God's essence, a content which is utterly different from the literal or historical content of the text, which merely serve

---

1. Scholem, "Revelation and Tradition as Religious Categories in Judaism," 294.

to mediate the expression of God's essence. This then becomes meaningful for us in the ongoing dialectic with history which means that the words of Torah effectively have a constantly developing and shifting meaning.

The Zohar puts it more poetically:

> Rabbi Shimon said, "If a man looks on the Torah as merely a book presenting narratives and everyday matters, alas for him! . . . The Torah, in all of its worlds, holds supernal truths and sublime secrets . . . The tales related in the Torah are simply her outer garments and woe to the man who regards that outer garb as the Torah itself, for such a man will be deprived of portion in the next world . . . The words of the Torah are garments; the inner message lies within."[2]

## THE STRUCTURE OF INTERPRETATION IN CHRISTIANITY

The Christian mystical tradition does not occupy the synchronic or diachronic continuity which can be claimed for Kabbalah, so in this section I will concentrate on the Western tradition, although many of the points would hold true for the other strands of Christian mystical thought also.

To this day, much of the vocabulary of Western Christianity is a result of the decisive synthesis with classical Greek philosophy that took place in Christianity's formative centuries, and this is no less true when we come to examine the mystical tradition, the most typical and influential representative of which is Pseudo-Dionysius the Areopagite. Indeed, Denys Turner points out that in Western mystical thought this can be typified by the concern in the tradition with the story of the ascent of Moses to Mount Sinai and the myth of the cave in Plato's *Republic*. Both of these were read as accounts of the Christian's assent to union with God in a way which sets the stage for the resultant interpretive strategy. This can be seen with particular clarity in the work of Pseudo-Dionysius the Areopagite, in his commentary on Moses's ascent of Mount Sinai:

> But then he [Moses] breaks free of them [things perceived with the eye of the body, of the mind], away from what sees and is seen, and he plunges into the truly mysterious darkness of unknowing. Here, renouncing all that the mind may conceive, wrapped entirely in the intangible and the invisible, he belongs completely to him who is beyond everything. Here being neither oneself nor someone else, one is supremely united by a completely unknowing

---

2. *The Zohar*, 3:152.

inactivity of all knowledge, and knows beyond the mind by knowing nothing.³

Note that here, as in the Kabbalistic view, the point of the text is primarily knowledge of God, that the words of the text are expanded upon, that a meaning different from that of the plain sense of the text is what becomes crucial, and that the literal and historical elements of the text are seen as mediating factors.

McIntosh, referring to Paul Ricoeur's formulation of the text as an event of meaning, however, introduces a new element into the equation by formulating the mystical view of biblical interpretation thus: "The biblical witness can be God's chosen 'site' for a new encounter between believers and the Incarnate Word."⁴

The important point here is not so much whether one agrees or disagrees with McIntosh's point that all interpretation is to be itself interpreted as essentially Christological, but rather, the fact that on a structural level, the meaning-event of interpretation is one which, in Christian terms, is an encounter with God, and in which meaning is rooted within God's self.

Scholem makes a structurally similar point in his essay, "Revelation and Tradition," in which he quotes the words of Meir ben Gabbai, who views the Torah as being the constant outpouring of the second emanation of the Tree of Life, the *sefirah Hokhmah*. As such, it is itself part of this flowing forth from God as God is in godself—as distinguished from God as God is in relation to us. In both cases, the act of interpretation becomes both an encounter with God and an encounter rooted in God. In both cases, the fullness of interpretation of the text lies in moving beyond the literal meaning of the text, which, if it became the term of the act of interpretation, would be simply, spiritually, missing the point.

Though this may seem a relatively arcane point in terms of the relationship between the modern disciplines of theology and biblical studies, it does possess considerable structural relevance. First, it underscores that the two disciplines do not need to find themselves locked in any sort of competition over the literal sense of the text as, quite simply, and—*pace* the growing ranks of fundamentalists of all stripes—in this mystically

---

3. *Dionysius the Areopagite on the Divine Names and the Mystical Theology*, 1000c–1001a.

4. McIntosh, *Mystical Theology*, 140.

based analysis, the question of the historical events which lie behind the text is not where theology's gaze should be primarily directed.

Equally, the discipline of historical-critical study, along with the relevant archaeology and ancient history, have done theology a very considerable service by disabusing it of the notion of the historicity of the texts conceived in a positivistic way, thus liberating it for a full engagement with the texts *qua* texts which are sites of revelatory meaning—rather than further embroilment in disputed questions of historicity.

Of further relevance here is the mystical insistence that God is not one object alongside others, as this concept seems to be behind a considerable amount of the anguish generated in biblical literalists by the findings of historical critical scholars. If some things *qua* things are shown to be untrue by biblical research, then other things—including the particularly big thing, which is God—might also be debunked. Yet, such a view is inimical to both traditional Judaism and Christianity and, in mystical terms, is seen as being an obstacle to true knowledge of the Divine. Hence Meister Eckhart prays, "I ask God to rid me of God."[5]

Thus, it becomes possible to see the advent of historical-critical scholarship—from a mystical perspective—as a necessary stage of purgation from an attachment to the literal and historical sense of the text interpreted in modern positivistic categories, which has been and still is widespread within Christianity, thus opening the way to entering into a fully theological, and therefore spiritual, engagement with the text *qua* revelatory word.

## STRATEGIES FOR INTERPRETATION

In the light of the above points, however, several questions arise. Firstly, given that the history lying behind the text is not the crucial locus of meaning in this view, what is? Secondly, is there anything which prevents a purely subjective reading of the text in such a way that no reading can be deemed illegitimate? Thirdly, given that the texts do manifestly seek to interpret historical events, what is the significance of history in all of this?

To deal with the first of these questions inevitably involves some foray into the field of hermeneutics, and while a comprehensive survey is impossible here, I would like to suggest what I deem to be three lines

---

5. Eckhart, *German Sermons and Treatises*, GS 292.

of fruitful inquiry. The crucial point in all three is simple: the locus of meaning in theological interpretations of the Biblical text is, in point of fact, the text itself as interpretive world and not any reality lying behind the text. Paul Ricoeur is at pains to point out that in the text, while an experience is not transmitted, its meaning, whatever that may be, is. In this view, the text itself becomes an invitation to a participatory knowledge through entry into its world, and its literary character *qua* text becomes of crucial importance. Ricoeur states, "The mistaken assumption . . . would be to take these forms of discourse as simply neutralized so we can extract their theological content. . . . To uproot this prejudice, we must convince ourselves that the literary genres of the Bible do not constitute a rhetorical façade which it would be possible to pull down to reveal some thought content that is indifferent to its literary vehicle."[6]

Thus, the primary locus for interpretation is the text itself. Obviously, this is an approach which can claim a very ancient provenance in both Christianity and Judaism—from Augustine's hermeneutical reflections in *De Doctrina Christiana* to both the halakhic and aggadic exegesis present in the writings of the Rabbis. In its modern form, this approach has been decisively influenced by the emergence of literary theory in the secular academy, and in particular, by the adoption of what George Lindbeck terms the "cultural-linguistic" approach in parts of the world of theology.

In his study of post-critical interpretation of the Torah, Peter Ochs sums up the cultural-linguistic position as follows:

> According to the "cultural-linguistic" alternative, "meaning is constituted by the uses of a specific language." Scriptures therefore display their meaning intratextually, which means within the context of Scripture as a system of symbols. These symbols are to be interpreted by the community for which they are meaningful as rules of conduct: first, the conduct of scriptural reading itself, and, then, the everyday conduct that is enjoined by this reading.[7]

In this formulation, then, the return to the text, so to speak, has to be anchored by being located within an interpretive community, whether that of church or synagogue. The risk here, however, is a lack of a hermeneutical suspicion towards the interpretive communities themselves. It is not as if, after all, religious communities exist outside historical, social, and

---

6. Ricoeur, cited in McIntosh, *Mystical Theology*, 142.
7. Ochs, *The Return to Scripture in Judaism and Christianity*, 53.

political conditions; class interests; gender hierarchies; etc. Here again, the helpfulness of the historical-critical approach comes to light as the rigorous clarification of the meaning of the words of the text in historical context can provide some kind of safeguard against eisegetical tendencies that could serve to distort the meaning of the text.

This strategy does provide at least some kind of answer to our second question: the location of the play of textual meaning in an interpretive community, with the historical-critical clarification of the meaning of the plain sense of the text acting as a control on the interpretation of the community, does mean that interpretation does not become some kind of post-structuralist free-for-all.

The third question then becomes that of the significance of history in interpretation. With Ricoeur and Lindbeck, we can certainly agree that the texts present us with an interaction between the perspective of the author or community which produced the text and the historical events alluded to. This meaning may be a question of textually creating a desired historical reality or of reading present circumstances back into past events. One way or another, the structure is that of dialectic between the horizon of the author and history. As we have seen, this notion of the dialectic with history in which revelation assumes its meaning for us was crucial to Scholem. Further, the postmodern critique of the disembodied rational self of modernity has the merit of pointing out that, when we come to interpret, we too are involved, either explicitly or implicitly, in such dialectic.

History, then, becomes the "other term" in the dialectic which generates meaning both in the production and the interpretation of texts. In terms of sites of contested meaning, however, the question then becomes "Whose history?"—and this not simply in the somewhat facile manner of extreme postmodern perspectivism. One anecdote which can illustrate what is at stake is the reflection in the Basic Christian Communities (the groups of Christians who were formed as part of the flowering of Liberation theology) in Chile on the singing of the *Te Deum* in the cathedral at Santiago at the news that General Augusto Pinochet was to become the president of Chile. Clearly both responses saw themselves as being faithful to the Gospel, but coming as they did from different social locations, their responses to the event were diametrically opposed.

Looking at this difficulty in the context of the Christian mystical tradition, Mark McIntosh suggests that we evaluate the legitimacy of any standpoint in terms of the effects it produces, and he endorses the Liberation theologian's call for a privileging of the hermeneutical location of the poor and oppressed. As Dorothee Soelle puts it in her book *The Silent Cry: Mysticism and Resistance*, "The hermeneutics of the poor is one of hunger for bread and liberation. The Bible is read as the answer to what oppression, illness, lack of education, and apathy inflict on human beings."[8]

Thus, in a mystical view of interpretation—in which the text is the locus of encounter with the Divine, read within an interpretive community, and bestowing meaning in a dialectical relationship with history—we as interpreters have to look and answer the question posed by the Jewish poet, Adrienne Rich: "With whom do you believe your lot is cast?" The process of interpretation does not allow for ideological neutrality, a fortiori, in a global context of starvation, inequality, and oppression.

To sum up then, my aim here has been to advocate an embrace of the interpretive strategy emerging from the Jewish and Christian mystical traditions in which the revelation embodied in the text is God's self-revelation and in which the historical and literal elements in the text are the mediations of this revelation. The disabusing of theology of the notion that the texts represent pure history opens the way to this encounter with the divine in which the interpreter brings her social location and existential commitment as a crucial element in the dialectical structure of the generation of meaning. This encounter with the divine, finally, becomes interpreted in the light of history, and meaning emerges. Seen in this way, it becomes possible that both historical-critical Biblical Studies and theology, albeit in their very different ways, may yet have something to say to a world increasingly populated by those who see too clearly to see well.

---

8. Soelle, *The Silent Cry*, 48.

## BIBLIOGRAPHY

*Dionysius the Areopagite on the Divine Names and the Mystical Theology.* Vol. 3. Translated by C. E. Rolt. Translations of Christian Literature, Series 1. London: SPCK, 1920.

Eckhart, Meister. *German Sermons and Treatises.* Vol. 2. London: Watkins, 1979.

McIntosh, Mark Allen. *Mystical Theology: The Integrity of Spirituality and Theology.* Challenges in Contemporary Theology. Oxford: Blackwell, 1997.

Ochs, Peter. *The Return to Scripture in Judaism and Christianity: Essays in Postcritical Scriptural Interpretation.* Theological Inquiries. New York: Paulist, 1993.

Soelle, Dorothee. *The Silent Cry: Mysticism and Resistance.* Translated by Barbara and Martin Rumscheidt. Minneapolis: Fortress, 2001.

Scholem, Gershom. "Revelation and Tradition as Religious Categories in Judaism." In *The Messianic Idea in Judaism, and Other Essays on Jewish Spirituality*, 282–303. New York: Schocken, 1995.

Sperling, Harry, and Maurice Simon, translators. *The Zohar.* Vol. 3. London: Soncino, 1931–1934.

www.ingramcontent.com/pod-product-compliance
Lightning Source LLC
Chambersburg PA
CBHW062023220426
43662CB00010B/1454